D1453546

DATE DUE

THE MOST PROMISING YOUNG OFFICER

THE MOST PROMISING YOUNG OFFICER

A LIFE OF RANALD SLIDELL MACKENZIE

By Michael D. Pierce

UNIVERSITY OF OKLAHOMA PRESS : NORMAN AND LONDON

This book is published with the generous assistance of
The Kerr Foundation.

Library of Congress Cataloging-in-Publication Data

Pierce, Michael D. (Michael Dale), 1940–
    The most promising young officer : a life of Ranald Slidell
Mackenzie / by Michael D. Pierce.
        p.   cm.
    Includes bibliographical references (p.   ) and index.
    ISBN 0-8061-2494-6 (alk. paper)
        1. Mackenzie, Ranald Slidell, 1840–1889. 2. Indians of North
America—Wars—1866–1895. 3. Generals—United States—
Biography. 4. United States. Army. Cavalry, 4th—History.
5. Mackenzie, Ranald Slidell, 1840–1889. I. Title.
E83.866.M33P54   1993
973.8′092—dc20
[B]   92-32281
                                                                      CIP

The paper in this book meets the guidelines for permanence and durability of the Committee on Production Guidelines for Book Longevity of the Council on Library Resources, Inc. ⊗

1   2   3   4   5   6   7   8   9   10

To my parents

CONTENTS

ILLUSTRATIONS

FIGURES

MAPS

PREFACE

THE idea for writing this book grew out of a series of conversations with my colleague Craig Clifford. At the time, Craig was putting together his collection of essays about Texas that was published as *In the Deep Heart's Core: Life, Letters, and Texas* (Texas A&M University Press, 1987). In our discussions about the process of making Texas, Ranald Mackenzie's name cropped up from time to time. I knew a little about Mackenzie, but I became curious to learn more. It was then that I found that no full biography of Mackenzie had been attempted and began to think of trying my hand at writing it. Craig put me in touch with his friend Myles O'Donovan, who had accumulated a large amount of material on Mackenzie along with the rest of the Indian fighting army. Myles generously loaned me this collection, and I was off and running.

I would not have gotten far, however, without a substantial amount of help and encouragement from friends and strangers. I was surprised and gratified at the willingness of people throughout the country to supply me with information, help me locate new sources, or simply wish me luck. The following acknowledgments are just a token of the debt I owe.

Byron Price, while director of the Panhandle-Plains Historical Museum, encouraged me to undertake the project and helped me locate materials. Since then Byron has moved to the National Cowboy Hall of Fame and Western Heritage Center, but he has read my manuscript and has made valuable comments. Byron also put me in touch with Mr. and Mrs. Ed Harrell, who graciously allowed me to visit their ranch and view the Palo Duro battlefield. My colleague in the English Department at Tarleton

State University, Tom Pilkington, has taken time from a busy schedule to read and comment on my work. Chris Guthrie, who is really a European historian, used his different perspective to write a detailed critique of the manuscript. I did not always agree with his suggestions, but he forced me to think carefully about what I had done. Sherry Smith of the University of Texas at El Paso generously shared her research and thoughts on Mackenzie's depression with me.

Marie Capps and her successors at the U.S. Military Academy Archives were most helpful in steering me to relevant materials. Mary Elizabeth Sergent, whom I met at West Point, made several helpful suggestions and encouraged me to keep working. Roberta Y. Arminio, director of the Ossining Historical Society, went far beyond my expectations in locating materials to help in my understanding of Mackenzie's boyhood. The same is true for Ruth Neuendorffer at the Historical Society of the Tarrytowns. Susan Gulick and the staff at the Joint Free Public Library of Morristown and Morris Township made it easy for me to locate sources there. Richard J. Sommers, archivist-historian at the U.S. Army Military History Institute, took an active interest in finding relevant documents. Arline Denosey of the Morris County Clerk's Office supplied important information about the Mackenzie household. Sharon Brand, librarian of the Williamsiana Collection at Williams College, answered several inquiries and allowed me to roam the library at will when I visited.

Richard A. Thompson was generous in supplying me with copies of material to which I did not have easy access. Katherine Skinner-Klee unearthed the records of Mackenzie's land holdings as well as copies of the Mackenzies' wills filed for probate in Kendall County. Kate also arranged a tour, guided by Bille Busby, of the 7-11 Ranch, which incorporates much of the land once owned by Mackenzie. Wanda Hoffman introduced me to the alternate version of Mackenzie's romance. Paul A. Hutton answered an inquiry about research possibilities. Stanley Graham answered some of my questions regarding discipline in the frontier army. Jim Clark of Annapolis, Maryland, found a useful source for me and fed me crab and chicken when I visited. Robert A. Calvert and John Lenihan of Texas A&M University gave me useful advice and boosted my morale at a crucial time.

The staff of the Southwest Collection at Texas Tech University was very helpful. The same held true for the staffs at the Library of Congress and the National Archives. The librarians at the Dick Smith Library of Tarleton State University, especially Glenda Stone and Jane Dickson, who handle interlibrary loans, rendered important aid. The staffs of the following institutions supplied requested materials in a prompt and friendly manner: Stanford University Libraries, Staten Island Institute of Arts and Sciences, the Thomas Gilcrease Museum, the Texas General Land Office, and the Hagley Museum and Library.

Rosiene Robertson, ably aided by Barbara Thurman, Tracey Hoadley, and Konay Bradshaw, was invaluable in preparing the manuscript for publication. Grants from the Organized Research Committee of Tarleton State University helped make travel possible and provided release time.

It is customary at this point to absolve all of those named above of any guilt associated with errors of fact or interpretation, and I do so in the strongest terms.

My wife, Aleta, and my two children, Martha and Bill, didn't much care about Ranald Mackenzie one way or the other, but they continued to love and support me anyway.

MICHAEL D. PIERCE

Stephenville, Texas

THE MOST PROMISING YOUNG OFFICER

INTRODUCTION

THE scene has been replayed countless times in books and movies and on television. The wagon train, isolated ranch house, or small army patrol is surrounded by hundreds of painted Indians yelling fearsome war whoops and circling closer and closer. Just as the end seems inevitable for the emigrants, ranch family, or patrol, a sound is heard in the distance. A bugle! It is the cavalry come to the rescue just in the nick of time. The image of the horse soldiers protecting the advancing frontier is an indelible part of American folklore. Given the familiarity of this picture, it is especially ironic that the average person, if asked to name one leader of the army that waged war against the Plains Indians, can only come up with the name of George Armstrong Custer. Bolstered by an active publicity machine, as well as having suffered the most spectacular, if not the worst, defeat of the army at the hands of Indians, Custer remains well known today.

Custer is virtually the only high ranking officer to be portrayed in books or films. Typically, the hero of the cavalry story is a junior officer—often a maverick who goes against the book—or a civilian scout. Senior officers are presented as stodgy, rigid, unimaginative, and ineffective old men. The most successful of the leaders of the army in the West, Nelson A. Miles, George Crook, and Ranald Slidell Mackenzie, have rarely, if ever, appeared as characters in popular depictions of the Indian wars.

Officers such as these were well known in the nineteenth century but are little heard of today. One reason for their faded reputation is that the army as an institution does not fit easily into the myth of western settlement. Popular imagery depicts the

tamers of the West as rugged individualists who braved the unknown seeking a better life. The heroes of the West are cowboys, ranchers, sodbusters, miners, sheriffs, gunfighters, and
lower ranking army officers. Custer, for example, escapes ano-
nymity by virtue of his colorful personality and flouting of regulations. Generally, however, the army, with its regimentation,
strict discipline, and bureaucracy, is not consistent with that picture. A faceless, nameless soldier taking orders from an equally
unknown officer fails to satisfy the demands of romanticism.

Modern opinion regarding the treatment of the Indians has
also colored the popular view of the army in the West. Once
pictured as savage barbarians capable of any atrocity, Indians
are today presented almost as innocents living in communion
with nature who became victims of the white man's greed and
lust for land. The army's role in confining the Indians to lives of
poverty and squalor on the reservations has played a part in
causing its leaders to be forgotten.

There is also a tendency among historians today to play down
the role of the army in the defeat of the Indians. Other factors
are cited to account for the Indians' demise. Causes most com-
monly mentioned are the slaughter of the buffalo, the extension
of modern technology, especially the railroads and telegraph,
and the sheer numbers of white people. By way of contrast, the
army is often presented as unimaginative and ineffective in dealing with the Indians. Officers who lived through the gore and
glory of the Civil War had trouble taking the Indian wars seriously and only rarely developed innovative approaches to deal
with a different kind of enemy.

Still, the army performed commendably, considering the problems that handicapped it. The determination of Congress to hold
down governmental expenses kept the army undermanned and
often underequipped. Divided counsels on the best way to deal
with the Indians also limited the army. Eastern reformers, convinced that the Indians could be "civilized" by peaceful means,
sometimes blocked the army's efforts to control the tribes. To
others, it seemed that the army could only move to suppress

hostilities after the Indians had initiated them and that reservations often served as sanctuaries where raiders could escape punishment.

In spite of the limitations on their freedom of action, some officers performed very well against the Indians. A few, such as Crook, advocated unconventional approaches to Indian warfare. Others were more conventional and achieved success through dogged effort.

Of the successful officers, Mackenzie was arguably the best, and he combined elements of the traditional and the nontraditional in his leadership. He had an outstanding Civil War career, rising to the rank of brevet major general of volunteers before he was twenty-five. In his sixteen years as a field commander in the West, he suffered only a few minor setbacks and no major defeats. He fought four large scale engagements against the Indians, inflicting large numbers of casualties as well as considerable property damage. Two of his victories were instrumental in bringing major Indian wars to a close. His understanding of, and sympathy for, peaceful Indians was important in keeping the Kiowa and Comanche Indians on their reservations once they surrendered. His forceful personality prevented a serious outbreak among the Utes when they were forced to move from Colorado to Utah.

Undoubtedly Mackenzie's career would have been even more illustrious had he not, at age forty-three, suffered mental breakdown, which forced him out of the army. His death six years later ended the life of a man who might well have finished a normal length career as commanding general of the army. Short as it was, Mackenzie's life deserves to be better known. His intelligence, determination, and willingness to act on his own reflect well on the American heritage of individualism as well as on the best traditions of the United States Army.

CHAPTER ONE

A BRIGHT LOOKING CHILD

RANALD Slidell Mackenzie was born June 27, 1840, the son of Alexander Slidell Mackenzie and Catherine Robinson Mackenzie. Alexander Mackenzie was the son of John Slidell, a successful businessman in New York City. Slidell made his fortune as a soap and tallow chandler, then branched out into other ventures as well as taking part in civic and church affairs. Life as a middle-class merchant did not appeal to Slidell's sons, however, and none of them followed him into the trade. The unpleasant aspects of the chandler's trade sent them in other directions.[1]

Slidell's oldest son, also named John, became an idle young man about town and was forced to leave New York after dueling a theater manager. Young John moved to Louisiana and, after marrying into an established Creole family, became active in politics, serving in Congress and later acting as a diplomat for the Confederacy. Another Slidell son, Tom, also moved to Louisiana and eventually became chief justice of the state supreme court.[2]

Alexander Slidell (he would adopt his mother's maiden name in 1837) was born in 1803. His way of rejecting his father's trade was to join the navy. In 1814 the marriage of his sister Jane to Matthew C. Perry brought the Slidells into intimate contact with the great war hero Oliver Hazard Perry. The latter appointed Alexander as a midshipman when the boy was not quite twelve years old. Besides a distaste for his father's trade, Alexander had an adventurous nature inspired by his mother's Mackenzie forebears.[3]

John Slidell married Margery Mackenzie, who as a child had immigrated from Scotland with her parents. The Mackenzies were of noble blood and supporters of the Jacobite uprising of the 1740s. When the Battle of Culloden ended the Stuart fantasy, the Mackenzies moved to America. There was a wild, romantic strain in Alexander that belongs more to the tradition of the Scottish Highlands than to the middle-class world of the Slidells. He was involved enough in his Scottish heritage that he visited the head of the clan while touring Great Britain. His addition of the Mackenzie name to his own was also motivated in part by an uncle's promise of a large legacy if he did so.[4]

Ranald Mackenzie absorbed pride in his Scottish ancestry from his father. Years later, when he was a well known army officer, he became furious at an attempt to honor him by decorating his coach with an Irish flag and spelling his name McKenzie. In the words of a witness to that incident, "It put him out of humor for half a day."[5]

Alexander Mackenzie was constantly on duty from 1815 to 1824. In the navy he was introduced to a world of danger, brutality, and boredom. Serving with both the Perrys, he learned the combination of harsh discipline and genuine concern that went into commanding a U.S. naval vessel. An attack of yellow fever almost killed him in 1824, and during the extended leave he took in order to recuperate, he toured Europe, ending with a stay in Spain.[6]

In Madrid, Mackenzie met Washington Irving, already famous as the foremost American author, and Henry Wadsworth Longfellow, who would soon be almost as well known. Mackenzie helped Irving deal with the technicalities of sailing while the latter was writing his biography of Christopher Columbus. In return, Irving encouraged Mackenzie's literary efforts and edited and found an English publisher for *A Year in Spain*, the novice's first book. Irving's enthusiastic support helped to make Mackenzie's book a popular success in both England and America.[7]

Mackenzie pursued writing as an avocation for the rest of his life. None of his later works were as successful as *A Year in*

Spain, but he did sustain a growing literary reputation. He engaged in public controversy with James Fenimore Cooper after the latter's attack on Mackenzie's *The Life of Commander Oliver Hazard Perry.* Longfellow remained a close friend and read the proofs of a biography of John Paul Jones for Mackenzie. Longfellow also did Mackenzie's literary reputation a service by advising against the publication of a fictional work called *Piña de los Enamorados,* which he thought not up to the standards of Mackenzie's nonfiction.[8]

Writing offered Mackenzie certain pleasures, not the least of which was entrée into America's highest literary circles. Nevertheless, he always considered the navy to be his real calling. He was especially concerned with upgrading the morals and character of the sailors and improving shipboard conditions. One of his ideas, developed in association with Matthew C. Perry, was for school ships to train young midshipmen in the ways of the navy while preventing their exposure to the crude lower class that comprised the crews.[9] Mackenzie's and Perry's efforts bore fruit when the *Somers* was commissioned as a training ship in 1842.

Mackenzie was an obvious choice to command the *Somers,* and on September 13, 1842, he took the ship on her first voyage. One of the crew was a troubled youth named Philip Spencer, son of Secretary of War John Spencer. Young Spencer began to incite crew members to take over the *Somers* and turn pirate. Upon learning of this mutinous talk, Mackenzie arrested Spencer and several of his coconspirators. The *Somers* had no brig, so Mackenzie decided that it was necessary to hang the leaders of the plot immediately to prevent its spread. After consulting with his officers, the captain had Spencer and two others swung from the yardarm.[10]

The events on the *Somers* created a furor when the ship returned to New York. A hasty court of inquiry, a sort of naval grand jury, decided no action needed to be taken, but Mackenzie asked for and obtained a full court martial in order to clear his name and forestall possible action in civilian courts.

The court martial's verdict of not guilty was less than satisfactory to Mackenzie because it was a negative judgment and not a positive affirmation of his action. Although "respectable" men expressed public approval of his deed, Mackenzie went into a kind of self-imposed exile at his Tarrytown, New York, farm, where he devoted himself to the life of a scholar, farmer, and family man.[11]

War with Mexico in 1846 brought Mackenzie back into active naval service. President James K. Polk selected him to act as agent in negotiating with former Mexican president Antonio López de Santa Anna for an early peace settlement. That mission over, Mackenzie returned to the United States eager for military action. Longfellow's wife was put off by Mackenzie's enthusiasm, noting that he "really seemed glad of this war as a proof that we have not lost the tiger and wolf nature."[12]

Commander Mackenzie saw active service for the rest of the war. He participated in the blockade of Mexico, was present at the surrender of Veracruz, and took part in the capture of Tabasco. He returned to Tarrytown in April 1848 with his health much deteriorated. One September day, young Ranald opened the gate for his father to go on one of his usual solitary horseback rides. It was his last ride. When the horse returned alone, a search was made, and Alexander Slidell Mackenzie was found dead of a heart attack at age forty-five.[13]

In 1835, Alexander Slidell Mackenzie married Catherine Robinson. Her father was Morris Robinson, a prominent New York banker. Such a marriage not only enhanced Mackenzie's social position (navy officers were not high in the social register) but also strengthened the warrior tradition in the Mackenzie heritage. Catherine was descended from William Alexander, Lord Sterling, the only American who served as a general in Washington's army who claimed noble descent.[14]

Catherine Mackenzie was a generous and open-hearted woman who impressed all who came into contact with her. Washington Irving described her as "noble hearted." The marriage was one that moved the romantic Mackenzie to poetic flights. In a letter to Longfellow, he described his marriage as one of "happiness, contentment, and enchantment." In April 1840 the couple moved to a farm overlooking the Hudson River between Tarrytown and Ossining, New York. The actual site was between the Hudson River and the Albany Post Road in the community of Mount Pleasant. They purchased about 150 acres of the old Beekman estate which contained "a small old farmhouse." When not at sea, Mackenzie pursued his literary interests there and played the role of gentleman farmer. The choice of location was easy for the Mackenzies. Washington Irving had already taken up residence at "Sunnyside" just to the south of Tarrytown, while Mackenzie's brother-in-law, Matthew C. Perry, had a large dwelling nearby, as did other friends. As a bonus, the farm was less than thirty miles from New York City, increasing the ease of reporting for duty.[15]

Ranald was the couple's first child. The choice of his given name suggests again the elder Mackenzie's involvement with his Scottish heritage; Ranalds were often associated with Mackenzies in the Highlands. Ranald was followed by four other children: Alexander, Junior, in 1841; Harriet and Mary; and Morris in 1847. The little evidence available shows that they enjoyed a strong and happy family life. When not at sea, Alexander Mackenzie followed his father's habit of reading aloud to his family in the evening. After a visit to the Mackenzies' farm, Irving was moved to comment that, if he were Mackenzie, he "would not have exchanged his lot for that of the richest man of my acquaintance."[16]

Ranald Slidell Mackenzie had a relatively normal childhood. Irving described him as a "bright looking child." At age three, according to reports, he suffered a "slight sunstroke" which left him rather frail for several years. A memorialist, using information from Mackenzie's family, said that as a result of this childhood experience, "any long confinement to the house was certain to bring on headache and depression." This last symptom sounds more like a young boy's longing to get outdoors and play than the result of an illness. At any rate, young Ranald seems to have recovered with no lasting ill effects.[17]

The Mackenzie farm was rather isolated, and Ranald had only his younger siblings as playfellows. Whether alone or in the company of others, Ranald engaged in the abundant outdoor activities available to a child in the Hudson Valley. With the river so near, Alexander Mackenzie instructed his sons in the rudiments of sailing; two of them would follow naval careers. Probably, too, Ranald was old enough to be taught riding by his father, although, according to later reports, he was not a particularly adept horseman. Fox hunting with hounds was a popular sport in the region. Young Ranald might not have been able to participate at that time, but in later life he would keep a pack of hounds to run game. Winter sports were available in abundance. Others who grew up in the region mention coasting, sledding, and ice skating as well as snowball fights by organized sides. These last presented Ranald with his first leadership opportunities.[18]

Ranald was sent to a local school, the Mount Pleasant Academy, in 1845 or 1846. There were several schools in the area, but the academy was chosen not only for its academic reputation but also because it included military training in its curriculum. It had been founded for the dual purpose of training boys for college and a life as active citizens and to prepare them "to contribute their share toward the defense of their country." It is clear that at this early date Alexander Slidell Mackenzie determined that his firstborn should have a military career.[19]

Ranald Mackenzie enthusiastically embraced the profession chosen for him by his father. In his biography for the records of Williams College he would list Mount Pleasant Academy as his college preparatory school in spite of the fact that he could not have attended it for more than three or four years and in fact received more of his early education at the Morris Academy in Morristown, New Jersey. This emphasis on his first school shows the importance that the military training had for Ranald.[20]

At Mount Pleasant, Ranald wore his first uniform, blue with silver buttons, and received his introduction to military discipline. Students were known by number, not by name, and excessive misconduct or poor academic performance might result in expulsion. Those students who were slow to adjust to the regimen were placed in the "awkward squad." At West Point, Ranald would earn large numbers of demerits, so it would be surprising if he had yielded completely to the discipline at his first academy. He did not display any promise of academic distinction, and his boyish exuberance was a major part of the reason why.[21]

Mackenzie's character at this early stage of life was not clearly formed. One of his biographers has written, "He was very shy and reserved, his speech slow and a little indistinct, his manner diffident and hesitating." His younger brother seemed to overshadow him. In contrast, another biographer claims that "he was noted for courage and character" and that he was quick to resort to fighting when he felt pushed. Perhaps the contradiction was in his attitude toward schoolwork as opposed to extracurricular activity. He may have been bored by the classroom but stimulated by the outdoors.[22]

Ranald was too young to have been aware of the notoriety of his father's actions on board the *Somers*, but he learned of it as he grew older. The lesson his father would have taught was unswerving devotion to duty and honor regardless of the cost. Certainly one of Ranald's distinguishing characteristics as an officer was his willingness to accept responsibility and act on his own without reference to higher authority. It was part of the heritage passed on by his father.

Alexander Mackenzie's literary ability was not inherited by his children. None of them would be a writer. Ranald later showed a reluctance even to write reports for his superiors. Still, according to later testimony, he acquired a taste for reading and managed even on active duty "to keep *au courant* with literature of the best class, of which he was an acute and discriminating critic." This, too, was part of the legacy left by his father and was a comfort to Ranald in his later career. It also helped him move in society and gain respect and affection for reasons other than his purely military achievements.[23]

There is no written record of Ranald's reaction to his father's death, but that loss must have been a severe blow. The death of Alexander, Junior, in 1867 struck Ranald with great force, and he undoubtedly had felt the loss of his father even more. As the oldest child, Ranald began to assume a protective relationship with his mother and his siblings. The whole family was drawn closer together. They were consoled by the admiration expressed for Alexander Slidell Mackenzie by those who joined in the mourning. Longfellow declared that "few remain so brave, so good, so gentle as he!"[24]

For a variety of reasons, Catherine Mackenzie decided to move to Morristown, New Jersey, following her husband's death. Mrs. Mackenzie loved her husband deeply, and she may have wanted to move to escape the strong emotions evoked by their pleasant farmhouse. Financial problems also influenced the decision to move. According to one report, Alexander Mackenzie had suffered sharp losses with the collapse of the Bank of the United States. The revenue from the sale of the 150-acre farm could certainly have helped to relieve any financial strain. Finally, there was the attraction of being closer to members of her family, some of whom had settled in Morristown. This move broadened Ranald's horizons and helped to prepare him for a wider world.[25]

CHAPTER TWO

ALL THAT IS GOOD AND NOBLE

IN 1848, Morristown, New Jersey, was a growing town of about two thousand people. The iron industry was the source of its early prosperity, but by the 1820s the foundries had declined in importance. Other small industries moved in to sustain the economy, and Morristown began to attract attention as a place to live to escape the pressures of living in New York City while still being near enough to retain close contact with the metropolis.[1]

When the Mackenzies moved to Morristown, the citizens were making a conscious effort to transform it from a small pioneer town that still had traces of the frontier about it to a genteel city of "culture and refinement." As if to illustrate the contrast, one issue of the local newspaper had a story about the opening of a fancy new hotel next to another about a dog that killed thirty-four rats in ten minutes in the stable of the same hotel. At the same time that Morristown was grappling with the problems associated with its growing population, it was possible to go a few miles out of town and regain the wilderness. A bear hunt could be staged within five miles of town.[2]

The move to Morristown brought Ranald out of the semi-isolation of Mount Pleasant and introduced him to a wider range of people and experiences. One lure of the town for Mrs. Mackenzie was the presence of William A. Duer, her uncle. Duer had retired as president of Columbia University in 1842 because of ill health and had moved to Morristown in search of a quieter life-style. After regaining his strength, he took an active role in civic affairs as well as maintaining his interest in judicial matters. Duer, like Alexander Slidell Mackenzie, was a friend of Washington Irving and other literary figures. He carried on Ranald's literary education and tried to influence him in the direction of law.[3]

Duer took part in religious affairs to the extent that he participated in a revolt against the local Episcopal church and helped to establish a new one. Other family members joined the move, and one of Ranald's brothers later served as a vestryman for the new church. None of this religous activity seems to have influenced Ranald, and there is no indication that he ever developed any strong concern about religion. The use of the Episcopal service at his mother's funeral seems to have been a matter of form.[4]

Catherine Mackenzie moved into a large house on the corner of Oak Street and Macculloch Avenue where she presided over a household of eleven assorted sons, daughters, sisters, nieces, and nephews and four Irish immigrant servants. In spite of the large number of dependents, Catherine Mackenzie prospered. The census of 1860 gave her occupation as "lady" and listed her total wealth as twenty thousand dollars. In a few years the Rodgers family moved in next door, expanding an already large extended family. The Perry family often visited Morristown, adding to Ranald's sense of belonging to the town. The presence of a large family created the kind of milieu in which Ranald functioned best. A visitor in the early days of the Civil War described each member of the household and declared that it was "the happiest family that I ever saw."[5]

There is no record to indicate that young Mackenzie's leadership ability began to emerge at this time, but he did leave a long lasting impression. When the youngest Mackenzie brother, Morris, retired to Morristown in 1915, a newspaper article stated that he would be remembered as "one of the Mackenzie boys, as they were called." The "Mackenzie boys" joined others in the neighborhood in the typical escapades of youth. Quite likely they played at war. Once the Civil War had begun, and with

Ranald already in the Military Academy, the younger playmates he left behind formed their own mock unit of zouaves. Before the war was over, most of them would experience the real thing.[6]

Morristown was something of an educational center. With a population of 2,306, the town supported seven schools and two libraries. The best of the schools was the Morris Academy, which Ranald attended until he left for Williams College at the age of fifteen. Tuition was cheap enough, five dollars a quarter, that Mrs. Mackenzie probably sent all three of her sons to the school. The academy offered a wide variety of courses intended to ensure a good background for the student going on to college. Among the courses offered were English grammar, geography, history, algebra, geometry, trigonometry, Latin, Greek, modern languages, a variety of sciences, music, drawing, and painting. If the instructors were at all competent, a graduate of Morris Academy would have no trouble with college.[7]

Ranald Mackenzie was not an exceptional student at the academy. His performance was such that many who did not know him well doubted his ability to do well in higher education. The family clergyman, conditioned by Ranald's work at the school, later expressed something like shock to learn of the youth's high standing at West Point. He admitted to Mrs. Mackenzie that he had predicted failure for Ranald.[8]

The primary problem was that school failed to fully engage Mackenzie's attention. Like most other schoolboys, Ranald found more attraction in games with his fellows and roaming the woods and fields that surrounded Morristown than parsing sentences or solving equations. Some, however, were not deceived. Acute observers could see an intensity beneath Ranald's casual demeanor that indicated great ability. Ranald's family, of course, expected him to succeed, and one of his teachers, noting the determination just below the surface, wrote that "he will always be equal to what is required of him."[9]

At age fifteen, Ranald enrolled in Williams College in Williamstown, Massachusetts. Ranald's uncles, unaware of his resolve to pursue a military career, or thinking it not a good choice, encouraged him to attend Williams to prepare for the study of law. William A. Duer and Ranald's Slidell uncles were lawyers, and they tried to steer him in a direction familiar to them. William Johnson Slidell, a cousin who later became a capable lawyer, was already attending the college, a circumstance which helps to explain Ranald's choice of schools. Williams's good reputation was also an attraction. Ranald was too young for West Point, so he went to Williams willingly, but with the reservation in his mind that he would transfer when the time came. [10]

Williams College was founded as an independent liberal arts college in 1793. In the 1850s it was a small school with about sixty students in each class. Many of the buildings dated to the American Revolution. The campus was designed to promote tranquillity and dedication to studies. A description from the 1880s pictures wide expanses of green lawns with the sidewalks shaded by "a profusion of old elms and maples." Dormitories provided housing for the exclusively male student body. [11]

Williams was headed by Mark Hopkins, who not only served as president but also taught "moral and intellectual philosophy." Hopkins had some reputation as a philosopher and educator. He was also an ordained Congregational minister who preached often, served on the Board of Commissioners for Foreign Missions, and attempted to encourage independent thought in his students while establishing a firm theological foundation. The other faculty were not so well known as Hopkins, but they shared his basic values. At least one teacher during this period, and usually two or three, besides Hopkins prefaced his name with the title Reverend. In the 1840s, new students were required to take an oath to obey the rules of the college and, in particular, "avoid the use of profane language, gaming and all disorderly behavior." The oath appears to have been abandoned by the time Mackenzie entered Williams, but attendance at chapel continued to be required on a daily basis. [12]

There is some evidence that neither Williams's reputation for intellectual quality nor its piety was fully deserved. The four-year course of study, which seems demanding on the surface, included Greek, Latin, mathematics, history, science, political economy, philosophy, and theology. One student, Washington Gladden, who would become famous for his role in the development of the concept of the social gospel, recorded that the entrance examinations "were not formidable." Gladden also stated that the level of instruction was not particularly high. Another student complained that he was hindered in his studies by the majority of the students, who had no respect for the serious students or the faculty. [13]

The oath of good conduct and required chapel tell of an enforced piety of a traditional nature. Deviation from the somewhat staid Congregationalism of New England prompted harassment from the student body. James A. Garfield, the future president, was a Campbellite and as such was subjected to much unfriendly criticism until he proved his abilities by determined effort. [14]

The presence of Greek-letter fraternities at Williams also challenged traditional standards of piety as well as diverting attention from scholarly pursuits. The first of these organizations appeared in 1833, and by 1860 seven more had been added. The fraternities attracted about 50 percent of the students during the 1850s, and their existence generated some controversy. An article in the student quarterly in 1855 described fraternity men as drunks and wastrels. The anonymous author went on to say "their estimate of character is founded upon a peculiar bias. How much can he drink? Has he got the rocks? Does he smoke and chew? Can he brag of his intimacy with those who disgrace the sex of she who bore him?" In that year two of the Greek-letter fraternities challenged the Social Fraternity, which had been formed to offer an alternative social organization, to a debate on the merits of the Greeks. When the antifraternity group selected Garfield, who had developed into a formidable debater, to represent them, the Greeks withdrew the challenge. Bickering between pro- and antifraternity groups continued into the 1860s. [15]

Two facets of Ranald Mackenzie's personality began to come into focus at Williams. Gladden described him as "very quiet, modest to shyness, and with a little lisp." This basic shyness, perhaps intensified by a feeling of being overshadowed by the "great brilliance of his younger brother," helps to explain Mackenzie's later stern, forbidding manner that drew comment from even the most admiring junior officers.[16] Mackenzie's natural reserve was reinforced by the training he received at West Point and made him seem unapproachable to many of the lower ranks.

On the other hand, Gladden continued his remarks by saying that Mackenzie was very likable and popular. Mackenzie joined the Kappa Alpha Society and took full part in its more robust activities. On at least one occasion he was fined for harassing a freshman. There is no evidence that Mackenzie drank, but it seems likely that he did indulge to some extent. He certainly smoked, as this would be an offense which would cost him many demerits at West Point. The record is silent about any sexual escapades, but that proves little. Proper people in nineteenth-century America did not talk of such things unless they became a public scandal. Given Ranald's shyness, sexual adventures seem unlikely, yet some scholars link his later mental problems with syphilis, so it is possible that he was not as innocent as he seemed. Whatever the extent of his involvement in collegiate adventures, it is clear that Ranald could overcome his shyness in the company of those with whom he felt comfortable. Later, when many saw him as cool and aloof, his letters would show him to be open and sociable with his equals.[17]

There were no organized athletics at Williams, although a variety of activities was available. Gladden mentions kicking "a football rather aimlessly about" and also occasional baseball games. Mackenzie was most likely attracted to the sports he had grown up with, which were individual pursuits instead of team activities. He climbed Greylock, the most popular target for student mountain climbers, and roamed the wooded hills nearby. The winter sports he had known along the Hudson were available, too, at Williams. There are no indications that he participated in other extracurricular activities, but it is not hard to imagine him participating in "chip day," the last Monday of the term, which was always reserved for a schoolwide effort to beautify the campus. Nothing in his later life, however, suggests that he might have been willing to participate in dramatics or the glee club, and it seems unlikely that he did.[18]

Mackenzie did not join either of the two rival literary societies at Williams, although he was a good scholar. No official records remain to give his class standing, but unofficial sources indicate that he did well, if not brilliantly. The Williams alumni obituary record stated that he "took good rank in his class." Gladden remembered that Mackenzie was "a good scholar," although he admits that no one at Williams fully recognized his ability. Mackenzie was competent enough as a scholar to be one of those selected to present a paper at the Junior Exhibition, but he did not deliver the paper because of the death of his uncle, William A. Duer. Mackenzie did not graduate from Williams, because he dropped out to accept an appointment to the U.S. Military Academy at West Point. After he began to attract notice in the Civil War, Williams restored Mackenzie to the class roll and granted him the A.B. degree. Still later, in 1873, the college awarded him an honorary A.M. degree.[19]

It was significant that Mackenzie's Junior Exhibition paper was to have been on military tactics, a subject somewhat removed from the usual concerns at Williams. By that time Mackenzie had already begun the process of applying for an appointment to West Point. His uncles may have thought he was preparing for the law, but Ranald was determined on an army career, and he had begun to prepare for it even before he secured admission to the Military Academy. Dorst, writing in the 1880s, stated that Mackenzie decided to try for an appointment in order to ease the financial burden on his mother. Expense was possibly a minor factor, although Mrs. Mackenzie was not poor, but he would have chosen the academy in any case. Dorst's claim that Mackenzie made the decision to leave Williams on his own without consulting anyone does, however, ring true. Throughout his career he would show a tendency to make his decisions without consultation.[20]

In 1843, Congress had passed a law authorizing the nomination of a cadet from each congressional district as well as establishing ten at-large positions. The tradition quickly arose of appointing the sons of military officers to fill the at-large vacancies. In the absence of competitive examinations, social, political, and business connections were important influences on the selection process. Mrs. Mackenzie initiated the application process by writing to the secretary of war in January 1858. She was rather reluctant to do so but complied with her son's wish because she wanted him to follow the career of his choice. Ranald also enlisted the support of his uncle John Slidell, now a senator from Louisiana. Along with the formal application, Slidell wrote a separate note to John B. Floyd, the secretary of war, in which he stressed that "it was one of the last requests" of Alexander Slidell Mackenzie that his son secure an appointment to West Point. Slidell recruited the support of Congressman John Appleton, who wrote directly to President James Buchanan in favor of the application. Mackenzie signed a formal acceptance of his appointment on March 18, 1858.[21]

In an effort to fully prepare her boy for the move to West Point, Mrs. Mackenzie wrote to her friend Sophie, the wife of Admiral Samuel duPont, whose nephew, Henry, was already a cadet. Mackenzie left Williams College before the term was over in order to have a few months to prepare before reporting to the academy in June. There was no real need for this preparation according to Henry duPont, who reported that the entrance examinations were "not very redoubtable" and that anyone with Mackenzie's training could prepare for them in only a few hours. DuPont offered practical advice on extra clothing and warned that to report early would only expose the new cadet to "a pretty disagreeable fortnight" while serving no good purpose. "He has got to make up his mind," continued duPont, "to meet with a great many unpleasant things at first, which however will in a great measure cease after the first month or six weeks."[22]

Hazing at West Point appears to have been of a rather mild variety, hardly differing from that at Williams College. Mackenzie was exposed to such things as being dragged out of bed in the middle of the night or having the ropes of his tent cut. One cadet, writing in 1860, described efforts to take the gun of a plebe on guard duty by creating the "Great Hyankydank": two cadets—one on another's shoulders—draped with a sheet. Mackenize took such harassment with good humor, and Henry duPont reported to his aunt that young Mackenzie was "getting on very well." Judging by his record at Williams, Ranald did some hazing of his own once his plebe year was over.[23]

West Point accepted the task of character building and moral guidance adopted by most colleges during the period and, perhaps, took its obligation more seriously than most. The schedule was designed to minimize opportunities for the cadets to get into trouble by keeping them busy most of the day. Reveille was at 5:00 A.M. in the summer, and the officers-to-be were kept at drill in various arms, on parade, and policing the grounds and barracks for most of the day until supper at 8:00 P.M. In winter the cadets were granted an extra half-hour's sleep, but the schedule was as crowded as in the summer. Taps sounded at 9:30 in all seasons.[24]

Much of the daily routine was occupied by classes or study periods, and for many students the competition for class standing was one of the most exciting aspects of West Point life. Ranald Mackenzie entered into this competition with zest. At the end of his first year, he stood fifth in a class of fifty-six. He climbed to second the next year, ranking number two in mathematics and English and seventh in French. He then slipped to twelfth in his third year, taking a high standing only in philosophy and falling to twenty-first in drawing. This drop in academic effort may have been a result of the excitement generated by the secession of the southern states and the onset of the Civil War. Mackenzie was in Company D, which contained many Southerners, and even though he did not become involved in any of the arguments about the war, relations between Northern and Southern cadets were severely strained.[25]

Once the initial excitement that accompanied the beginning

of the war and the resignation of most of the Southern cadets had diminished, Mackenzie applied himself to his studies with new dedication. Mackenzie's class, which was to have taken a five-year course, was graduated in four years because of the demands of war. This acceleration required compression of the course content and increased the number of courses to be taken in the final year, which imposed a heavy academic burden. The pressure on Mackenzie was increased when he was designated an acting assistant professor of mathematics. Mackenzie's ability to concentrate his energies became evident when he graduated number one in his class. He stood first in engineering and ordnance, with his lowest ranking being number nine in chemistry.[26]

Mackenzie's academic record was all the more remarkable because of the large number of demerits he received throughout his cadet years. Those who served with Mackenzie in the Civil War and the campaigns against the Indians would have been astounded to see his disciplinary record at West Point. Mackenzie became known as a strict, sometimes harsh disciplinarian, but he gave little indication of deep-rooted concern with rules and regulations while at the academy. Instead, he showed a marked disregard of the fine points of military conduct. A plebe of 1860 complained in a letter home that the cadets were "a swearing, immoral, boisterous set, very vulgar in their language and excessively given to a petty teasing habit." Mackenzie fit the description exactly. In his first year he compiled 110 demerits. The number climbed to 154 in his second year and 185 in the third (the year disrupted by the beginning of the Civil War, when he fell to number twelve in class standing) and finished with 122 in his final year. He was never the worst but was always far from the best in terms of "proper" cadet decorum.[27]

Young Mackenzie's offenses were never serious, but they were constant. A sampling of his offenses shows something approaching disdain for higher authority. Typical of his misdemeanors were talking on parade, absence from parade (many violations), "not carrying piece properly at parade after being repeatedly spoken to about same," having his stock out of place, many cases of being late, talking on guard, smoking on guard, "laughing in ranks," having another cadet answer for him at roll call, "trifling conduct," "using profane language," and many cases of talking and visiting at improper times. Ranald would have attained high cadet rank except for his conduct. He did, in fact, earn promotion to lieutenant in the summer of 1861 but was reduced to private almost immediately.[28]

Mackenzie's good nature and love of fun and sports countered to an extent his intense dedication to his studies and his career. He took advantage of the available diversions with gusto. The end of each summer camp created one such opportunity. The cadets armed themselves with clubs and, when the wooden floors of the tents were raised, attacked with vigor the hundreds of rats that had sought refuge beneath. This activity generated, wrote one cadet, "such a yelling, chasing and slaughter of rats it was never my fortune to behold heretofore." Another, unplanned, episode also offered opportunity for excitement. In February 1861, Cozzen's Hotel, which adjoined the academy, burned, and the cadets were called out to help extinguish the blaze. Many of the cadets took advantage of the confusion to sample Cozzen's supply of wine, some to the extent that they were overcome and placed under arrest for drunkenness. Whether or not he helped to reduce Cozzen's liquor supplies, Mackenzie enjoyed the break from routine. In the context of the unmilitary side of his personality, the nickname given him by his fellow cadets, "Mack," was more than a convenience. It was a mark of genuine affection.[29]

West Point absorbed Ranald Mackenzie into army life and created a sense of belonging in him that ended any lingering doubt about his career. Every phase of life at the academy had its counterpart in the regular service, and Mackenzie thrived on it even if he did not enjoy it. Whatever the demands of the Point or of his career later, he met them without complaint and, usually, with enthusiasm. With the other plebes he spent his first summer sleeping on the wooden floor of his tent; with all the cadets he subsisted on the dull, barely nourishing food served by Cozzen's (any help given by the cadets at the February fire must have been halfhearted at best); with the others he underwent the rigors of the drill field, the riding and fencing schools; and through it all he was creating those bonds of friendship that helped the young officers sustain themselves throughout their careers.[30] The army became Mackenzie's second family, the close support group that enabled him to overcome his shyness and reach the full potential of his talents.

The family feeling that Mackenzie experienced at the academy was enhanced by fairly frequent visits from his mother and sister. Accustomed to a large family circle, Mrs. Mackenzie had no trouble enlarging it to take in many of her son's classmates. Those who later saw him only from a distance could not appreciate the warmth and humor that Ranald could display when he was with those to whom felt close. His class photograph shows a slender, solemn-faced young man with a slightly down turned mouth and serious eyes. This was his public expression, the one presented to awestruck young second lieutenants. Those who knew him, however, remembered his "sweet smile" and that he was "all that is good and noble."[31]

Mackenzie's character as a child was considered to be remarkable. He did not lie or make excuses. He was brave and loyal. These traits stayed with him, and by the time he graduated from West Point they were fused to a personality that attracted love from friends and admiration even from rivals. He loved sports and the society of those he knew well. He was not easily angered except by an insult to his honor or the failure of others to fulfill their duty. In spite of impressions to the contrary, these traits, even the sociable nature and good humor, remained with him until his mental disorder overcame him. In the 1870s the frequent pain from old wounds and arthritis, as well as his initial reserve with strangers and junior officers, sometimes hid his more attractive qualities. They stayed with him, however, and often emerged at unusual times. Even his rival for a brigadier's star, the self-promoting and not very likable Nelson A. Miles, was quick to come to his defense when Mackenzie was slurred by an Oregon newspaper at the time of his breakdown.[32]

Ranald Slidell Mackenzie as a firstclassman at West Point. His solemn features give no hint of the sporting "Mack" who almost led his class in demerits as well as in academics. *(Courtesy Archives, U.S. Military Academy)*

Mackenzie and a group of classmates just before leaving West Point to take up their active duty stations in 1862. Mackenzie is seated second from the left. *(Courtesy United States Army Military History Institute)*

When Ranald Mackenzie graduated from West Point in 1862, he was partially realizing a boyhood ambition. Now he was prepared to carry it to completion, to earn high rank in his chosen profession. The Civil War then tearing the country apart offered him the opportunity to show his ability. The intensity and drive masked by his odd mixture of shyness and sociability gained him rapid promotion and recognition. In the crucible of war he found challenge and exhilaration that brought out the best in him.

CHAPTER THREE

THE MOST PROMISING
YOUNG OFFICER

TOP-ranking graduating cadets at West Point were traditionally given commissions in the Corps of Engineers. This was the case with Ranald Slidell Mackenzie. The young second lieutenant was assigned first to Major General Ambrose Burnside's staff and then, in a few weeks, to the staff of Brigadier General Jesse L. Reno as assistant engineer of the Ninth Corps. The Corps of Engineers were considered to be the elite of the peacetime army. Service with them offered escape from the dull life of the typical army post and the chance for adventure in exploring the West or assignment to the East Coast working on coastal defenses. Lucrative civilian jobs were often available to army-trained engineers. For most officers, service with the engineers in wartime meant laboring in obscurity on important but little recognized tasks. Because of his drive and ability, plus a good helping of luck, Mackenzie would use his assignment as a path to fame and success.

Mackenzie received his first combat experience as a member of Reno's staff at the Battle of Second Manassas. On the afternoon of August 29, 1862, while Reno's corps was joining the assault on Stonewall Jackson's position along an unfinished railroad cut, the newly commissioned lieutenant was called upon for courier duty. When he stopped to ask directions of another soldier, Mackenzie was struck by a rebel bullet. Apparently he had presented a profile to the enemy, as the projectile "entered at the right shoulder, passing over the shoulder blade and spine without breaking the skin, and grazing the left shoulder blade as it went out making a serious and painful but not dangerous wound." Two of Mackenzie's assailants approached him with the intent of robbing the corpse. Still conscious, he asked for water. The rebels claimed to have none and took his pistol and money, leaving his watch. After lying without shelter all night, Mackenzie was found the next morning and sent to a hospital in Washington. There his brother found him and notified their mother. As she would do many times in the next three years, Catherine Mackenzie came to care for her wounded son. Mackenzie's first words to his mother were, "I am wounded in the back, but I was not running away."[1]

Fear of being thought a coward was not unusual in this war. Men forced to retreat would sometimes walk backward to avoid the possibility of a wound in the back which might, in the eyes of some, brand them as cowards. Mackenzie's concern was not, therefore, unusual. Still, that he was so quick to deny the possible conclusion speaks strongly of his concern for honor. For his service at Second Manassas, Mackenzie was awarded his first promotion by brevet for "gallant and meritorious services."[2]

Mackenzie returned to Morristown with his mother to convalesce and luckily missed the bloody carnage of the Sharpsburg campaign, in which General Reno was mortally wounded. Mackenzie recovered rapidly and reported for duty on October 19, 1862. He served with the U.S. Engineer Battalion for a few weeks; then he was posted as assistant to the chief engineer of the Right Grand Division when General Burnside reorganized the Army of the Potomac.[3]

As the army moved toward the fatal engagement at Fredericksburg, Lieutenant Mackenzie was kept busy at engineering duties. Chief Engineer Cyrus Comstock selected him to scout fords across the Rappahannock River and to decide where the support artillery should be posted to cover a crossing. Mackenzie was one of the supervising officers on December 14, 1862, when attempts were made to lay a pontoon bridge to allow the Federal troops to march through Fredericksburg. Enemy sniper fire prevented the completion of the task until infantry had crossed in boats and routed the enemy. Mackenzie seems to have played no other role at this battle, but his prompt obedience to orders and coolness under fire earned him a mention, along with others, in Brigadier General Edwin V. Sumner's official report of the battle.[4]

Mackenzie neglected to inform his mother that he had survived the Battle of Fredericksburg unscathed. She wrote Tully McCrea in January, telling him that she was ready to come nurse him or her son if they had been wounded. Mackenzie's failure to keep his mother posted is a bit surprising, given the attachment he seemed to have had to her. Joseph Dorst wrote that Mackenzie's love and respect for his mother caught everyone's attention. Yet, even later, when he had had time to mature, he would still be guilty of failure to write regularly. Mrs. Mackenzie at least once complained to his superior officer about the dearth of mail from her son. One reason for the lack of communication with his mother was that Mackenzie simply did not have the inclination to write. His superiors in later years would also press him to report more often and in more detail, but his correspondence was sporadic throughout his career.[5]

In later years, Mackenzie would become well known for his opinion that junior officers should not marry. His early reluctance to maintain contact with his mother was in keeping with that feeling. Family attachments imposed hardships and distracted from duty. It was better, in Mackenzie's view, to rigidly separate military duty from the charms of family life—at least in the formative stages on one's career.[6]

Major General Joseph Hooker reorganized Burnside's dispirited army shortly after the Battle of Fredericksburg, and Ranald Mackenzie was assigned to the headquarters of the Army of the Potomac. He spent the next several months working on fortifications along Aquia Creek and, later, Potomac Creek. This was the standard duty expected of the Corps of Engineers—the kind Mackenzie complained of until he received a combat command.[7]

By May, Mackenzie was serving as an aide to Major General Gouverneur K. Warren, who was for a while chief engineer of the Army of the Potomac. It was in this capacity that Mackenzie received his second brevet, to captain, for service at the Battle of Chancellorsville. There is no exact record of what the young engineer did to earn his promotion. He may have been the aide sent by Warren to warn Major General Daniel Sickles of the collapse of the Eleventh Corps on the Union right on May 1. Such a ride, under fire, might have earned the honor, but his service record merely states that he was promoted for gallantry.[8]

Brevet Captain Mackenzie played a more noticeable part in the Battle of Gettysburg. After the Union and Confederate armies accidentally bumped into one another near the small Pennsylvania town, Major General George Gordon Meade sent Warren to evaluate the situation. Mackenzie accompanied Warren as an aide. Meade based his decision to fight at Gettysburg, rather than his fall-back position on Pipe Creek, partly on the findings of the engineers.

Warren and Mackenzie had a more important role to play on the following day, July 2, 1863. Meade had posted the Third Corps under General Sickles on the Union left. Sickles had, without orders, moved his troops forward to prevent the Confederates from occupying ground that would give the rebel artillery significant advantage. This move uncovered the Union left flank and made it susceptible to destruction should the Southerners become aware of the blunder. Uneasy about Sickles's new troop dispositions, Meade sent Warren with Mackenzie and Lieutenant Washington A. Roebling to survey the situation. When Warren discovered that Little Round Top, the hill which was the key to the entire Union position, was unoccupied by Federal troops and about to be taken by the Confederates, he acted immediately by sending Mackenzie to Sickles to request a brigade to secure Little Round Top. Sickles, already pressed to the limit, had no troops to spare. Mackenzie then rode to Major General George Sykes, who commanded the Fifth Corps. Sykes responded by sending Mackenzie to lead the brigade of Brigadier General James Barnes to the hill. Unable to locate Barnes, Mackenzie gave the order to Colonel Strong

Vincent, whose brigade thus became the vital plug to stop the Confederate flood on the Union left. Mackenzie was slightly wounded and received his third brevet for bravery under fire.[9]

Mackenzie's gallantry did more than earn him a wound and a citation. His conduct cemented the good opinion of General Warren. Warren had taught Mackenzie mathematics at West Point, a circumstance that explains why the lieutenant was on his staff. Warren was so impressed by the young officer's coolness under fire that he would support Mackenzie for a combat command in 1864.[10]

Mackenzie was active in the pursuit of Lee's retreating army after the Battle of Gettysburg, serving as a scout for Major General John Sedgewick in an attempt to locate the defeated enemy. On July 31, 1863, Mackenzie supervised the construction of a bridge across the Rappahannock against light opposition, and later he spent more time building and improving roads. During the winter and on into the spring of 1864, when the Army of the Potomac began its southward move to open the Wilderness Campaign, he served as a scout.[11]

For all of his work and scouting activity, Mackenzie still had time to relax and savor the company of his friends. One advantage of the Corps of Engineers was that they were semi-independent and had more opportunities to make their lives more comfortable than did those in the combat arms. Tully McCrea, Mackenzie's good friend at West Point, had the chance to visit several times and on each occasion came away envious of the good life he saw. McCrea noted that on Thanksgiving the engineers ate turkey and drank fresh milk from the cow they led with them. Shortly after Fredericksburg, McCrea joined Mackenzie and others for "playing cards, smoking, talking & etc." After a visit in August 1863, Mackenzie's friend complained that the engineers always got the best of everything.[12]

Mackenzie was zealous in his duties as an officer of the Corps of Engineers. His quick obedience and ability to act on his own won him the good opinion of his superiors. Like many other young officers, however, he was not content with what was essentially a noncombat position. He had an insistent craving for command and glory. This yearning for fame was generally suppressed and never took the form of blatant self-promotion, as was the case with some of his contemporaries such as George Armstrong Custer and Nelson A. Miles. His ambition was nevertheless a driving force, and he knew it could not be fulfilled as an engineer. In letters home, Mackenzie complained "of pontoons as a 'bore' and a pontoon train as his 'pet aversion.'" The spring offensive of the Army of the Potomac offered him the opportunity to demonstrate his abilities and make contacts that moved him toward achieving his ambition. [13]

As the army moved south in early May 1864, Mackenzie and Lieutenant Charles W. Howell were assigned to a cavalry column as scouts to map the point of advance. Mackenzie was attached to Brigadier General David M. Gregg's cavalry division and took part in fighting around Todd's Tavern. When the Engineer Battalion was assigned to act as infantry in conjunction with General Warren's Fifth Corps, Mackenzie rejoined his company. He, along with the rest of the battalion, engaged in constructing defensive works while under fire from the enemy. The next day, when the Confederates attacked the Fifth and Sixth Corps, the battalion was "under fire but not engaged." [14]

Mackenzie was sent for duty with headquarters on May 7, after the battalion was relieved of its infantry duties. On May 10, he was detailed to scout for weaknesses in the enemy's lines near Spotsylvania Court House. He helped Brigadier General David Russell select the point of attack for Colonel Emory Upton's famous effort to break through Confederate lines at the Bloody Angle. Upton's attack was unsuccessful, but the attempt so pleased Lieutenant General U. S. Grant that Upton was promoted to brigadier general on the spot. This honor was portentous for Mackenzie, because it brought him to Upton's attention. The two young officers had been at West Point at the same time, Upton a year ahead of Mackenzie. They had known each other only slightly then, but the Spotsylvania episode was the beginning of a close relationship. In less than a month, Upton would have the chance to recommend Mackenzie for a combat command.[15]

For the rest of the month of May, Mackenzie continued to serve as an engineer officer engaged in the same variety of activities as before. His main duties were scouting enemy positions and guiding Union troops. The Volunteer Engineer Battalion, which often worked in conjunction with the regulars, engaged almost constantly in building bridges and tearing them down (in order to use the materials again), and it is likely that Mackenzie supervised some of this activity.[16]

On June 3, 1864, General Grant ordered the attack that created an opening as combat commander for Mackenzie. One of the regiments in the attack that Grant sent against Confederate lines at Cold Harbor was the Second Connecticut Heavy Artillery, a volunteer regiment that had been raised in the summer of 1862. Originally intended to be used as infantry, the unit was designated as heavy artillery in November 1863. It never trained in that capacity, however, and it still served as infantry in the spring of 1864. The Second Connecticut was commanded by Colonel Elisha S. Kellogg, who was somewhat unusual for a volunteer officer commanding volunteers in that he maintained strict discipline and was ready to administer summary punishments in the harsh fashion of the regular army. In spite of his strict rule, Kellogg was popular with his troops. In the middle of the fighting at Cold Harbor, the regiment suffered 335 casualties, including Colonel Kellogg, who was killed leading the charge against the Confederate entrenchments.[17]

After hearing of Colonel Kellogg's death, the governor of Connecticut sent a colonel's commission to the regiment's second-in-command, Lieutenant Colonel James Hubbard. Hubbard refused to take the responsibility, saying that he "was *worn out*" and that he would not order men "into the jaws of hell." The Second Connecticut Heavy Artillery was part of the Second Brigade of the First Division of the Sixth Corps. The brigade commander was newly promoted Brigadier General Emory Upton, who reacted to Hubbard's refusal to assume command by recommending to the regimental officers that they request that a regular army officer be assigned to take over. Ranald Mackenzie was Upton's choice. After some debate, and urged on by Hubbard, the officers united to petition the governor to appoint Mackenzie to the vacant position. The petition was favorably endorsed by Upton, Corps Commander Horatio Wright, Commander of the Army of the Potomac George G. Meade, and Ulysses S. Grant, commanding general of all the Union armies. General Warren also supported Mackenzie's promotion even though it meant he was losing "a gem of a man."[18]

General Meade officially ordered Mackenzie to take command of the Second Connecticut on June 10, 1864, with the rank of colonel of U.S. volunteers. Mackenzie now had the opportunity he had sought since the outbreak of the war. Boyish dreams of glory were now about to be realized, although Mackenzie was not much more than a boy still. He was not quite twenty-four years old when he assumed command.[19]

The Second Connecticut was at that time a dispirited, disorganized group of men. The punishment it had sustained at Cold Harbor, along with the loss of its stern but loved commander, had left it barely effective as a fighting unit. Colonel Mackenzie spent a few days observing his new command and realized that strong action was needed to restore its fighting qualities and to create for himself an instrument with which to demonstrate his own abilities. His training at West Point and his own instinct told him that discipline was the key to success in war. Mackenzie began to tighten the screws of discipline after allowing his regiment only a brief respite. Then, wrote one of the historians of the Second, Colonel Kellogg was missed all over again. "That commander had chastised us with whips, but [Mackenzie] dealt in scorpions."[20]

Many means of enforcing his will were at Mackenzie's disposal. Officers of the period had large discretion in administering physical penalties for violations of good military order, and he used most of them. A member of a neighboring regiment remembered cutting down a private of the Second Connecticut who had been suspended by his thumbs for some infraction. The rescued offender was so weak that he could not walk. Angered by straggling on the march from Washington to the Shenandoah Valley in August, Mackenzie punished the entire regiment by having them drill with logs after a full day's march.[21]

Mackenzie was not cruel or arbitrary, nor was he any harsher than the average officer of the period. He knew that troops with discipline fought better and lived longer than those without it. He saw too that pushing the men to their limit would distract them from their demoralizing memories of Cold Harbor. He may have deliberately set himself up as an object of hate to unify his men. The young colonel was not without mercy. During the Shenandoah Valley Campaign, Mackenzie, enraged over some offense, threatened to reduce a sergeant to the ranks. His anger cooled rapidly, however, when he learned that the soldier had earlier served in the navy under Alexander Slidell Mackenzie. The sergeant escaped without penalty.[22]

Ranald Mackenzie now began to develop the public personality that would come to be associated with him and to create the appearance of a soldier who was more a machine than a human. He made no attempt to cultivate the affection of his troops. Popularity was not a requisite for good leadership, he believed, nor did the leader's popularity ensure a competent combat unit. Mackenzie was always proper and correct around enlisted men and junior officers. "No enlisted man ever saw him laugh or smile except in a fight," wrote one of his subordinates. At other times, he continued, it was "very uncomfortable to those around him." Another memorialist noted that Mackenzie did not care to be popular with his men as long as he was respected and obeyed. Many observers accepted Mackenzie's public face as being the whole man, but he would continue to be friendly and sociable throughout most of his career.[23]

The Second Connecticut was soon in motion as part of Grant's ambitious effort to shift fronts and take Richmond from the south. With the rest of the Sixth Corps the regiment moved after dark on June 12. The march was delayed when the Sixth became entangled with the Second Corps, but once the tangle was cleared, the regiment marched all day June 13. After six more days of marching and waiting to march (during one of which waits the men of the Second Connecticut got their first chance in several weeks to bathe), the Sixth Corps entered entrenchments in front of Petersburg, just south of Richmond and the key to the capture of the Confederate capital. The position was exposed to intermittent fire, and any soldier who showed himself above the trenches was risking death from sniper fire. The restlessness of the soldiers, who were not happy under the ground, increased the danger. Mackenzie tried to keep his troops under cover, at one point ordering a private to "stop putting his head over or he will get it knocked off." Half of the regiment was on the line and half in the rear, but the danger was equal in either place. So great was the hazard that Mackenzie ordered his staff to set up their tents separately to reduce the chance of all being shot at once.[24]

General Grant was not content simply to besiege the Confederates, but also attempted to break the lines. The Second Connecticut was a part of the effort. On June 18 the regiment was moved out of the trenches to support an attack which did not take place. Then, on June 22, it joined a two-corps effort against the position of Confederate General James Longstreet. Upton's brigade was not directly engaged, but it did come under enemy fire and suffered several casualties. One of them was Ranald Mackenzie, who was struck in the right hand when he pointed with it while giving an order. Two fingers had to be amputated, and the colonel, against his will, was forced to take sick leave while his regiment dug in to wait out the enemy.[25]

Mackenzie was on leave for a little more than two weeks, which barely gave him time to return to Morristown. At home he found his old friend Tully McCrea nursing a leg wound. Mrs. Mackenzie had become surrogate mother and nurse to many of her son's classmates, and McCrea took advantage of her hospitality several times. Mackenzie enjoyed the reunion, but his intense drive and dedication to service made him restless, and he hastened back to the front as quickly as was feasible. On July 10, 1864, Mackenzie rejoined his regiment "with a rag around his abbreviated fingers" to return to his duties.[26]

The commander was encouraged to rejoin his regiment early because news was being spread that Lieutenant General Jubal Early was leading a large rebel force into Maryland. Indeed, as Mackenzie landed at City Point, Virginia, the major staging point for the Army of the Potomac, he met the Second Connecticut along with the rest of the Sixth Corps about to embark on a rush trip to Washington, D.C., to shore up defenses there. Early was following orders from Robert E. Lee to create a diversion by menacing the Federal capital. The hope was that Grant would withdraw a major portion of his forces at Petersburg, opening the possibility that the siege could be broken. Lee's plan worked to the extent that two Federal corps were dispatched to protect Washington, but Early's force was too weak to draw off more troops, and the situation south of Richmond remained essentially the same.[27]

Mackenzie boarded the troop ships with his men at 2:00 P.M. on July 10, and they arrived at 6:00 P.M. on July 12. The troops were immediately marched up Seventh Street toward Fort Stevens, one of several redoubts constructed to defend the capital. Some troops slipped out of the column to take advantage of "the luxury, liberty, and whiskey of Washington," a fact noted by the Second Connecticut's commander, who stored the knowledge away for a later reckoning. As the Sixth Corps veterans filed into Fort Stevens, they found a rag-tag crew of defenders commanded by Major General Christopher C. Augur already engaged with the enemy. The Second was one of the regiments ordered to join the fray, and after a sharp skirmish, it helped to drive the enemy back. Mackenzie then marched his regiment to nearby Fort Kearny and bedded it down for the night.[28]

Early withdrew during the night of July 12–13, and in the early hours of the thirteenth the Union forces set out in pursuit. On the march, Mackenzie began "to be disagreeable." He gave vent to his wrath over the straggling in Washington and continued to punish his men in the heat of the chase after Early. He broke a sergeant who allowed a corporal to fill his canteen. A member of Company G yelled for coffee at a rest stop, and the entire company had to stand at attention throughout the break. Mackenzie was disturbed by what he saw as potentially disastrous conduct in the presence of the enemy. The heat and pace of the march were too much, however, and straggling was common. Not until the corps stopped for a thirty-hour rest did the regiment reassemble. At this stage some of the men began to talk of killing their colonel in the next battle in order to relieve themselves of their oppressor. It is not clear whether this plot was genuine or merely camp talk, but apparently no attempt was made to carry out the plan.[29]

The chase after Early continued until July 22, when the Sixth Corps was ordered back to Washington. At the capital, the Second Connecticut was detached from the corps and stationed in the defenses surrounding the city. This period of inactivity did not last long, however, for General Early still occupied the Shenandoah Valley and offered a continuing threat to the Union north of the Potomac. At the end of July, Early sent to Chambersburg, Pennsylvania, two brigades of cavalry which burned much of the town when it failed to deliver a ransom. The threatening presence of the Confederates in the valley finally prompted the organization of a new Army of the Shenandoah to be commanded by Major General Philip H. Sheridan. The heart of the new army was the Sixth Corps, and the Second Connecticut joined it in moving back to western Maryland.[30]

Somewhat overshadowed by William Tecumseh Sherman's conquest of Atlanta and subsequent march through Georgia and the Carolinas, Sheridan's Shenandoah Valley campaign was nevertheless of great importance. The victories over Early's forces sustained the North's growing sense of success initiated by Sherman. Union success in the valley further damaged Confederate morale and weakened Lee's army by depriving the South of foodstuffs that were crucial to continuing rebel resistance. All of the troops under Sheridan were full participants in the campaign, but a special role was played by the Second Connecticut Heavy Artillery and its commander.[31]

Sheridan's superiors had saddled him with a delicate job, and his valley campaign got off to a slow start as a result. Northern politics—Abraham Lincoln was up for reelection—made it imperative that Sheridan not lose a battle and almost as important for him to win one. His mixed mission, plus uncertainty about Confederate numbers, led Sheridan to act with some caution at first. From August through September he played a hide-and-seek game with Early's army. Sheridan's force, made up of the Sixth and Nineteenth Corps, the Army of West Virginia, twelve batteries of artillery, and three cavalry divisions, was kept on the move almost constantly roaming throughout the lower Shenandoah Valley, seeking an advantage over the enemy.[32]

In the early morning hours of September 19, 1864, Sheridan sent his cavalry splashing across the Opequan River to begin what was called the Third Battle of Winchester or the Battle of the Opequan. This battle saw as fierce fighting as the war produced, and Ranald Mackenzie and the Second Connecticut were in the very heart of it.

A traffic jam in a narrow ravine on the approach delayed the beginning of the main attack until nearly noon. At 11:40 A.M. a signal gun fired, and the Union assault began with a charge by two divisions of the Sixth Corps and one of the Nineteenth Corps across a terrain of open fields, wooded areas, and occasional ravines. The Second Connecticut was a part of the Sixth Corps' First Division, commanded by Brigadier General David A. Russell, which was held in reserve. The advance by the leading elements of Sheridan's command met bloody resistance, and, after a bit of success on the right, those units were forced into a retreat that a strong rebel counterattack threatened to turn into a rout. Sheridan acted quickly and ordered Russell's reserve division into the fight. General Russell already had his troops moving, and this salvaged the battle for the Union force. Two of the division's brigades slowed the enemy's advance, while the third,

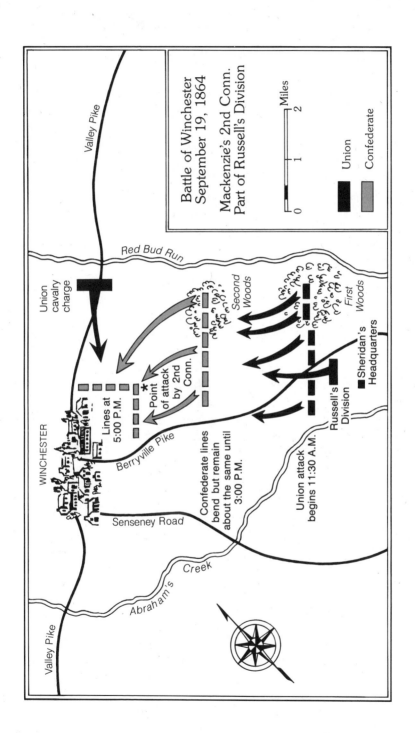

Battle of Winchester
September 19, 1864

Mackenzie's 2nd Conn.
Part of Russell's Division

Miles

Union
Confederate

Valley Pike

Red Bud Run

Union cavalry charge

Second Woods

First Woods

Sheridan's Headquarters

Point of attack by 2nd Conn.

Russell's Division

Lines at 5:00 P.M.

WINCHESTER

Berryville Pike

Union attack begins 11:30 A.M.

Confederate lines bend but remain about the same until 3:00 P.M.

Senseney Road

Creek

Abraham's

Valley Pike

Upton's, charged into the Confederate flank and forced a with-drawal. Upton's move was led by Mackenzie's regiment, with the colonel himself riding at its head. Mackenzie encouraged his men by placing his hat on the point of his sword and riding back and forth to show his troops that he was still leading them. According to the Sixth Corps' commanding general, Horatio Wright, the effort of the Second Connecticut saved the day.[33]

The day, however, was far from over. After the enemy was driven back, Upton advanced his brigade in order to position it for a counterattack. Mackenzie marched the Second Connecticut to a spot within killing range of the Confederate rifles. There he awaited events under more or less constant fire from the rebels. While his men tried to blend into the earth, the young colonel stayed mounted and exposed himself to the enemy "in a very reckless manner." One of his lieutenants heard him remark, "I guess those fellows will get tired of firing at me by and by." Mackenzie was not hit, but many of his men were.[34]

Sheridan ordered a new advance of the Sixth Corps when Brigadier General George Crook's attack from the Union's far right began to stall. Some of the bloodiest fighting of the day was about to occur. Mackenzie again placed his hat on his sword as a guide for his men. The regiment advanced to a woods under heavy fire but cleared it of enemy forces. It then advanced against the main line of the enemy, engaging in a fierce stand-up fight—"the deadliest spot of the day" for the Second Connecticut. Mackenzie suffered a skinned leg when a solid shot cut his horse in two. Halting briefly for a bandage, the colonel joked, "That's dismounting without the numbers."[35]

Mackenzie continued to lead his men afoot. By that time the enemy had bent its lines into an L shape to meet both Crook's and the Sixth Corps' attacks. Mackenzie led the Second Connecticut straight toward the angle formed by the two lines. At first the weight of the rebels' fire drove the regiment back. Many of the men lay down for protection, and others ran. But the rattled troops rallied around Mackenzie, and with a second effort they carried the enemy's breastworks. Weakened by all-day fighting, the Confederates began to waver. A classic cavalry charge ordered by Sheridan smashed into the rebel lines and forced a withdrawal.[36]

It had been a near thing, but the Third Battle of Winchester was a Union victory, and Ranald Mackenzie had played an important part in it. Mackenzie's conduct had won the respect of his troops. If, indeed, some had planned to shoot him in the first battle, that resolution was overcome by his bravery on the field. "The men hated him with the hate of hell" but could not kill him.[37]

On a larger level, Mackenzie's quick response to orders and his handling of the regiment marked him as worthy of higher command in the Union Army. General Upton mentioned the colonel in his report, remarking not only on Mackenzie's "fearlessness" but also on the "ability he displayed in commanding [the regiment] during the entire action. His regiment on the right initiated nearly every movement of the division and behaved with great steadiness and gallantry." General Wright, the corps commander, echoed Upton's remarks and mentioned Mackenzie, along with others, as one "whose gallantry . . . deserves some mark of recognition." General Grant's statement that Mackenzie advanced on "his own merit and without influence" was true. Unrecognized merit, however, does not lead to promotion. With the Third Battle of Winchester, Mackenzie began to gain the influence that his merit warranted.[38]

Sheridan's army closely followed Early's retreating rebels. Three days later, the Union forces caught up with the defeated, but not demoralized, Confederates just south of Strasburg, about twenty miles up the valley from Winchester. Early placed his troops on Fisher's Hill, where earlier in the campaign he had successfully defied Sheridan to attack. This time, the little Federal general would not be deterred. Sheridan called for a council of war with his subordinates. One of them, General George Crook, who like Mackenzie would gain his greatest fame as an Indian fighter, recommended a flanking movement through heavily wooded country cut up by numerous ravines. This terrain was so rugged that Early had taken only minimal precautions to protect that end of his line. Crook's proposal was adopted, and while he moved his Army of West Virginia—who referred to themselves as "buzzards"—the other two corps of Sheridan's army menaced Early's front to hold him in place and distract his attention from his left flank.[39]

When Crook burst upon the rebels' lightly guarded left, the Sixth and Nineteenth Corps launched a frontal attack. Ranald Mackenzie, as part of the Sixth Corps' movement, led his regiment up the steep, rocky slope. The Confederates at first poured a heavy fire into the Union ranks, but resistance faded rapidly under the influence of Crook's yelling divisions. The historian of the Second Connecticut claimed that Mackenzie's men were the first to plant the Union flag on the top of Fisher's Hill "from the direct front." It was an easily won victory, one which Sheridan thought ended Early's ability to do any further damage.[40]

Sheridan was so convinced that there was little threat remaining from Early's army that he passed up opportunities to smash it completely. He also ignored broad hints, but not direct orders, from General Grant that he take advantage of his strength to do greater damage to the rebel army. Instead, he contented himself with destroying as much of the bounty of the valley as possible to deny the Confederacy one of its most important sources of food. Meanwhile, the Confederates' commanding general, Robert E. Lee, out of stubbornness or optimism, sent reinforcements to Early, who began to look for an opportunity to strike back.[41]

On October 15, 1864, Sheridan, still believing that Early was unlikely to take up the offensive, decided to accept an invitation from Secretary of War Stanton to come to Washington for a personal conference. He left his army encamped between the small village of Middletown and a twisted stream called Cedar Creek near its confluence with the North Branch of the Shenandoah River. Sheridan warned his troops to be prepared for anything—there was a possibility that Lee had sent Lieutenant General James Longstreet's corps to buttress Early's army—but no one really expected trouble.

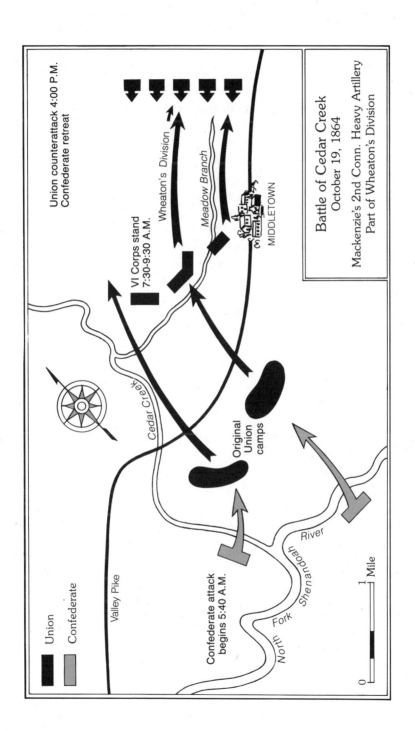

Union counterattack 4:00 P.M.
Confederate retreat

VI Corps stand
7:30–9:30 A.M.

Wheaton's Division

Meadow Branch

MIDDLETOWN

Cedar Creek

Original Union camps

Confederate attack begins 5:40 A.M.

Valley Pike

North Fork Shenandoah River

Union
Confederate

0   1 Mile

Battle of Cedar Creek
October 19, 1864

Mackenzie's 2nd Conn. Heavy Artillery
Part of Wheaton's Division

Jubal Early, at about the same time, realized that because of a shortage of provisions, he had either to attack or to retreat. Early was a fighter, so he did not hesitate to go on the offensive. He assigned General John Brown Gordon, probably his most able subordinate, to devise a flank attack on Sheridan's forces at Cedar Creek. Gordon came through brilliantly, forming a plan that would have, with just a bit of luck, forced Sheridan out of the valley.[42]

In the early morning darkness of October 19, Gordon's plan was put into action. Gordon himself led the main attack against the Union left from across the Shenandoah River. This move was supported by another rebel thrust from across Cedar Creek, and together the two attacks quickly brought about a near collapse of Sheridan's army. Two-thirds of the Federal forces broke under the surprise assault, the effectiveness of which was increased by a heavy fog that made it difficult for the bluecoats to discover what was happening. At this stage the bravery and skill of Captain Henry A. duPont, Mackenzie's friend from West Point, was all that saved the Union army from destruction. DuPont's handling of his artillery gave the Sixth Corps time to form defensive lines and prevent what had for a time seemed a complete rebel success.

The sound of firing alerted the men of the Sixth Corps, and Mackenzie, like most of the commanders, began to order his troops into combat formation. As the crash of musketry and artillery increased, Mackenzie marched his regiment toward the noise of battle and placed it in line with the rest of the First Division. The ground in front of the Second Connecticut sloped down to a small stream, then up to a patch of woods. Mackenzie had his men lie down and fire as the Confederates began to charge out of the woods. The combined regiments of the First Division inflicted numerous casualties, but they, in turn, suffered heavily. The Second Connecticut took four-fifths of its day's losses in this action. The troops around Mackenzie began to withdraw, and he was informed that General Wright had ordered a retreat. At first Mackenzie balked, in spite of the heavy casualties his unit was taking. "This line will break if I do," he declared. But the other regiments were leaving the position, and there was no real choice but to follow suit. At that time, Mackenzie's horse was struck in the head and killed. Mackenzie had already been wounded in the heel, and he now ordered a retreat which he led on foot. What began as an orderly withdrawal quickly turned into a rout.[43]

Mackenzie helped in establishing a new line about eight hundred yards behind the first. He had become acting commander of the Second Brigade, as Brigadier General Joseph E. Hamblin had been wounded. After securing another horse, Mackenzie led the brigade in a slow retreat until the enemy ceased to follow, then he advanced again. Mackenzie was hit once more and knocked off his horse. He ordered his men to help him back on his mount and, being temporarily paralyzed, had the horse led by a sergeant. By that time Sheridan had rejoined his troops after making his famous ride from Winchester, and after a few hours' respite—Early's attack had expended its initial force—the general ordered a counterattack all along the line. Mackenzie led the Second Brigade in the attack and was wounded for a third time. In spite of his wounds, the young colonel stayed with his troops until it was clear that the Confederates were beaten.[44]

Sheridan got the public credit and public adulation for turning the near defeat at Cedar Creek into a convincing victory, but it was his officers and men who truly deserved the praise. The momentum of the battle had begun to shift before most of the troops were aware of their general's presence. Not the least of the many heroes of the day was Ranald Slidell Mackenzie. He was mentioned in General Wright's report as having "behaved admirably." More importantly for his career, Mackenzie this time attracted the personal notice of Sheridan. Mackenzie's style of bravery was the first thing Little Phil looked for in an officer. After Cedar Creek, Sheridan would play an increasingly large role in Mackenzie's fortunes.[45]

The kind of courage Mackenzie displayed was remarkable but not unusual. At times it almost seems as if the rank of colonel in the Civil War armies was designed to select out men to sit on their horses and inspire their regiments by getting shot. Mackenzie certainly calculated his chances. He once remarked to a subordinate that he expected to be wounded but not killed. He considered and then registered the possibility of being shot as part of the price to be paid for a military career. What made Mackenzie stand out from most of the "boy generals" Sheridan took as protégés was the intelligence and military ability he brought along with his "rashness and foolhardiness." In the Civil War and later in the Indians campaigns Mackenzie relied as much on intelligence and careful planning as on reckless charges.[46]

Sheridan was not the only one to note Mackenzie's ability. After the Valley Campaign ended, Sheridan and most of his army were transferred to the Petersburg front. James H. Wilson, one of Sheridan's cavalry commanders who had graduated from the Military Academy two years ahead of Mackenzie, was instead sent west to reorganize the cavalry there. Wilson probably knew Mackenzie at West Point, but he also had seen how the younger man handled troops in the valley. Quoting General William T. Sherman as authority, Wilson specifically requested Mackenzie's assignment to the West. Wilson's request was not granted because Sheridan had prior claims.[47]

Mackenzie again recovered from his wounds in a remarkably short time. When he rejoined his unit on November 11, 1864, he found himself commanding the Second Brigade, First Division, Sixth Corps. On December 1 the entire corps began a movement back to Petersburg. The trenches in front of Petersburg had by this time become so elaborate and comfortable that the returning soldiers thought at first that "there must be some mistake." The war there had settled down into a stalemate made even more fixed by the cold of winter. Except for a few excursions, the men of the Second Brigade were able to catch up on their rest and work to make their trenches even more habitable. One change was noted by the men at inspection in January. "Mackenzie appeared in stars." He was now Brevet Brigadier General Mackenzie.[48]

Mackenzie as a brigadier general looking hardly older than in his class picture at West Point. The sideburns are an attempt to establish adulthood but are still skimpy, indicating his relative youth. *(Courtesy Western History Collections, University of Oklahoma Library)*

There was little opportunity for Mackenzie to improve on his reputation in the dull winter days of 1864–65, but he was not forgotten. As spring approached and the prospect for action improved, General Grant, probably acting on Sheridan's suggestion, asked General George Meade if he could "possibly spare General Mackenzie." Grant had decided that the newly promoted general would be a good cavalry officer and wanted him to take over the Cavalry Division of the Army of the James. Meade consulted with the commander of the Sixth Corps, who resisted the transfer, saying, "I can't replace him by so good an officer." General Wright's objections were fruitless, and orders were issued implementing the change.[49]

There is no indication that Mackenzie's shift to another command was because of any shortcomings of the Cavalry Division's previous commander. Brigadier General A. V. Kautz appears to have been the victim of influence. While it is possible that Kautz had offended the commander of the Army of the James, E. O. C. Ord, in some way, it seems that he was reassigned primarily to make room for a favorite of the higher command. The historian of one of the division's regiments wrote that the change was made "much to the regret of the regiment."[50] Mackenzie might have actually angled for the promotion. He was never as open and relentless in his ambitions as many of his contemporaries were, but he always pressed his advantage when the opportunity came.

Movement of the two opposing armies came with the spring thaw. In late March, Mackenzie began to prepare his new command for combat—getting rid of excess baggage and issuing ammunition and rations. On March 28 the Cavalry Division, Army of the James, marched to the extreme left of the Union lines southwest of Petersburg. Mackenzie's first assignment as cavalry commander was guarding trains, a dispiriting business made worse by frequent rains. Action came on April 1, however, when his division was detached from the Army of the James and assigned to Sheridan's command.[51]

Mackenzie's division was to be a part of a movement by Sheridan to cut off the last railroad still bringing supplies to Petersburg. To counter this move, Lee sent Major General George Pickett with a force of eleven thousand men to hold the crossroads of Five Forks. Sheridan became concerned that Lee might send more troops which could take him in the flank as he moved against Pickett. He therefore ordered Mackenzie to ride up from Dinwiddie Court House to Five Forks, then turn east on the White Oak Road to deal with any rebels coming from that direction. Shortly after turning east, Mackenzie's cavalry struck enemy pickets, who, when charged, retreated to join "a considerable force strongly posted in rifle pits." Mackenzie lined up two squadrons to feel out the enemy, but a young officer from Sheridan's staff urged haste, so Mackenzie led his men in a full charge, which "drove the enemy out in confusion."[52]

The Cavalry Division then paused for a breather before Mackenzie led it back to Five Forks to seek further orders. Sheridan, pushing the attack against Pickett with all of his forces, ordered the cavalry to swing around to the east in an attempt to hit the enemy on the flank and rear. Thick woods slowed and scattered Mackenzie's men, and they were unable to reach Hatcher's Run, which had guarded the rebel front, until after the enemy had been dislodged by Union infantry. Mackenzie was able to take many prisoners, and his force prevented Pickett from attempting a return to the Petersburg lines.[53]

Mackenzie's first action as a cavalryman was not spectacular. It was, though, a solid success, proving that his smooth handling of infantry, which had led to his transfer to the mounted arm, was no fluke. Sheridan gave him "great credit" for his success at Five Forks. Almost as important for Mackenzie's future success, his men, who had at first somewhat resented him, now felt that he had "won his spurs."[54]

In the next eight days, Sheridan, followed by the rest of Grant's huge army, hurried to cut off the retreat of Lee's rapidly dwindling army. Mackenzie's cavalry had an active role in this pursuit. Assigned to serve under Major General Wesley Merritt, the Cavalry Division followed Lee closely, picking up numerous prisoners and fighting several skirmishes to drive enemy guards away from river fords. Mackenzie led the march to Prince Edward's Courthouse, which blocked Lee's access to the fleeing Confederate government at Danville.[55]

On April 7, 1865, the small Cavalry Division was redesignated as a brigade and assigned to General Crook's division. The next day, Crook led his command to the Lynchburg Pike west of the village of Appomattox Courthouse to stop any breakout attempt by Lee. On the morning of April 9, the effort came. A large force of rebel infantry came up the pike. Mackenzie deployed his men across the pike alongside those of Colonel Charles H. Smith, blocking the advance. The rebels were too strong for two brigades of cavalry, and the men in blue were forced back. They retreated slowly and in good order. Mackenzie knew infantry was being sent to back up his force and that it was imperative that the road be held until its arrival. Mackenzie and Smith retreated about a mile before being supported by enough Union troops to stop the Confederates. While preparations were being made for a Union counterattack, word arrived that hostilities had been suspended.[56]

Four years of bitter warfare were coming to an end for the United States, and Ranald Slidell Mackenzie had made a good start in his chosen profession. From May 1862 to April 1865 he had risen from second lieutenant to major general. In less than a year he had gone from captain to the two-star rank. Although such rapid rises in rank were common in the Civil War, Mackenzie's progress was especially remarkable in that he did not have a combat command until June 1864. No wonder, then, that Ulysses S. Grant referred to him as "the most promising young officer in the army."[57]

CHAPTER FOUR

GONE TO TEXAS

LEE'S surrender effectively ended the fighting for the Army of the Potomac, but there was still much work to be done collecting captured equipment, paroling prisoners, and rounding up the Confederates who had slipped through Union lines before the surrender. Mackenzie's first duty after the fighting stopped was to keep his division at Appomattox to maintain order and protect public property. He was also charged with overseeing the collection of rebel cavalry equipment. This duty had lasted only two days when he was ordered to march to Lynchburg as part of the Twenty-fourth Corps to take charge of enemy stores and elicit the surrender of rebel cavalry that had moved there before Lee's capitulation. [1]

As Mackenzie's division, leading the move, approached Lynchburg, it was met by a delegation of city officials who surrendered the city to the general. Mackenzie then ordered the band to take the lead, and the division made a "triumphal entry." Grant's orders were that private property should be carefully respected if there were no resistance. Mackenzie carried out this directive by ordering that any person caught pillaging would "without trial be hanged." This tactic apparently worked, as there is no record of any citizens being molested while the town was occupied. [2]

At Lynchburg, Mackenzie made contact with Confederate cavalry that had slipped away from Appomattox and had thus avoided being included in the surrender terms. Mackenzie sent a message to the rebel commander, Brigadier General Thomas T. Munford, asking that he report to Lynchburg. Munford replied that he was not sure that he was included in Lee's surrender and would not "accept your polite invitation until I can ascertain my status." Munford meant to fight if he was not covered by Lee's action. Major General John Gibbon, commander of the Twenty-fourth Corps, joined the correspondence at this point. After checking with Grant, Gibbon found that any troops who had broken out of the Union net were not included in the surrender. Munford would have to judge his position for himself. Further fighting was prevented when Munford decided to yield.[3]

Even before Munford's surrender, which was accepted by General David M. Gregg, the Twenty-fourth Corps had left the Appomattox-Lynchburg area and had moved toward Richmond. Mackenzie's cavalry accompanied the move, primarily to guard against straggling and pillaging. As the war wound down, many Union soldiers sought to take advantage of the situation and fill their pockets with loot and souvenirs. Gibbon's orders to Mackenzie made clear that he did not intend for his troops to add to the misery of the defeated Virginians. Mackenzie was enjoined to appoint "trustworthy officers" to command troops on the flanks and rear to pick up stragglers and prevent looting. Adding emphasis to the orders, Gibbon expected Mackenzie to preserve the corps "from the disgrace which a few bad men" would bring on if allowed the opportunity.[4]

Mackenzie's tenure in Virginia after this point seems to have been uneventful. He continued to command his division, now under orders from the Department of Virginia. On May 31, 1865, he was named to a special board to consider which officers were fit to serve in the regular army. By August, affairs in Virginia were so quiet that Mackenzie was relieved of duty while the army was being reorganized. He went to New York and stayed with his Duer relatives, apparently until January 1866, when he was mustered out of the U.S. Volunteers as brigadier general. He then took a month's leave before reporting for duty in his new permanent rank of captain of the Corps of Engineers.[5]

Mackenzie's new post was Portsmouth, New Hampshire,

where he assisted in the reconstruction of the forts guarding the harbor. Naval bombardments during the war revealed that America's coastal defenses needed strengthening to withstand attack by ships that might take advantage of the latest technological developments. Mackenzie's assignment offered promise of a lengthy stay in the East, for Congress appropriated funds for the construction of a new fort at Portsmouth as well as refurbishing of the old ones. One advantage of the post was that Mackenzie's family could join him and live in comfort. For a man less ambitious and dedicated to advancement, the situation might have seemed ideal. Mackenzie might have rested secure in the knowledge that he had served his country well in its crisis and might have regarded his scars as excuses from seeking more active service. But service in the Corps of Engineers, no matter how appealing in some ways, offered little hope for promotion and less for glory. Ranald Mackenzie wanted both and exerted himself to secure a transfer to a combat arm in order to advance his career in the West.[6]

In the spring of 1867, Mackenzie visited Washington and pressed his claim to active service to General Grant in person. He joined several others waiting to beg favors from the commanding general and grew somewhat discouraged. He persisted, however, and told Grant that he was willing to accept any appointment that would take him to the field. The commanding general told him to come back in two days. Mackenzie met General Sheridan outside of Grant's office and explained his mission. Sheridan then added his considerable influence to Mackenzie's cause. When the young engineer officer met with Grant two days later, he was offered the colonelcy of the Forty-first Infantry Regiment.[7]

The Forty-first was one of the Negro regiments mandated by Congress after the Civil War. Although service with a black unit offered the opportunity for more rapid promotion—Mackenzie went immediately from captain to colonel—few white officers were willing to be assigned to such units. The post had already been rejected by several officers before it was offered to Mackenzie. That he took the position shows that Mackenzie was relatively free of racial prejudice and reveals, too, the intensity of his ambition. Even though the black regiments were looked down upon, taking the command was a definite upward move for Mackenzie. There is no direct evidence, but it is likely that Grant and Sheridan promised a more prestigious position for him when an opening should appear. Taking a less desirable post was an important first step toward more prominent command.[8]

In March 1867, Mackenzie underwent physical and professional examinations to qualify for service as an infantry officer. He passed both with no apparent trouble. Of particular interest is the fact that Mackenzie's Civil War wounds seemed to have had no permanent disabling effect. Within a few years Mackenzie would be suffering numerous physical ailments which seem to have been largely the result of his war service. That he passed the physical with no qualifications suggests a less than thorough examination or, quite possibly, deliberate concealment on Mackenzie's part. His ambition for fame and promotion was intense enough that he might have hidden any potentially disqualifying problem. Three days after the tests, Mackenzie formally accepted his new appointment.[9]

Mackenzie officially took command of the Forty-first Infantry in Baton Rouge, Louisiana, on May 25, 1867. Although black regiments did not have good reputations, he set out to raise the Forty-first to a high level of efficiency. The key to the improvement Mackenzie brought to the regiment was to elevate the quality of recruits. The new colonel was able to get the unit's recruiting stations changed. In June he sent recruiting officers to three northern cities with orders "to enlist only such men as can read and write." With better material to begin with, it did not take long for Mackenzie's stern discipline and emphasis on drill to bring a sharp improvement in the regiment's performance. When the Forty-first reported to duty stations in West Texas, the post surgeon at Fort Concho noted that the black company stationed there was "decidedly superior" in drill to the white troops stationed at the same post. By that time the Forty-first was recognized as one of the best units in the army, with one of the lowest desertion rates. The medical officer went on to say that the black musicians also excelled, although in sounding the calls "sweetness of execution" took precedent over "military exactness." Mackenzie was well known for demanding strict adherence to regulations, so it is unfortunate that there is no record of his reaction to improvisation by the regiment's buglers.[10]

Fortunately for Mackenzie his regiment did not remain on Reconstruction duty for long. Such service produced no glory and often hurt, rather than helped, an officer's career. New orders sent the Forty-first to the lower Rio Grande valley of Texas to replace a volunteer regiment about to be mustered out of service. The shift to the west opened up new career opportunities, and Mackenzie undertook the assignment gladly. The Forty-first served at several border stations, ending at Fort Clark, where Mackenzie was designated as commander of the Subdistrict of the Rio Grande. The regiment was to guard against border incursions but apparently spent most of its time in drill, working for that excellence that Mackenzie expected. There was enough time also for Mackenzie to begin to explore the variety of hunting opportunities available in the West and which would provide him recreation throughout his days on the frontier.[11]

Mackenzie's real western service might be said to have begun when he was ordered to Fort McKavett, Texas, in March 1869. He also assumed command of a new regiment, the Twenty-fourth Infantry, created by congressional action out of a combination of his Forty-first and the Thirty-eighth Infantry, which also was composed of black soldiers. The shift brought Mackenzie into close contact with two men who would have an effect on his career in the future. His new Lieutenant Colonel was William R. Shafter, a short, rather stout soldier who seemed to have an affinity for black troops. The two officers got along well, being in many ways much alike both in manner and dedication to service and career. Shafter would be ridiculed during the Spanish-American War because his great size would require that he travel in a buggy, but in the late 1860s he was still very energetic and effective. Shafter and Mackenzie would cooperate several times in dealing with Mexican border troubles. Assigned to the new unit as quartermaster was First Lieutenant Henry Ware Lawton. Lawton, a civil war veteran, would prove to be an extremely able quartermaster who was apparently able to work miracles to deliver supplies. Mackenzie kept Lawton with him as long as he had a field command, and Lawton must be given great credit for his commander's successes on the Llano Estacado.[12]

Fort McKavett was first established in 1851 near the sources of the San Saba River. Abandoned in 1860, the fort was reoccupied in 1868 as the people of Texas again began to push westward and demanded protection from the Indians. At McKavett, Mackenzie served as commander of the Subdistrict of the Pecos as well as colonel of the Twenty-fourth Infantry. This position gave him responsibility for a large, if indeterminate, area of West Texas. It was galling to Mackenzie that his administrative duties took so much time and that he rarely had the opportunity to lead troops in the field. Indians from both sides of the Texas-Mexican border were active in the territory under Mackenzie's charge, and he regularly kept troops out on scouts. The nature of the country dictated that most of the scouts be made by cavalry while the infantry stayed to protect fixed installations.[13]

The young colonel got his first taste of Indian warfare while leading a mixed force consisting of a detachment of the Twenty-fourth Infantry and a company of the Ninth Cavalry under Captain John M. Bacon. On June 7, 1869, the bluecoats confronted a force of about one hundred Lipan and Mescalero Apaches. In the first clash, two Indians were killed and the rest were driven from the field. Mackenzie's troops gave chase until their horses tired and then burned the Indians' *rancheria*. This was not a major engagement, but it was important for introducing Mackenzie to a new kind of war. He began at this time to think seriously about the problems of war in the West and generated ideas which contributed to his later success.[14]

Ranald Mackenzie's West
1869–1883

Scale in Miles

0   100   200

The June 1869 expedition was the only one led by Mackenzie while he commanded at Fort McKavett. The rest of the scouts and expeditions were led by others. In September, Captain Henry Carroll led a force of about one hundred men composed of infantry and cavalry on a month-long scout. Carroll's unit had a two-day fight with Indians on the Salt Fork of the Brazos River but "were unable to make any impression upon the savages." Mackenzie sent out another expedition in October that had better luck. This force, under the command of Captain Bacon, had a two-day fight with a large body of Indians and defeated them soundly, burned their camp, and took prisoners. One female prisoner was taken to Fort Concho by Lieutenant George E. Albee, who intended to "civilize" her. The attempt came to an end when she had to be treated by the post surgeon "for old organic disease." Other scouts sent out by Mackenzie in 1870 were not as successful as Captain Bacon's. [15]

The task of rebuilding Fort McKavett was one problem that demanded Mackenzie's attention and prevented him from taking a more active part in the field. When the fort was reoccupied in 1868, it was almost in ruins. Mackenzie's predecessor began the process of rebuilding, but because of a lack of craftsmen and materials, the work was largely incomplete when the command changed. Mackenzie brought with him a civilian work force of five carpenters and six masons and, using the unskilled labor of his regiment, soon had work on the reconstruction well under way. The importance of Mackenzie's energy in directing the construction was indicated by the slowdown in work when he was called to San Antonio for court-martial duty. Most of the buildings were of stone, and by the time Mackenzie left Fort McKavett, the post was one of the best in Texas. [16]

Encounters with civilians also distracted Mackenzie from his duties. One case involved election disputes in Mason, Kimble, and McCulloch counties. The details of the case are not clear, but apparently the citizens of those counties, not happy with the results of local elections, asked Mackenzie to select the officials from a list of candidates provided. Not being personally acquainted with any of the prospects, Mackenzie made inquiries among the citizens and selected the men who seemed most respected in the counties. He also recommended that Kimble and McCulloch counties be combined with adjoining counties for some purposes. Mackenzie seems to have settled the difficulties to the general satisfaction of everyone involved. This was a minor episode, but it illustrates the vexations facing army officers on the frontier as well as the growing respect that Mackenzie commanded in Texas.[17]

Ben Ficklin, a stagecoach entrepreneur, caused considerable difficulty for Mackenzie. Among other enterprises Ficklin operated a stage line from San Antonio to El Paso. In 1869, Ficklin requested that cavalry patrols from Mackenzie's command be ordered to escort the stage runs. Mackenzie complied with this request according to the availability of troops, although he thought it a waste of manpower as far as any long term settlement of Indian problems was concerned. Mackenzie even temporarily stationed a detachment of cavalry at Kickapoo Springs some distance north of Fort McKavett. In May, however, Mackenzie sent the detachment back to its regular duties, whereupon Ficklin complained to the commander of the Department of Texas, Brevet Brigadier General Joseph J. Reynolds. More sensitive to the needs of prominent citizens than Mackenzie, Reynolds ordered the troops to be returned to the springs on June 16 during Mackenzie's absence on patrol. Captain John Carroll obeyed the order, although he pointed out that Kickapoo Springs lay within the jurisdiction of Fort Concho, not Fort McKavett.

When Mackenzie returned, he was enraged to discover his superior's tampering with his command. In a letter of complaint, he stated that he regarded Reynolds's action as a censure of his own conduct. He then wrote that "the best way to guard the mail and the people of the country is in my opinion to keep the Infantry at the posts and the Cavalry a great part of the time scouting." Mackenzie was forced to keep the troops at Kickapoo Springs but was able to deflect Ficklin's demand for a permanent subpost there. This altercation with Reynolds suggests that the later troubles between Mackenzie and the general were intensified by personal animosity. [18]

Texans in the area of Fort McKavett did not particularly care for the black troops stationed at the post, but they were generally pleased with Mackenzie's control. The colonel treated his black troops just as he would whites. As far as he was concerned, they were soldiers of the United States and would conduct themselves as such. As he would in other posts, Mackenzie kept his charges busy on construction projects and drill when not in the field, and there was little trouble between the black troops and the white citizens. The glaring exception involved a settler named John M. Jackson. [19]

Jackson was an old settler who had come to the San Saba country before the Civil War and had stuck it out on the frontier after the army was withdrawn during that conflict. Jackson, known as "Humpy" because of a physical deformity, was a good farmer and began to gain a measure of prosperity by selling produce to the army after Fort McKavett was reactivated. Trouble came when a sawmill was established not far from Humpy's farm to provide lumber for construction at the fort. Black soldiers from Mackenzie's command were stationed there to run the operation. One of the soldiers was attracted to Jackson's daughter, Narcissus, and one day he passed her a note declaring his affection. Jackson, who shared the general dislike of blacks held by many Southern whites, was outraged and determined to shoot the offender. Because of either his fury or his ignorance of who had written the message, Jackson shot and killed the first black soldier he saw. It was the wrong man. [20]

Whether the victim was innocent or guilty of offending white mores made no difference to Mackenzie. The dead man was a soldier of the U.S. Army, and the murderer had to be caught and punished. Mackenzie first ordered Lieutenant John Bullis to take a detachment and arrest Jackson, but the killer managed to escape. As long as he was in command at Fort McKavett, Mackenzie doggedly kept troops on Jackson's trail. Jackson usually was able to elude his pursuers, but he was captured once and, with the aid of friends, escaped, killing two more soldiers in the process. Mackenzie posted a reward for the capture of the men who had aided Jackson. Mackenzie's frustration was alleviated some when an army patrol killed one of Jackson's friends, but Jackson himself remained free until after the colonel assumed command of the Fourth Cavalry and left Fort McKavett. Once Mackenzie was gone, Jackson either surrendered or was captured. After being indicted for murder, Jackson stood trial and was acquitted by a sympathetic jury.[21]

Perhaps the most telling thing about this episode was the determination with which Mackenzie kept troops in the field after Jackson. This kind of determination became one of the hallmarks of the officer's career. Whether chasing renegade whites or Indians, he pushed to the limit of his and his men's endurance. His reputation as a field commander had just begun to grow, but he established it on a firm foundation. As early as November 1869, one Texas newspaper praised Mackenzie for his drive and energy. Mackenzie was on his way to becoming the most respected army officer in Texas.[22]

Mackenzie went on a leave of absence in April 1870—a leave extended, at his request, until October of that year. He spent most of his leave visiting family and friends in Morristown, although he most likely visited Washington also to keep his name before his superiors. The young colonel had hardly returned to Texas when he was ordered back East to serve on a special board to deal with the surplus of officers created by the consolidation of some regiments to meet a congressionally mandated reduction of the army. Boards such as this were known as "benzine boards." Apologists claimed that the name was applied to them because of the cleaning properties of benzine. A more likely explanation for the name is that many officers were involuntarily retired because of excessive drinking, and benzine was "the jocular name of certain other liquids," whiskey specifically.[23]

Mackenzie used his off-duty time in Washington to maintain his contact with important patrons, and it was at that time that President Grant told him he was to get command of the Fourth

Cavalry. Joseph H. Dorst later said that although Mackenzie had greatly desired a cavalry regiment, he could take pride that the transfer had come without "the slightest personal solicitation." Dorst was either naive or was being disingenuous. Mackenzie's effort to secure a transfer to a combat arm has been noted. He had been given at least an implied promise that his acceptance of the less desirable Forty-first Infantry would ensure a more promising appointment later. Mackenzie was not as blatant in his search for publicity as were some of his contemporaries, but he was just as ambitious as they and had no scruples about advancing his prospects.[24]

Throughout his career, Mackenzie made sure that his superiors were aware of his claims for preference. In Grant and Sheridan he had two of the three most important men in the army looking out for him. They had seen Mackenzie in action firsthand and needed little persuasion to support his case. Nevertheless, they, as well as William T. Sherman, after he became commanding general, received regular reminders. Sherman came to regard all of the young ambitious officers as pests or worse. He singled out Nelson A. Miles and Mackenzie as being particularly "ambitious and troublesome." That the two officers mentioned were natural rivals was well known throughout the army. A widely repeated story tells of Mackenzie gazing at the night sky when an officer "remarked laughingly, 'I'm afraid, General, that there's Miles between you and that star!' The General turned away, snapping his fingers nervously."[25]

Mackenzie wrote a revealing letter in 1875 in response to a proposal by General John Pope to divide control of the Indian Territory between Mackenzie and Miles. Mackenzie professed to being "very much hurt by even such a proposition being made." He continued:

I wish to have control of this territory and honestly think I ought to have it. I have no word to say against Colonel Miles on the contrary I regard him as a very fine officer. I am not in the slightest degree jealous of him. I regard him not as my superior in any way and in some particulars I am sure he is not my equal. . . .

Nor do I feel that it is the desire of any of my Superiors to slight me. I believe honestly that in breadth of views, and in a certain power which can only be acquired by time, acquaintance with a subject, and a knowledge of many men I am far superior to any officer commanding any of the Posts in the Indian Territory or Texas and have the power to combine in a way no one else can readily acquire, at the same time I do not at all think that I am invaluable.[26]

Mackenzie clearly saw his ability and made sure that his superiors were aware of it. In view of his assertions of his ability, the last phrase quoted rings somewhat hollow.

Concern for promotion, of course, lay in the future. For the time being, Mackenzie could exult in the knowledge that he was one of the youngest colonels in the army and in command of a regiment with a good, if not glorious, reputation. He knew that in the Fourth Cavalry he had the key to his own fortune in his hands.

CHAPTER FIVE

A NEW START

RANALD Mackenzie arrived at Fort Concho, Texas, on February 24, 1871, and officially assumed command of the post and the Fourth Cavalry the next day. The regiment had originated in 1855 as the First Cavalry and was redesignated as the Fourth in the general reorganization of 1861. It had on its original muster rolls the names of several officers who became well known in the Civil War. During the war the Fourth engaged the enemy seventy-six times, and following the war it was sent to Texas and its companies were scattered among several posts in the usual manner of the frontier army. The regiment had, altogether, a solid but not distinguished record. Mackenzie would change that. Within a short time Mackenzie turned the regiment into one of the best Indian fighting units in the army. He asserted to his family shortly after taking command that "it shall not be on account of any laziness of mine if it falls below any other."[1]

Laziness may, indeed, explain why the Fourth had not accomplished much on the Texas frontier before Mackenzie took over. Lieutenant Robert G. Carter, who served as the regimental adjutant from time to time, noted that before the colonel's arrival the officers at Fort Concho had spent as much time hunting and fishing as scouting for Indians. Mackenzie's arrival, he wrote, "sent rifles and shotguns to the rear to rust in their covers" while the Fourth Cavalry devoted itself to protecting the frontier. Because of slow promotion and dull assignments at isolated posts, officers sometimes showed little interest in their profession. Whether or not a particular unit could successfully ward off the frontier doldrums often depended on the quality of its commander. Mackenzie's energy and discipline provided the driving force to make the Fourth Cavalry a cohesive fighting outfit.[2]

Mackenzie was only thirty when he took command of the Fourth Cavalry and apparently was little changed in appearance since the Civil War. Carter described him as "about medium height, slightly built with side whiskers." This description fits the portrait of Mackenzie made during the Civil War. There is no indication that Mackenzie's wounds had begun to cause him any serious trouble, although later he would suffer regularly from their effects. Carter wrote in this diary that the colonel appeared to be "very sociable" and that he expected the two of them to get along.[3]

Mackenzie still had the shy public appearance that he had shown throughout his life. As he entered a new situation, his stammer became more pronounced and he "at times appeared embarrassed." The contrasting images stand out: "sociable" and "embarrassed." No doubt some observers were misled by the apparent reserve and perceived Mackenzie as cold and aloof, but as always, when Mackenzie became familiar with his situation the sociable side became more apparent. He had little trouble fitting in with his associates, whether military or civilian.[4]

When he took over the Fourth, Mackenzie began to establish the authority that was required to mold an effective fighting regiment. After his first meeting with the Fourth's officers, Carter noted that Mackenzie "seems to be quite a disciplinarian." Mackenzie would develop a reputation as a harsh taskmaster, but as was the case in the Civil War, strict, often cruel discipline was the standard for the army. Courts-martial were rare in the regiment, for Mackenzie preferred to deal with most offenses within the unit. Except for major offenses, company commanders were allowed to apply punishments following guidelines laid down by the commanding officer. Such punishments included solitary confinement, walking post carrying a thirty pound log, and, for drunkenness, extended dunkings in any convenient waterhole. Mackenzie watched such punishments to see that they did not go so far as to inflict permanent injury. In one case, Lieutenant Carter had a total of sixteen prisoners strung up by their thumbs. The colonel approved the action after cautioning that the miscreants' feet should touch the floor.[5]

The companies of the Fourth were drilled regularly both to maintain their responsiveness to orders and, also, simply to keep the men busy and out of trouble. The latter purpose was not always achieved, but Carter stated that the result overall was to create "perfect discipline." Regular inspections were instituted, with Mackenzie conducting them in person. Carter wrote that Mackenzie was "very particular about the appearance of the men."[6]

In his memoirs, Carter emphasized Mackenzie's concern with his troops' uniforms by relating the story of Lieutenant Boehm's hat and thereby did the colonel an injustice. As Carter recalled it, Peter M. Boehm was in charge of the Tonkawa scouts and, apparently with Mackenzie's permission, wore a "*white* sombrero hat with a low crown and very wide brim," which excited the jealousy of the other officers. Carter, appointed as the officers' spokesman, approached Mackenzie requesting permission to adopt similar headgear. "The answer was snapped out. 'No! Boehm is in command of the Indians. As such he is outside the marching column, a sort of free lance, and somewhat of an independent and picturesque character.'" Carter failed to see the subtle humor in Mackenzie's answer and helped to create the image of a soldier who demanded strict dress and displayed no sense of humor. Both parts of the image are misleading, if not completely erroneous. Carter's diary presents a somewhat different picture. An entry made during the summer of 1871 noted the heat, then stated that "we are allowed to wear white pants and straw hats which adds greatly to our comfort."[7]

Instead of Mackenzie, it was Carter who had little sense of humor. Carter seems to have remembered only the rebuff and not the definitely nonregulation straw hats. Carter similarly

Fort Concho still under construction in 1871. The large building in the center is the hospital. The buildings to the right are officers' quarters. All the buildings are built from standard army plans. (*Courtesy Fort Concho National Historic Landmark*)

Fort Concho in the 1880s. The main corral is to the left, enlisted men's barracks in the center, and officers' quarters to the right. The particularly desolate appearance of the landscape in this photograph may be a result of the prairie fires that periodically swept the area. (*Courtesy Fort Concho National Historic Landmark*)

failed to appreciate Mackenzie's wit in another episode. When Mackenzie led his men into the gypsum country of the eastern part of the Texas Panhandle during the chase after Kicking Bird in 1871, men and horses suffered acutely from the heat. The men's lips were cracked and bleeding, and both men and animals suffered violently from drinking water infused with alkali. Many of the horses died, and some of the men appeared to be approaching death. Mackenzie was as sick as anyone but managed to keep his sense of humor. Sitting around a campfire one night, he declared, "'Gentlemen, we shall all have a new stomach when it gets thoroughly coated with a crust of gypsum,' and measuring on his finger added, 'I think my coating is now about *that thick!*'" Then the colonel stumbled off into the bushes to be sick.[8]

Carter may have been so sick himself that he failed to appreciate Mackenzie's attempt to lighten the moment a little. Yet Carter himself felt at home enough with his commander to attempt practical jokes. On another expedition, Carter, acting as adjutant, and Mathew Leeper, Mackenzie's interpreter, felt that they were being worn out by constant demands on their time. The two of them resolved to pretend to be asleep and not hear the the next time Mackenzie called them. A violent thunderstorm blew down the tent housing them all, and still Carter and Leeper feigned sleep. Later, when Mackenzie demanded to know how they could sleep through such weather, Leeper replied, "I am always a very heavy sleeper in the field—it takes more than a storm like that to wake me." It is difficult to believe that Carter would have played such a joke had he not been aware that Mackenzie would take it in good humor.[9]

Mackenzie was sometimes hard to get along with, sense of humor or not. Carter's recollection in his memoirs that the colonel "was fretful, irritable, often times irascible" is borne out by his diary entries for 1871. Carter noted several times that Mackenzie was "very irritable." Other officers also testified to occasions when Mackenzie was snappish, moody, or otherwise hard to get along with. Lieutenant James Parker, for example, described the experience of dining alone with him in a letter to the homefolks. Mackenzie was not, Parker wrote, "the most convivial person in the world." Parker continued that when he and Mackenzie sat down to eat, "we are full of meditation, and we meditate and eat and meditate." This was especially true when the "Old Man" had had something go wrong. [10]

It is clear from the writing of both Carter and Parker that much of what was disagreeable about Mackenzie's personality was the result of the pressures of his duties. Once, when commenting on the colonel's irritability, Carter made clear that it was evidenced "in his Office" and that otherwise Mackenzie was "inclined to be very sociable." In his memoirs Carter emphasized his belief that Mackenzie's snappishness was caused by his work and pain from his old wounds. Parker's letters to his family also stress the influence of pressure upon Mackenzie's personality. A revealing glimpse of Mackenzie's impatience was provided when the Fourth Cavalry was transferring from Fort Concho to Fort Richardson. When a large herd of buffalo blocked the path, the colonel snatched up a carbine and began to fire into the air in an effort to speed up the progress of the shaggy beasts. This performance was typical of a man driven to excel and was characteristic of Mackenzie throughout his adult life. He was a relatively small man with no notable physical attributes. Like many men with this makeup, he drove himself to show that he was the equal of anyone. Anything that interfered with his advancement, whether it was paperwork, buffalos, or Indians, stimulated his aggressive nature. [11]

The unpleasant parts of Mackenzie's personality did not prevent his officers from admiring and respecting him. As shown by the writings of Carter, Parker, and others, Mackenzie made a profound and lasting impression of his younger officers. One reason was that he worked hard for their promotion. At the time, promotion through the rank of captain was within the regiment, and Mackenzie did what he could to clear the deadwood to open the path for deserving officers. Moreover, Mackenzie took an almost fatherly interest in the welfare of his subordinates. When Lieutenant John A. McKinney reported to the Fourth Cavalry, he was five hundred dollars in debt. Mackenzie paid the full amount when he learned of it, telling the young officer that he could repay the sum as he was able. Mackenzie impressed both Parker and Charles Crane with his concern when they were physically incapacitated. After a serious illness, Parker wrote of his commander's compassion, not, he said, "kindness as an officer but as a friend." Crane, a lieutenant in an infantry regiment under Mackenzie's command, accidentally shot himself and was promptly visited by the colonel. Earlier, Parker had been surprised to be ordered to accompany Mackenzie on a visit to the departmental headquarters in San Antonio. Parker offered to stay with the regiment to fulfill the duties of adjutant, but Mackenzie, to the amazement of all observers, "snapped his fingers and replied that he wanted me to go to San Antonio 'to have a good time.'"[12]

Mackenzie expected his officers to maintain the high standards that his own conduct exemplified. He tried to prevent those who did not meet his criteria from advancing their careers in the army. When Captain Charles D. Beyers was caught in financial misdoings in the Twenty-fourth Infantry, Mackenzie attempted to block his transfer to another regiment, writing that "he is not fitted to remain in the service." At the same time, if there were doubt, or if he saw the possibility of improvement, Mackenzie was generous in extending a second chance. In two cases of drunkenness and other misbehavior at Fort Clark in 1874, Mackenzie dropped charges—in one case out of regard for the officer's past good service and in the other because of the difficulty of proving the charges. The colonel expressed his wish to both men that their future conduct would justify his action. In yet another case, Mackenzie supported an officer's application for a staff position in hope that the change would help him deal with his drinking problem.[13]

Young officers stood in awe of Mackenzie, and statements in regard to his irritability were widespread, but there are many cases in which these young officers took extraordinary liberties with their superior without repercussions. Carter told of a banquet at which Mackenzie hesitated upon being called to take his seat, and a young lieutenant "slapped him on the back," urging him to move on and cease delaying activities. Lieutenant Crane was on a receiving board that had to account for the loss of spoiled potatoes. The members of the board thought the loss natural, but regulations required that the responsibility be assigned, so they "found General Mackenzie accountable and assessed the loss, or damage against him!" There was no official reaction, although Mackenzie's adjutant did demand to know "what in the h——l were you people thinking of?" These examples suggest that Mackenzie was not quite as awesome as his stern adherence to duty often suggested.[14]

Whatever his exact relations were with his officers personally, Mackenzie commanded their strong loyalty. There were no cliques for and against the commander in the Fourth such as those that existed in Custer's Seventh Cavalry. Mackenzie worked to maintain good relations among his officers. On at least one occasion he urged James Parker to patch up a quarrel with the regiment's major. The major, Mackenzie wrote, was a gentleman, and the trouble probably was the result of mutual misunderstanding. For the sake of his career and personal honor, Parker was advised to settle the disagreement. Mackenzie was willing to admit his error if he misjudged an officer. For example, when he first assumed command of the District of New Mexico (Department of Missouri), he requested the removal of the district quartermaster. After examining the situation, Mackenzie decided that the incumbent was doing a good job and withdrew his request.[15]

The attitudes of the enlisted men of the Fourth toward their commander varied, as might be expected. One report says that the men called him "Mad Mackenzie," but it is not clear from the context whether the expression referred to his often angry appearance or to his intensity in the field. The few available bits of testimony suggest that many of the enlisted men admired and respected their commander. One veteran of the Fourth's winter campaign against the Cheyennes wrote that the men would "go with him to the last ditch." A sergeant who had a long and ambivalent relationship with Mackenzie had great regard for his commander but admitted that "he got on my nerves terribly at times." The same sergeant described a curious experience. Mackenzie, on his way to swim in a stream, invited the sergeant to join him. The sight of the colonel's bullet-scarred body gave the noncom a sense of the pain the colonel lived with every day and increased his respect for his commander. [16]

Mackenzie certainly exerted himself to see that his men were well supplied and cared for. When the Fourth Cavalry stopped at Fort Griffin, Texas, on the way from Oklahoma to Fort Clark on the Rio Grande, Mackenzie commandeered large amounts of supplies for his troops, using his superior rank to override the objections of the post commander. Another time, Mackenzie endorsed the efforts of his quartermaster to secure higher pay for teamsters serving in the field. When enlisted men of the Fourth reported stories of the entertainments they concocted to amuse themselves at Fort Sill, they credited the regiment's officers, "especially the commanding officer," for supporting their efforts. Mackenzie obviously recognized that maintaining morale was crucial for a top-quality fighting outfit. [17]

Mackenzie got along well in society outside of the army and was a popular public figure. Part of his popularity was a result of his reputation as an Indian fighter, but his quiet, dignified manner enlarged his image. He did not have the exuberant and outgoing style that gave some officers their reputation. Instead, his manner promoted confidence and friendship. At Fort Richardson, Texas, the post guide, a man named Dozier, was kept on in spite of his sparse knowledge of the country. Mackenzie enjoyed his conversation and retained him while relying on others to supply intelligence. A resident of Jacksboro, the town that grew up alongside the fort, recalled that her grandmother had a piano that attracted a regular group, including Mackenzie, for "many pleasant evenings," and the young colonel became a "warm personal friend." [18]

In San Antonio, Mackenzie belonged to the Army and Civilian Social Club, which periodically held dances at the Menger Hotel. A dance with the dashing young colonel was considered to be a great coup by the young women of the town. In Santa Fe, where he served as the commander of the District of New Mexico, Mackenzie was a regular part of the social scene. He participated in such public events as the Fourth of July observance and other ceremonial occasions. In October 1882 he was honored at a "complimentary dinner" of "rare magnificence" made more enjoyable by the congeniality of the company. The colonel also participated in ceremonies honoring prominent citizens of Santa Fe. On one such occasion, his response to a toast to himself and the army would have done honor to a more celebrated orator. So popular was Mackenzie in Santa Fe that practically the entire population of the town turned out to honor him when he was promoted to brigadier general. "All hoped that he would be retained in Santa Fe in command of the district."[19]

Mackenzie was almost handsome as a young man, although his lean, hawklike features gave him a stern, forbidding countenance. He put on weight as he grew older, and the added flesh softened his face and made him more attractive. His good looks and the aura of glory attached to high rank attained at such an early age made him a tempting target for young women. The lure of romance, however, failed to turn Mackenzie from his ambitious path. Some of his letters show that he could overcome his shyness and be charming to the ladies, but only one brief affair marked his adult life.[20]

Mackenzie probably had unrecorded flirtations on his numerous leaves to the East, but still he adhered to his view that a young officer should not encumber himself with a bride. The life of a soldier was too uncertain, and the responsibility of a family was too distracting for a man who aspired to be a general. His attachment to his mother, too, was a factor in his decision to remain unattached. Marriage would double his obligations and increase the unspoken need to avoid danger for the sake of loved ones. When high rank and a certain stability could be assured, he might commit himself to marriage, but not before.

An image of abstemiousness has grown up around Mackenzie that is somewhat misleading. Lieutenant Carter's picture of the colonel has led some historians to portray Mackenzie almost as if he were a cloistered monk. To the contrary, he was a very convivial man once he felt comfortable with the society around him and occasionally consumed alcohol and smoked cigars. Twice while involved in the Powder River campaign, Private Earl Smith, Mackenzie's orderly, recorded in his diary that his chief was tipsy from drinking with other officers. An old Civil War companion, on meeting Mackenzie at Fort Sill in 1872, remembered his taste for cigars and presented him with a box of them. Clearly, Mackenzie did not often indulge to excess, nor did he easily abide those who did, but just as clearly he was no ascetic and enjoyed the pleasures of the senses from time to time.[21]

One old-timer's reminiscences are particularly revealing of Mackenzie's popular image. According to the story, Mackenzie was hunting with Sam Wells, who had been involved with Lieutenant Henry Lawton in attacking a group of Indians responsible for massacring a white family. During a rest break "the General punched Sam in the ribs" and asked what had been done to the Indians. Wells elicited a promise from Mackenzie not to repeat the story and told what had happened. Mackenzie responded, "The Damn Rascal. He [Lawton] did just right." While it would be interesting to know just what fate Lawton dealt to the Indians that brought such enthusiastic approval from Mackenzie, the important part of the story is the picture of the two men sitting under a tree swapping stories. Whether Mackenzie really punched Sam in the ribs is not as important as the fact that his popular image allowed him to be pictured doing so. This is a great contrast to the cold, aloof impression often conveyed by Mackenzie's subordinates.[22]

Mackenzie's love of hunting certainly did nothing to diminish his acceptance by the frontier population. The abundance of wild game in the West in the 1870s was beyond the imagining of the twentieth-century hunter. Carter remembered that hunting was "unsurpassed," and another contemporary claimed that Texas had a greater variety and abundance of game than any other part of the Union.[23]

Oddly enough, Mackenzie did not hunt buffalo. Carter states that this was because he was "a poor rider." More likely, the hard horseback chases that were the approved method of taking buffalo aggravated his war wounds. The colonel's preferred method of hunting was with dogs. He sometimes kept two packs, one for bear and a second for swifter game. Within a short time of assuming command of the Fourth Cavalry at Fort Concho, Mackenzie was reported to be following the chase. Although he had probably acquired the dogs earlier, this was the first recorded mention of their use. Henry W. Strong was Mackenzie's frequent hunting companion after the Fourth was transferred to Fort Richardson. Mackenzie was so impressed with Strong's tracking ability that he hired Strong as a scout. Strong claimed that he and Mackenzie once filled two army wagons with turkeys in only two days of hunting.[24]

At Fort Sill, Indian Territory, Mackenzie kept a special pack of fox hounds for "running wild cats and bears." The dogs were cared for by his orderly, a Russian named Strobel, who seems to have had a way with animals. Lieutenant James Parker described an incident in which a mule balked at being loaded into a railroad car and kicked Strobel, who immediately returned the kick. At that, the mule gave up and boarded without further resistance. Both Strobel and Mackenzie were enraged if the dogs did not perform as expected, as was the case when the pack trailed a herd of pigs instead of wild game. Parker often went along on the hunts and as the youngest officer present was delegated to climb the trees to dislodge cornered quarry. The hunts, Parker wrote, were "thrilling."[25]

Such was the man who was about to become one of the best known and most effective Indian fighting officers in the army. He was young, tough, and dedicated. He had the ability to create a disciplined fighting regiment while retaining the respect, if not the love, of those who served under him. At the same time, he had a public presence that allowed him to be an effective ambassador for the army with the general public. If he at times seemed moody and irascible, he was able to balance that temperament with a sly sense of humor and an open and dignified public demeanor. Above all, he had the intelligence and drive to find the Indians in their own country and to defeat them.

CHAPTER SIX

BAD HAND

THE whole of the Texas frontier was threatened by increasing Indian attacks when Mackenzie assumed command of the Fourth Cavalry. Since the beginning of the Civil War, the Comanches and Kiowas, long-time allies and among the most belligerent of the Plains Indians, had taken advantage of weakened frontier defenses to make their raids deeper into the state. Relentless pressure from the Indians resulted in the depopulation of large areas of the frontier and pushed the line of settlement back almost a hundred miles. By 1869, Jack County had only one quarter the number of white settlers it had in 1860, and the population of Wise County, just to the east, had declined from 3,160 to 1,450 in the same period.[1]

The federal response to the anguished cries of Texans took two different tracks. On one, efforts were made to negotiate agreements with the Indians to abandon their nomadic ways and learn to live as white men. This approach resulted in the futile "Peace Policy" of the Grant administration. At the same time, the government sent troops to Texas and revived the system of forts that had been initiated after the state was annexed in 1846. Neither policy did much at first to abate the storm of Indian raids on the frontier.[2]

At Fort Concho, Mackenzie was reintroduced to the frustrations of trying to deal with the fast-moving "lords of the South Plains." Small patrols sent out by scattered garrisons were easily eluded by the Indians. It was equally futile to wait until reports of a raid came in to the post and then send a detachment after the raiders. Usually a day, sometimes more, had passed before the news of an attack was received, and the delay rendered the chance of successful pursuit very small. Lieutenant Carter's diary entries for March 1871 record the lack of effectiveness of either approach. On March 1, Captain N. B. McLaughlin's company responded to an attack on a ranch eighteen miles from Fort Concho. By the time the troopers arrived, they found only a cold trail and were forced to return to Concho empty-handed. Three days later, Carter accompanied Major Joseph Rendlebrock's detachment in pursuit of Indians who had attacked the Fort Griffin stage. After four days the unit returned without having seen any Indians.[3]

On March 19, 1871, the commander of the Department of Texas ordered the Fourth Cavalry to replace the Sixth Cavalry at Fort Richardson as soon as possible. Jack County, the site of the fort, and the surrounding area were major targets of Indian raids because of the relative proximity of the Kiowa-Comanche reservation at Fort Sill, Indian Territory. Because the army was generally prohibited from entering the reservation, the warriors were able to make their attacks then retreat to the safety of the agency. The Sixth Cavalry had been notably ineffective in its efforts to halt the depredations, and that failure created the opportunity for Mackenzie.[4] The move was a great boost for his career. Not only would he be placed in one of the most visible areas of Indian conflict, offering greater opportunities to show his ability, but he also was ordered to concentrate most of his regiment at Fort Richardson, enabling him to experiment with his evolving ideas about the best way to fight the Indians.

On March 27, 1871, Mackenzie led his headquarters group plus Companies A and E out of Fort Concho. Many of the officers brought their wives with them, and the wagons carrying their household effects added to the companies' normal allotment of supply wagons made a large caravan. The resulting march, as described in the regimental journal and Carter's diary, takes on the appearance of a scene from a John Ford cavalry movie. Moving at a leisurely pace, Mackenzie was able to make notes about landmarks and traveling conditions. He was careful to note the quality of grass and water as well as potential danger spots along the way, such as "Mountain Pass," which was "a dangerous place in an Indian Country." Carter was less concerned with the military aspects of the march and recorded the ordinary events that took place. An attempt to break a recalcitrant horse that had repeatedly thrown its rider provided entertainment one day. Another day, a grass fire which threatened to burn the camp kept the troops from getting bored. There was at least one Indian scare, and every day great herds of buffalo sparked interest. Nights were passed almost as if the army was on a holiday excursion. One night, Carter wrote, "we made a large camp fire and Dr. H., Walton, Gen'l Mackenzie & the ladies sat around until quite late—a bright moonlight night." Near the end of the journey, as the group crossed the Salt Creek Prairie not far from Fort Richardson, Carter prophetically noted that it was "a dangerous place."[5]

A relatively new post, Fort Richardson lacked the refinements of older establishments. The post hospital was a fine stone building, but there were only a few frame houses available for officers. Most quarters for men and officers alike were of picket construction, in which poles were set upright in a trench dug for a foundation. The spaces between the logs were chinked with mud, which usually did not last long. Floors were of dirt, and although some of the roofs were made of shingles, tent canvas covered most of the buildings. These quarters were "dirty and filthy" and impossible to keep clean. Carter, who had his wife with him, considered the "wretchedness of our quarters . . . a disgrace to any govt."[6]

Ranald Mackenzie served at many posts where construction or reconstruction was necessary, but he had no time for such mundane work at Fort Richardson. He was there to fight Indians, and he devoted his efforts to that end. One observer noted the difference between Mackenzie and his predecessor, Colonel James Oakes. Oakes, he wrote, "could be found driving around the post in his carriage," while Mackenzie took to the field to lead his forces against the enemy. Mackenzie set to work trying to get all of his companies up to Richardson and planning an active campaign. Carter, serving as adjutant at this point, complained that he was "pressed from morning till night." Besides the planning for the summer expedition, Mackenzie kept him busy with boards of survey, courts-martial, and the "overhauling" of supply contracts.[7]

The anticipated arrival of the commanding general of the army, William Tecumseh Sherman, complicated activities further. Sherman had been deluged with stories of Indian raids and insistent pleas for more protection by the army. Unconvinced that the situation was nearly as serious as the Texans claimed, Sherman determined on a tour of the state to judge the situation for himself. Accompanied by Inspector General Randolph B. Marcy and a small escort, Sherman began his tour from San Antonio in early May and headed north for Fort Sill by way of the string of forts on the Texas frontier. What he saw did little to persuade him of the critical state of affairs. He saw no Indians himself and noted cases in which women and children were left alone in isolated cabins. What he saw, Sherman wrote, did not square with the stories he had heard. But Marcy, who had led an expedition through the region in the 1850s, saw that many ranches had been abandoned and that the population had declined. He expressed his concern that the whole area would be depopulated if the Indian raids were not stopped.[8]

Sherman's disregard for the danger of Indian attacks, as indicated by the size of his escort, was matched by his disregard for ceremony. Mackenzie ordered Carter to get up a party to meet Sherman some miles from the fort and escort him in proper military style. Carter scrambled to find crews for the regiment's two three-inch guns to fire a salute when the chief general of the army reached the post. All the effort was in vain, however, as Sherman dismissed Carter, ordering him to follow at his leisure. The salute was never fired. Sherman even rejected Mackenzie's offer of the use of his quarters and camped with his entourage on the parade ground.[9]

The day after his arrival at Fort Richardson, May 18, 1871, Sherman visited with the Fourth's officers, examined their quarters, and met their wives. Later on, he met with a delegation of citizens. Sherman remained doubtful of the seriousness of conditions despite the stories told by the civilians and their pleas for protection and aid in recovering stolen property. His doubts were largely dispelled later that night. In the midst of a heavy downpour, a wounded civilian named Tom Brazeal staggered into the post and reported the details of one of the most famous Indian raids in Texas history. Brazeal and eleven others in the employ of Henry Warren had been driving several wagons filled with corn bound for Fort Griffin southwest of Jacksboro. On the flat land known as the Salt Creek Prairie, crossed by Sherman only the day before, the wagon train was attacked by Indians. The large war party, consisting mainly of Kiowas and numbering 100 to 150 warriors, easily overtook the train and killed four of the teamsters almost immediately. Another was badly wounded. The seven uninjured whites broke through the circle of excited warriors in an attempt to reach the cover of timber. Kiowa pursuers killed two more of the whites, then broke off the chase, apparently fearful that they would miss out on the loot from the wagon train. The surviving wagoneers stumbled through the night to report the affair to the army at Fort Richardson. [10]

Sherman, less doubtful but still not convinced, ordered Mackenzie to take a detachment to investigate the incident and to pursue the raiders if the teamsters' story was verified. Mackenzie's instructions empowered him to follow the raiders onto the reservation in Indian Territory if on a fresh trail. Colonel William H. Wood, commander of Fort Griffin, was to send a strong force to cooperate with Mackenzie. It was still raining on the morning of May 19 when Mackenzie led a force of about two hundred men out of Fort Richardson to investigate the attack. Later that day, the cavalry reached the site of the attack and verified the teamsters' report, adding the grisly details of torture and mutilation. All of the victims except one, who was bald, had been scalped, and one had been badly burned, probably in retaliation for wounding one of the attackers. The corpses were buried in a common grave and covered with stones.[11]

After playing the role of coroner, Mackenzie set out in pursuit of the Indians, a task almost guaranteed to be fruitless. Not only was the cavalry already twenty-four hours behind the raiders, but the heavy rain handicapped troop movement and blurred the trail as well. The colonel later reported that he had followed the trail to within five miles of the Red River, where it was lost because of the rain and the tracks of a large buffalo herd. Several days were spent in trying to pick up the trail, but that was impossible. Mackenzie gave up and headed for Fort Sill, which seemed to be the destination of the hostiles. His troops did not spot any Indians, although the cavalry's camp was fired into one night and one horse was stolen by a daring brave who crawled along a ditch and cut the picket rope. Mackenzie and his men rode into Fort Sill on June 4, 1871, frustrated by their inability to catch the perpetrators of the raid.[12]

While Mackenzie and his weary troopers struggled with mud and high water, the Kiowas had returned to their reservation, and some of the ringleaders of the raid had been arrested in a dramatic confrontation. One of the most famous Indians in Texas history, a Kiowa chief named Satanta, had openly boasted to the Indian agent, Lawrie Tatum, that he had led the raid. Tatum was a Quaker and genuinely concerned with the welfare of the Indians. Nevertheless, he believed that raiding by his charges should be punished, and he called upon the commander of the Tenth Cavalry at Fort Sill, Colonel Benjamin H. Grierson, to arrest Satanta and his accomplices. In an episode that came near precipitating a general fight, Satanta and two others, Satank and Big Tree, had been arrested on the front porch of Grierson's house. Sherman, who had gone directly to Fort Sill from Fort Richardson, took a leading role in that arrest.[13]

Sherman was gone by the time Mackenzie arrived, but the general had left orders for Mackenzie to confer with Grierson about frontier defense and to escort the Indian prisoners to Jacksboro to stand trial for murder. The army commander was

Satanta, the best known if not the most important of the Kiowa war leaders. *(Courtesy National Anthropological Archives, Smithsonian Institution; photograph no. 1380a)*

Lawrie Tatum, Quaker Indian agent, with children freed from Indian captivity. Tatum's belief that Indians who raided off the reservation should be punished forced his resignation. *(Courtesy National Anthropological Archives, Smithsonian Institution; photograph no. 1420)*

concerned that fair and strict justice be accorded to the three: "They must not be mobbed or lynched, but tried regularly for murder," after which Sherman expected them to be hanged. Mackenzie rested his men for a few days while conferring with Grierson and Tatum. In spite of differences in personality and temperament, the three seemed to get along well and agreed that force had to be used to punish renegades who raided off the reservation. [14]

Mackenzie's return trip to Fort Richardson began on June 8, 1871. The prisoners were loaded into two separate wagons. Satank, an old warrior and a member of the exclusive Koitsenga soldier society, had been slipped a knife and would have attempted to use it if he had not been restrained by the younger Indians. Satank was determined to die, and as the wagons with their escort passed out of Fort Sill, he began to chant his death song. About three-quarters of a mile from the fort, while Mackenzie lingered to confer with Grierson, the old raider freed his hands and attacked his guards, who abandoned the wagon. Satank was cut down in a hail of gunfire as he tried to work the lever of a guard's carbine. Mackenzie arrived just as the confrontation ended. After ascertaining what had happened, Mackenzie ordered that Satank's body be left by the side of the road to be retrieved by his tribe later. The colonel refused to allow a Tonkawa Indian scout to scalp the Kiowa but gave him the old man's bloodstained buffalo robe. [15]

After Satank's death, an especially close watch was kept over the remaining two prisoners. Their shackles were checked regularly and at night they were spread-eagled and tied to stakes in the ground. The mosquitoes were so bad that one of the sergeants posted a sentinel over each Indian to wave the pests away. Mackenzie's main concern was to get his charges into Fort Richardson without incident and to prevent any violence to them until they could be tried and their sentences carried out. He was successful in this. With no fanfare he hastened them through Jacksboro and to the guardhouse at the fort before the citizens were aware that he was back. As word of the prisoners spread through the town, a great crowd gathered at the fort "and a strong guard had to be placed . . . to prevent the scoundrels from being killed." [16]

Satanta and Big Tree were tried for murder on July 5 and 6. Mackenzie's main role in the famous trial was to protect the Indians from mob violence and, as it turned out, to provide an escort for them to the Texas state prison at Huntsville. He may have been called upon to testify as a witness for the prosecution. If so, he could only have sworn to the bloody scene he found on the Salt Creek Prairie and that the trail of the marauders had seemed to be headed toward Indian Territory and Fort Sill when it was lost because of the rain. He had no certain knowledge of either Indian's involvement in the attack. That did not matter much, however, because the jury, made up of local citizens, would have returned a guilty verdict in any circumstances. The Indians were sentenced to be hanged, but the governor of Texas commuted the penalty to imprisonment for life at the behest of the Indian Bureau, Lawrie Tatum, and even the judge who had presided at the trial.[17]

Trying Indians in civil courts for actions committed on a raid could have changed the direction of Indian policy at that point. Deeds of war would have been transformed into criminal acts, and the entire relationship between the army and hostile Indians would have changed. As it turned out, however, such a change did not come about. The trial of Satanta and Big Tree did not become a precedent, and no major alterations of policy resulted from it. Some Kiowas did become advocates of peace, but others urged continuing the old ways. Although it attracted a great deal of publicity, most of it favorable, the Jacksboro trial had little lasting significance.[18]

Ranald Mackenzie believed that the trials were only a small step toward solving the Indian problem and that further and stronger actions had to be taken. "To obtain a permanent peace and to give Mr. Tatum whom I regard as an excellent man an opportunity to elevate these people, the Kiowas and Comanches should be dismounted and disarmed and made to raise corn etc. This of course is radical and requires the use of troops from the Department of the Missouri (including New Mexico and the Platt) as well as from Texas." He confided to Sherman that he had considered going after the Kiowas that had fled the reservation at the time of Satanta's arrest, but had decided to wait to see if the mules stolen from the Warren wagon train would be returned.[19]

While waiting to see if the stolen stock was restored, Mackenzie began to plan further operations. He was sure that the Indians mainly responsible for raiding into Texas came from the "head of the Brazos" or "the reserve," often in cooperation with each other. Mackenzie urged General Sherman to allow him to launch a large scale movement with most of his regiment against the Indians who raided from the direction of the Texas Panhandle and then against the Indians north of the Red River. The colonel had seen enough of the tactic of sending out small scout-ing parties, usually in response to attacks that had taken place hours or days before, to believe that they were inefficient. The policy should be to put a large force in the field and apply constant pressure on the hostiles. "If they are roughly-handled they will break up," and then smaller army units could do the mopping up. Mackenzie wrote a similar letter to General J. J. Reynolds, head of the Department of Texas, requesting permission to consolidate the companies of the Fourth for movement to the west to "if possible surprise the camps of Indians believed to be in that country."[20]

Mackenzie's ideas were not completely new. General Sheridan had carried out a campaign on this order in the winter of 1868. What made Mackenzie's suggestions different was the call to ignore departmental boundaries and maintain unrelenting pressure by large forces. If he did not originate the basic idea, Mackenzie did reinforce Sheridan's ideas. It was no coincidence that this was the basic strategy that would be followed in the Red River War of 1874.[21]

Reynolds responded to Mackenzie's proposal by authorizing an expedition with the timing of it at Mackenzie's discretion and temporarily extending the colonel's authority to cover Forts Griffin and Concho. Mackenzie was also given command of available transportation in the region. To enhance chances of success, the Fourth would be allowed to cross the reservation boundaries if in actual pursuit of hostile Indians. Anticipating approval, Mackenzie had already begun to make plans with Grierson at Fort Sill for a joint expedition aimed at catching the Kiowas who had fled the reservation on the day of Satanta's arrest. Sherman supported this plan and expressed his hope to Grierson that the joint expedition would "lay a trap to catch some party of horse thieves in Texas, near the line and hang everyone of them." The general predicted that such action "will stop this raiding."[22]

Heeding his own recommendation that large forces be used to campaign against the Indians, Mackenzie began to gather the scattered companies of the Fourth Cavalry at Fort Richardson in June. On June 29, 1871, he sent three companies of cavalry and one of the Eleventh Infantry under Major Clarence Mauck to establish a camp on Gilbert's Creek, which fed into the Red River between the Big Wichita and Pease rivers. This force was to scout the region for raiding Indians, especially Kicking Bird and his followers, Kiowas who had fled the Fort Sill agency in fear of general punishment for the Warren wagon train raid. Sending out this force also helped to relieve the overcrowding as the other companies of the Fourth began to arrive at Richardson. By the end of July, Mackenzie had brought together all ten companies of the regiment, making the fort the largest post in Texas. The facilities were so pressed that some companies were bivouacked in nearby Lost Valley.[23]

Overcrowding was not a problem for long. As soon as Mackenzie had his forces gathered, he put them into motion. On July 28, Captain N. B. Mclaughlin led Companies I and G ahead to prepare a crossing of the Little Wichita River. Two days later, the remaining companies underwent a mounted inspection to ensure their readiness to take to the field. On August 2, the regiment moved out. Mackenzie, Lieutenant Carter, who served as adjutant for the expedition, and Boehm, leader of the Tonkawa scouts, followed later, using the bright moonlight to find the trail. About eleven o'clock the command camped on the West Fork of the Trinity River about twelve miles north of Fort Richardson.[24]

As the expedition moved west, Mackenzie was introduced to some of the hazards of a large scale summer campaign in Texas. The weather was hot and dry; it had not rained appreciably since May 19, the day that he had investigated the episode on the Salt Creek Prairie. The land was baked to the hardness of concrete, and water supplies became chancy. Often when water was found, its quality was questionable, in spite of which "it beat nothing all to pieces." Much of the grass had been burned away by prairie fires, which made good grass almost as precious as good water. The terrain became increasingly rugged, and numerous arroyos and creeks delayed movement. The column halted frequently while creek banks were cut down or, in some cases, bridges improvised to allow the supply wagons to keep up. Mackenzie was lucky to have secured again the services of Lieutenant Henry W. Lawton, who acted as regimental quartermaster for this and most of the other expeditions of the Fourth. Lawton was a hard driver who applied large amounts of common sense to overcome natural obstacles to transport.[25]

The Fourth Cavalry was reunited at Gilbert's Creek on August 6, 1871. After resting the troops a day, Mackenzie led them toward a nearby crossing of the Red River. The colonel and his green troops still had lessons to learn about the problems of campaigning. There were no professional mule skinners with the column, and the half-broken mules caused delay and confusion. The extreme heat began to take its toll, and one officer was prostrated by it and sent on to Fort Sill to recover. These problems limited the first day's march to only twelve miles. A prairie fire sweeping towards the camp prevented the troops from getting any rest that night. In order to escape the blaze, which Carter called a "magnificent spectacle," the column was forced to hitch the wagons, load the mules, and struggle all night to get across the Red River to safety. The exertions of the river crossing limited the day's march, and the regiment camped early. Despite being slowed by a large buffalo herd the next day, the regiment covered twenty-five miles and camped on Otter Creek in position to link up with Colonel Grierson's Tenth Cavalry.[26]

For several days the regiments camped near each other, offering opportunities for the men and horses to rest and the

officers to socialize. Mackenzie and Grierson had several con-
ferences to work out plans for the coming campaign, and they
rode together over the beginnings of the routes they would
take. On August 15 the campaign resumed as Mackenzie led
the Fourth Cavalry—minus the "halt, sick, etc.," who were left
at Otter Creek under an officer who was sick. Matthew Leeper,
an interpreter from Fort Sill, thought that Kicking Bird might
have taken his band to Rainy Mountain Creek in the Wichita
Mountains and guided the regiment across the North Fork of
the Red River in that direction. Sand hills covered with shin oak
made travel difficult and required much back tracking and
weaving.[27]

Two days out of the supply camp, a courier bringing mail that
had accumulated since the regiment's departure caught up with
the column. One of the official messages greatly distressed Mackenzie. Adjutant Carter claimed later that Mackenzie seemed to
lose his heart for the enterprise. Carter believed that the dis-
patch in question had been concocted by Indian sympathizers
in Washington to keep Mackenzie from finding and attacking
Kicking Bird's village by placing him under Grierson's authority.
Ernest Wallace, who wrote a detailed study of Mackenzie in
Texas, thought that the colonel had received a copy of Sherman's message to Reynolds limiting the Fourth's operations to
Texas unless called upon by Grierson and a copy of Reynolds's
order denying the reservation as an area of campaign except in
hot pursuit. Neither theory seems adequate to explain a serious
mood change in Mackenzie. He was already cooperating with
Grierson, and the campaign was mapped out, so an order placing him under Grierson's authority would not have changed the
situation. On the other hand, Grierson was informed on the day
before Mackenzie left that Kicking Bird's people had made res-
titution for the mules taken in the Warren wagon train raid. A
similar letter was addressed to Mackenzie, so he knew that Kicking Bird was no longer the main target of the expedition.[28]

Possibly the message that disturbed Mackenzie related to the
route he was to follow. Grierson expected Mackenzie to follow

the Salt Fork of the Red River west to its head, then to drop south and return along the main stream of the Red. Instead, Mackenzie led his men north and northwest. Grierson later, in his report to Sherman, criticized Mackenzie for taking that direction. It is not clear whether the commander of the Tenth Cavalry was fearful, as Carter supposed, that Mackenzie might precipitate an Indian war or simply felt that there was a better chance of making contact with hostile Indians by moving directly west.

Whatever the case, the joint campaign amounted to nothing more than a valuable training exercise. The regiment moved through the very rugged gypsum belt along the Texas-Oklahoma border. The temperature was so hot that the troopers put sponges under their hats, keeping them moistened with water carried in an extra canteen. At one point Mackenzie ordered a night march, either to take advantage of the cooler temperature or to escape observation by Indian scouts. The maneuver turned into a shambles, and the all night march covered only seven miles. Other hardships endured by the Fourth included a violent thunderstorm that blew down many tents and drenched men and equipment and a stampede of the horse herd. The stampede was reckoned at first to have been caused by Indians, but Carter found out years later that the regimental surgeon had startled the horses by wandering around in a white nightshirt: "He had never dared [to tell the truth], at least while *Mackenzie lived.*"[29]

Twice the column made contact with a small party of Kiowas. The Indians were willing to parley, but they refused to give any hint of the whereabouts of their village. Some of Mackenzie's officers wanted to take them prisoner and force them to reveal their band's location, but Mackenzie took no such action. Carter claimed later that the regiment got within nine miles of Kicking Bird's camp on the Sweetwater River, but the scouts missed it, and Mackenzie broke off the campaign on August 25. A series of short marches brought the column back to the supply camp on Otter Creek on September 3. Mackenzie and his men had gained valuable experience but did not have the desired effect on the Indians. The Comanches and Kiowas were not impressed by the joint campaign and had gotten over the fear that the arrest of the Kiowa leaders had generated. As early as September 19, a Tenth Cavalry patrol was attacked, and on the twenty-second two civilians were killed and scalped by Kiowas. Tatum, at the Fort Sill Agency, felt obliged to send messages to Grierson and Mackenzie asking them to take punitive action.[30]

Mackenzie was forced to camp on Otter Creek for several days while wagons were sent to Fort Sill to bring back forage for the horses. The Fourth settled near four companies of Grierson's Tenth left under the command of Captain Louis H. Carpenter to patrol the border areas in a vain attempt to prevent raids from Fort Sill into Texas. Carpenter treated the officers of the Fourth to a dinner the like of which none had seen in the field. They were seated at a covered table, served in courses on "real dishes," and feasted on fish, turkey, quail, and buffalo, with prune pie for dessert. The dessert seemed to have a profound effect on Mackenzie. As his party returned to camp, the colonel snapped "his amputated finger stumps with more than usual vigor [and] emphatically exclaimed: 'prune pie! Well, I'll be d——d! *and in the field;* what do you think about that?'" Similar outbursts occurred on the ride to camp. Mackenzie's astonishment at the Tenth's luxury is a measure of the seriousness of his view of campaigning. Such extras slowed movement and reduced efficiency.[31]

The train with forage arrived from Fort Sill on September 6, and Mackenzie ordered the regiment on the road to its home base the next day. The lead elements reached Fort Richardson on September 13, 1871, but the Fourth Cavalry was not destined to get much rest. Mackenzie, frustrated by his meager results so far, was already planning a campaign in the direction of the Llano Estacado, the Staked Plain of the Texas Panhandle. General Sherman had authorized such an effort earlier, and Mackenzie was eager to take advantage of the opportunity to operate on his own with no restrictions. He intended to find and punish the Quahada Comanches, who had never agreed to accept the limits of a reservation and were believed to be major raiders of the Texas frontier.[32]

Within a few days of their return to Fort Richardson, the Fourth began preparations for another large-scale campaign. On September 19, the lead elements of the regiment left for the concentration point at old Camp Cooper near Fort Griffin. Eight companies of the Fourth as well as two of the Eleventh Infantry, along with twenty Tonkawa scouts, were in place a short time later under the command of Captain Wirt Davis. Davis had orders to keep the troops in camp in order to rest them and the horses. Even when Indians raided the Murphy Ranch about twenty miles away, Davis took no action, much to the disgust of the civilians who reported the attack. On September 29, Lieutenant Carter, with a small party, went ahead to scout out the beginning of a route to the headwaters of the Brazos River. The entire regiment moved out four days later, guided by Carter and with the Tonkawa scouts riding far ahead to guard against surprise attacks as well as to pick a trail. The troops were in a good mood and sang their regimental song as they headed west.[33]

The route taken by the column became the regular path of settlers heading for northwest Texas and was later known as the Mackenzie Trail. The trail left the Clear Fork of the Brazos and moved through present day Haskell, Jones, Stonewall, and Dickens counties. A supply camp was established on Duck Creek near the site of Spur. Each night as camp was made, precautions were taken to prevent surprise attacks by Indians, but immense herds of buffalo were a greater danger. At least twice the buffalo threatened to stampede the horse herd and, perhaps, overrun the camp. On one occasion disaster was avoided by the narrowest of margins when Carter and the night guard managed to turn a raging herd of the great beasts by waving blankets and shouting. Part of the horse herd was just brushed by the buffalo.[34]

The Tonkawa scouts were sent out by Mackenzie in the evening of October 7 to search for the Quahada village, which he believed to be in the area. The Indians were reluctant to go without an escort of whites, fearful that they might be taken for enemies upon their return to camp. Mackenzie's impatient nature kept him from waiting until the scouts could report. Instead, he sent Carter and a small detachment up Duck Creek. When the lieutenant reported the discovery of a "small trail," Mackenzie ordered a night march in hopes of surprising the Indians who had made it. This night exercise was no more successful than the one undertaken in August. After much stumbling around in a maze of ravines and creek beds, the regiment was trapped in a box canyon. Efforts to find a way out in the darkness failed, so the troops were forced to spend the night on the ground without fires and with only cold food to eat. At first light the column found a way out and marched to the Freshwater Fork of the Brazos, some miles south of present-day Crosbyton. Camp was made to allow the men to take advantage of what really was, to their surprise, fresh water. That afternoon, a scout led by Captain Edward M. Heyl made contact with the Tonkawas. The friendly Indians had spotted and driven off a small party of Comanches and came into camp worn out from their exertions. They reported finding the trail of a Comanche village, and Mackenzie quickly put his troops into the saddle to follow it. The regiment made only a little progress, partly because of the confusion created by the accidental discharge of a trooper's carbine. About dark, the cavalry made a crowded camp in a narrow valley.[35]

Mackenzie ordered special efforts to secure the horses and prevent a surprise attack, but the precautions were not enough to prevent a Comanche raid on the horse herd. About midnight a party of Quahadas rushed the camp yelling, shaking buffalo hides, and making every effort to stampede the cavalry horses. Mass confusion prevailed as the Indians whooped and hollered, troopers tried to restrain their mounts or took snap shots in the darkness, and officers shouted unheeded orders. When calm was restored and a count was made, it was found that sixty-six horses were missing, including Mackenzie's own "fine gray pacer which he prized very highly." It was not an auspicious beginning for a campaign.[36]

At dawn, Lieutenant Carter joined with parts of Companies K and G, led by Captain Heyl, to chase a dozen Indians who were making off with more horses. The Indians abandoned the horses and fled across a ravine, which halted all but a handful of their pursuers. The few who continued the chase followed the Indians up a bluff and onto a flat plain. There, the situation changed abruptly as the soldiers ran head on into a large body of Comanches, perhaps several hundred in number. Heyl cried, "Heavens, but we are in a nest! Just look at the Indians!" Carter saw at once that the jaded condition of the troopers' horses would not allow a headlong flight and that their only hope was to maintain a steady fire while withdrawing slowly. Heyl at first seemed to support the action but lost his nerve and ran, taking his men with him. Carter, left with only five men, faced the very risky chore of holding off the massed Indians while seeking cover. With cool courage Carter directed the men's fire, and their determination, plus the volume of fire put out by the repeating Spencer carbines they carried, saved the day. One man, Private Gregg, was killed when his horse gave out and a large Indian, with his face painted black, attacked him. The fight might have continued and still gone against the soldiers had not the Tonkawa scouts under Lieutenant Boehm arrived. There ensued a long-distance fire fight with neither group of Indians willing to come to close quarters. After a time this "grand, but rather dangerous circus" was ended by the appearance of Mackenzie and the main body of cavalry. The Comanches scattered, and the Fourth, its horses too fagged for pursuit, stopped to rest.[37]

Carter had seriously injured his leg when his horse had stumbled and slammed it against a rock. Mackenzie was very concerned about his adjutant's condition and offered to put him in charge of the dismounted men who were to be sent back to the supply camp. Mackenzie also asked about Heyl's conduct, and Carter, without actually condemning Heyl, let it be known that the captain's actions were questionable. Perhaps because he was not an eyewitness, and because Carter refused to make a positive statement, Mackenzie took no action in the matter. The colonel would have made every effort to remove Heyl from the regiment if there had been clear evidence of cowardice, but following his usual habit, he gave Captain Heyl the benefit of the doubt.[38]

While the Fourth Cavalry buried its slain comrade and rested, the Tonkawa scouts picked up the trail of the Comanche village. Mackenzie gathered the rest of his troops and spent the remainder of the day, October 10, following the sign up Blanco Canyon, which had been cut in the Caprock by the headwaters of the Freshwater Fork of the Brazos. After a while, the trail became confused, and the scouts discovered that the Comanches had doubled back, so the rest of the day was wasted in backtracking. The next day was equally frustrating. The Tonkawas led the regiment out of the canyon, back into it, and finally out onto the great expanse of the Llano Estacado. The men of the Fourth had the usual reaction to one's first sight of the Llano. It seemed to go on forever, with virtually no vegetation other than grass, no landmarks, no features at all. It seemed barren and mysterious, a vast, gently undulating plain that could only, rather tritely, "be compared to the ocean in its vastness."[39]

Now, however, Mackenzie made contact with the elusive quarry. Lodge poles and other debris began to mark the path of the retreating Indian village, and warriors became increasingly visible as they kept an eye on the pursuing cavalry. The growing evidence of closing with the Indians made this "the most exciting march of the expedition." October 12 was cold and dreary, but Mackenzie had his troops in the saddle early. The Comanche trail was now broad and obvious to even the most inexperienced eye. In their haste the Indians were now abandoning tools, buffalo robes, and even puppies too young to keep up. More Indians appeared to try to divert the pursuit away from the main body. The lead elements of the Fourth Cavalry caught sight of the village moving slowly in the distance late in the afternoon. Just about that time, a true Texas norther blew down upon the plains, driving a mixture of rain, sleet, and snow onto pursuer and pursued alike. The men of the Fourth expected Mackenzie to order increased speed to catch the Comanches before full darkness shielded them. No such order came, however, and, as the dim light faded and the cold grew more intense, Mackenzie halted the column and began to make defensive arrangements.[40]

The men were formed into a large circle, each holding his horse, and the pack mules were herded into the center of the ring. It was a long, bitter night. The cold was extreme, and most of the men had only their summer uniforms to protect them from the weather. Mackenzie himself had no shield from the elements until someone "wrapped his shivering form in a buffalo robe." From time to time Comanche warriors "rode in and fired upon us." Altogether, it was a miserable night. The storm blew itself out during the night, and the morning dawned bright and clear. Pursuit was resumed, but after about fifteen miles only a few Comanche scouts had been seen, and Mackenzie turned the regiment around and began to move it back toward the supply camp.[41]

Mackenzie's decision not to try to force a fight with an unknown, but large, number of Comanches in the fading light of October 12 is a prime example of the reason for his success as an Indian fighter. The young colonel's innate shyness may have made him a little less adept than his chief rivals at public relations, but he knew well that the key to advancement was a willingness and ability to find and give battle to the Indians. Nevertheless, Mackenzie refused to step over the edge of prudence. Possibly a hard push to catch the village could have resulted in a major victory and a severe blow to Comanche power in Texas, but it is just as possible that such a move would have brought disaster. It is not clear how many men followed Mackenzie up onto the plain, but the number was less than four hundred. These men, tired and riding worn, hard-used horses, would have faced several hundred Comanche warriors fighting to save their families. The odds, at best, would have been even. Even an initial victory for Mackenzie could have turned into a defeat. A hard fight would have dismounted many of the men, and the main supply camp was about eighty miles away on Duck Creek. Getting back to camp might have cost as many casualties as combat. Glory and high rank were not inducement enough for Mackenzie to take the chance. Characteristically, he chose caution rather than reckless abandon.[42]

An episode that took place on the journey back to the supply camp also brought a characteristic Mackenzie action. As the column moved back down into Blanco Canyon, the Tonkawa scouts spotted two Comanches and gave the alarm. The Comanche warriors were quickly surrounded by superior numbers, but, protected by good cover, they refused to yield. Mackenzie ordered Boehm to take fifteen dismounted troopers and root the Comanches from their hiding place. His Civil War habit of leading his men and his natural impatience prevented him from holding back, however, and he himself soon joined Boehm in directing the attack. The Comanches, fighting for their lives, loosed a barrage of arrows, one of which struck Mackenzie in the fleshy part of the thigh. It was not a serious wound, but the colonel's refusal to rest and let it heal almost drove the regimental surgeon to despair. The doctor, a contract surgeon named Gregory, threatened amputation if Mackenzie did not keep still and was almost brained with a crutch for his pains. Mackenzie's insistence on leading rather than directing from the rear earned the respect of officers and troopers alike. One enlisted man also was wounded in the scrape, and his was the only injury cited by Mackenzie in the official report.[43]

Mackenzie was not yet ready to end the campaign. He reasoned that the Comanches, no longer pursued, would double back to more favored camping grounds than were offered on the Llano Estacado. Accordingly, he determined to send the troopers who had lost their horses back to the supply camp on Duck Creek while he led the remainder toward the headwaters of the Pease River. This plan was put into action on October 24. Mackenzie's leg wound proved to be so painful, however, that he was forced to turn over command of the scout to Major Clarence Mauck and to return to the supply camp. The weather began to grow worse, and the condition of the men and horses dictated that the expedition be brought to a close. Mauck brought the scout column into the supply camp on November 6 without having found any Indians. His horses were so weak that the regiment could not start for Fort Richardson immediately. Mackenzie had earlier sent a wagon train to Fort Griffin for forage, and its return on November 8 enabled full feeding of the horses to resume. The entire command rested the next day, and in the afternoon of November 10 the return trip began. Three days later the regiment reached Fort Griffin, and the companies based at Fort Richardson reached their station on the eighteenth.[44]

It had not been a good year for Ranald Mackenzie. Lapsed time and bad weather had prevented him from playing a significant role in the aftermath of the Warren wagon train affair. Poor coordination, lack of knowledge of the country, and perhaps Grierson's deliberate efforts to avoid confrontation with the Indians had limited the effectiveness of the joint campaign. The recently completed campaign had achieved no measurable result, while the Fourth had lost one man killed and a large number of horses to both Indians and the weather. Nevertheless, some positive results had been secured. For one thing, both Mackenzie and his men had gained valuable experience in dealing with Indians and the terrain where future campaigns would be carried out. Mackenzie had done little to advance his ambitions but nothing to delay their fulfillment. His energy and determination retained the good will of General Sheridan and impressed Sherman, whom he had not known personally before. The Comanches and Kiowas had gotten their first look at the man who would play a major role in their loss of power and independence. It was probably during this year that the Kiowas began to refer to Mackenzie as Mangomhente, which is translated as "No Index Finger" or "Bad Hand."[45]

CHAPTER SEVEN

GIVE HIM A GOOD SWING

A BUSY season of campaigning had come to an end, and now Mackenzie had to turn his attention to the more mundane problems that faced a regimental commander. Foremost among these was a high rate of desertion by the men of the Fourth Cavalry. From April to December 1871, 171 men had decided to abandon the soldier's life. This was not an unusually high number, as desertion was a common problem in the frontier army. During the period 1871–1872, almost one-third of the enlisted men in the army attempted to desert. Low pay, dull routine, harsh discipline, and poor living conditions worked together to undermine the common soldier's devotion to duty. Hard service in a long campaign or exposure to combat further contributed to unauthorized leave-taking. A man who could take no more had an excellent chance for a successful escape. Commanders whose regiments were undermanned anyway rarely depleted their commands further by trying to bring back the runaways. Deserters could often count on assistance from civilians who cooperated out of sympathy or desire for profit. [1]

Mackenzie did not take the problem of desertion lightly, and as it threatened to reach epidemic proportions he resolved to take firm action. On November 29, ten men deserted from one company, and Mackenzie had had enough. He summoned Lieutenants Lawton and Carter and ordered each of them to take a detachment of two noncommissioned officers and eleven privates to search for the missing men. The two parties were to strike out in different directions under instructions to follow the trail of the deserters as long and as far as necessary, "even if it leads to Galveston and New Orleans, or, even, to New York." Other men who might be contemplating desertion had to be shown that escape was impossible. As it turned out, it was Carter who took the path the deserters had taken. Through dogged determination and sharp intuition, the lieutenant was able to capture ten deserters plus a civilian who had aided them in their flight. Carter also recovered the carbines that the men had sold to finance their journey. It was an impressive performance, and Mackenzie justly praised Carter. More important, the return of the prisoners had a decided effect on the number of desertions, which declined sharply.[2]

For those men who lacked the initiative to desert or whose patriotism prevented them from doing so, the most serious problem at Fort Richardson was trying to stay warm and avoid disease. The picket construction of the barracks left large gaps which allowed the winter wind to blow freely through the building, and the two wood-burning stoves did little to warm the men. Poor diet contributed to the susceptibility of the men to disease. Official rations consisted mainly of salt meat, beans, and hard bread. In these conditions, a variety of diseases, including typhoid fever, dysentery, pneumonia, and scurvy, struck the men. In the last two months of 1871, 20 percent of the troopers of the Fourth Cavalry were reported sick. Conditions improved as the weather warmed in the spring of 1872 and vegetables were procured to supplement the rations. Still, several men died of disease.[3]

Relations with the town of Jacksboro were another on-going concern for Mackenzie. One reason for discipline problems at Fort Richardson was the lack of activities for the men's leisure time. There were few amusements available for the men, and in particular no organized activities and no athletics. There may have been a small post library, but it offered little that appealed to the average trooper. To escape the dull monotony of post routine, the troopers resorted to Jacksboro, which had flourished greatly because of the increase in the numbers stationed at Fort Richardson. Henry W. Strong, who sometimes scouted for Mackenzie, thought Jacksboro was "one of the toughest towns in the United States." Ten army companies commanded a large payroll, and Jacksboro attracted a wide variety of frontier characters determined to get their share. At its peak Jacksboro had twenty-seven saloons and a proportionate number of supporting establishments. Whiskey was twenty-five cents a shot, gambling of all kinds was available, and prostitution was widespread. The bored trooper who crossed Lost Creek, which separated the fort from the town, was likely to lose his pay, lucky to avoid disease, and a prime candidate for company punishment for drunkenness.[4]

Given the volatile combination of disparate, often shady characters who converged on Jacksboro and the troopers hunting for excitement, it is surprising that recorded violence was relatively rare. Mackenzie's authority in the town and the respect in which he was held there helped to keep incidents to a minimum, but occasionally the need for order had to be emphasized. At least once Mackenzie was compelled to send armed troopers to arrest drunken cowboys shooting up the town. In another case the colonel's firm control of his own men and quick action prevented another incident from escalating into full scale hostilities between fort and town. A trooper from B Company was murdered in a bawdy house, and his messmates burned it in retaliation. Mackenzie moved quickly to put a cap on the episode. He visited his sergeants and charged them with responsibility for any incidents. The NCOs then, as one recalled later, "went to bed like good boys." Lieutenant Carter was then sent into Jacksboro with a small force to arrest any troopers who might have slipped into town. Carter was confronted by an armed mob of citizens, who were prepared to repel invasion. The officer was able to calm the mob, and the potentially explosive incident ended.[5]

Fortunately for Mackenzie, one problem, a troublesome and possibly career-threatening feud with his departmental commander, General Reynolds, was resolved in his favor. Reynolds was a West Pointer who had served in the pre–Civil War army, both on the frontier and as an instructor at the Military Academy, until 1857. During the war he became an officer of volunteers and rose to the rank of major general. He chose to stay in the army following the war, and he was given the permanent rank of colonel. As commander of the Department of Texas he had the authority of his brevet rank of brigadier general. President Andrew Johnson removed him from that position, but he was reinstated when his old classmate, Ulysses S. Grant, became president. For reasons that are not completely clear—perhaps the age difference or Reynolds's greater concern with Reconstruction policy than with Indian depredations—Mackenzie and his immediate boss did not get along.[6]

Trouble began as Mackenzie prepared for his campaigns in 1871. In his haste to complete preparations for taking the field, Mackenzie invoiced new pack mules to company commanders instead of the regimental quartermaster, as required by regulations. This was a technical error which Mackenzie rectified when it was pointed out to him. Meanwhile, Mackenzie suspended a contract with the company of Adams and Wicks to supply corn to Fort Richardson. The colonel had long suspected that Reynolds and the contractors were conspiring to defraud the government. When Reynolds ordered Mackenzie to accept the Adams and Wicks deliveries, Mackenzie's response was to inform the commander of the Division of the South, Henry W. Halleck, of his suspicions, including his belief that Reynolds had accepted the present of a house from the contractors. Mackenzie's failure to report the date of his departure for the field added to Reynolds's belief that the cavalry commander was being insubordinate and acting out of spite. Reynolds wrote a long letter to Halleck giving his side of the story and hinting of court-martial charges once Mackenzie returned from the field.[7]

An omen of the outcome of the dispute was given in General Sherman's endorsement of a letter from Reynolds complaining of Mackenzie's conduct. In sending the letter on to the secretary of war, Sherman declared that he did "not understand what Gen[.] Reynolds refers to." Following up his threat, Reynolds preferred charges against Mackenzie when the Fourth Cavalry came in from campaigning. He charged Mackenzie with disobeying orders, improper conduct, and disrespect for his commanding officer. After the charges had worked their way through channels, the judge advocate general ruled that it was "clearly not expedient to prosecute." Instead, Mackenzie was rather gently admonished by the secretary of war in early 1872. Mackenzie won in another way as well. On November 1, 1871, General Order Number 66 by the secretary of war reorganized the Department of Texas by adding Indian Territory to it and bringing it under the control of the Military Division of the Missouri. The order reassigned Reynolds and installed General C. C. Augur as commander of the Department of Texas.[8]

Clearly, Mackenzie's connections had made the difference. Reynolds was an able officer, although his reputation later suffered a severe blow by his conduct of a fight with a village of Northern Cheyennes in 1876. He had some claim to Grant's good will, but it was not strong enough to overcome the combined weight of Mackenzie's relations with the president; the commanding general of the army, Sherman; and the commander of the Military Division of the Missouri, Sheridan. The younger officer had not achieved spectacular results in his first year with the Fourth Cavalry, but the memory of his Civil War record plus his energy, drive, and youth carried enough weight with his superiors for them to retrieve him from hot water.[9]

By the spring of 1872, whatever restraining effect the confinement of Satanta and Big Tree had exercised on the Indians was dissipated. The first hint of spring was the traditional signal for the beginning of the raiding season, and both Kiowas and Comanches took to the warpath with renewed vigor. One party of Kiowas attacked a wagon train carrying government supplies at Howard's Wells in Crockett County, Texas. Seventeen teamsters were killed, and the Indians burned the wagons after taking what they could carry. Two troops of the Ninth Cavalry from

Fort Concho chanced by the scene later that day and pursued the raiders. The Indians had not expected such rapid pursuit and had not gone far before camping for the night. Taken by surprise, the Kiowas nevertheless held their own when attacked by the army. They killed two and held the cavalry off until dark. They then abandoned most of their plunder and retreated. Two Indians had been wounded, and that was enough casualties for one raid.[10]

The Howard's Wells raid was only the largest of a number of attacks that led Mackenzie to declare in June "that the outrages committed by Indians have been more frequent than I have ever known them here." Lawrie Tatum's request for troops to police the reservation confirmed Mackenzie's belief that most of the hostiles came from the Fort Sill Agency. As dedicated as he was to Quaker ideals, Tatum's experience taught him the lesson that many military men, including Mackenzie, had known from the beginning: most of the Indians would not settle down until they had been thoroughly defeated by the army. Tatum's growing disagreement with his superiors forced him to resign as agent early in 1873.[11]

Because it was clear that 1872 would be a year of hard campaigning, Mackenzie took special care in obtaining mounts for his command. Besides urging haste in the procurement of new horses, Mackenzie tried to maintain close supervision of the purchasing process. He sent a purchasing board of his own officers to ensure quality of the animals and declared that "no middlemen will be allowed." He stressed the selection of horses from within a 150-mile radius of Fort Richardson, an area which he thought would supply an adequate quantity as well as "the best horses in the state." Somewhat wistfully, Mackenzie speculated on buying the horses in Kentucky but saw that the expense would be prohibitive.[12]

Mackenzie needed men as well as horses. One measure he took was to assign men in the companies at Fort Griffin who were without horses to care for and guard the horses purchased by the board. For all of his reputation as a strict disciplinarian,

Mackenzie was willing to make allowances, especially when he needed every experienced soldier available. To this end he requested the remission of the sentence of Private John Comfort. Comfort's offense was serious, the colonel admitted, but the private had been drunk at the time. Besides, Comfort was, in many ways, an excellent soldier and would be "very useful for scouting purposes." The remission was granted. [13]

While making plans for another large-scale expedition to the Llano Estacado, Mackenzie responded to the increased raiding activity by stepping up the number of patrols sent out. As usual, most of these scouts ended without result, but occasionally contact was made. On April 21 a detachment surprised a band of hostiles and captured fourteen horses and two mules and chased the Indians for several miles until they scattered and the trail was lost. Another successful encounter occurred on May 12, when a party led by Lieutenant John McKinney had a stand-up fight with a band of Kiowas and Comanches. No Indian bodies were recovered, but the troopers saw three Indian warriors tied to their horses before the Indians broke off the fight. In late May, Captain Heyl had a less successful run-in with raiders in which he lost one man while apparently doing no damage to the Indians. [14]

These small-scale affairs were essentially holding actions while Mackenzie worked to complete arrangements for a major campaign. On June 14, 1872, the colonel led Companies A, B, and F out of Fort Richardson. At Fort Griffin the column picked up L Company, and two companies were dispatched from Fort Concho to join the regiment on the Freshwater Fork of the Brazos River. Mackenzie's command was filled out by the addition of two companies of the Eleventh Infantry and three of the Twenty-fourth, the latter under the command of Lieutenant Colonel William Shafter. The infantry was to guard the supply train and the base camp while the cavalry was to search for hostile Indians wherever Mackenzie thought he had the best chance of success. The aim of the campaign was not only to protect the frontier from Indian raids but also to break up the traffic in stolen cattle across the Llano Estacado. [15]

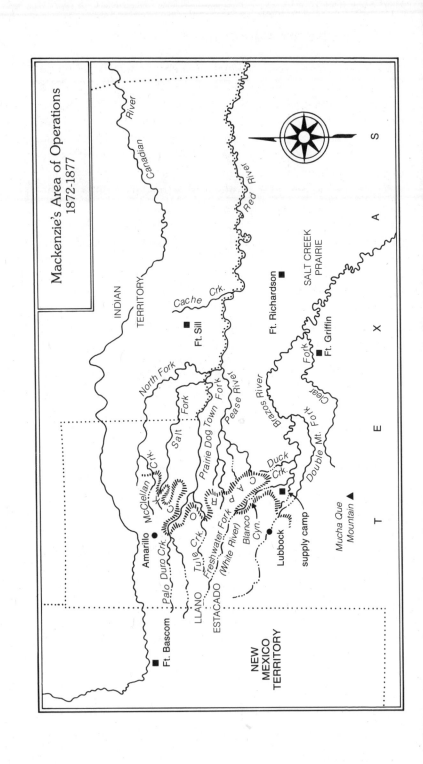

Mackenzie's Area of Operations
1872-1877

A fortunate break had revealed to the army the true extent of the commerce between the hostiles and the comancheros, illicit traders from New Mexico. A small patrol of the Fourth Cavalry out of Fort Concho, led by Sergeant William Wilson, had a brief fight with a band of raiders, killing two and capturing one. The prisoner turned out to be a New Mexican named Polónio Ortíz, who admitted belonging to a gang of comancheros that regularly crossed the plains to trade for cattle stolen by the Indians. Offered the possibility of a pardon for his crimes, Ortíz was induced to supply more information, including the fact that there were at least two routes across the Llano that had water at most seasons of the year. A scout from Fort Concho led by Captain N. B. McLaughlin confirmed the general reliability of Ortíz's statement. The patrol marched to Mucha Que Mountain and found evidence that it was the site of the rendezvous between the Indians and the comancheros. [16]

Armed with Ortíz's information, Sheridan authorized Augur to go after and end the traffic across the plains. Augur's orders were broad enough to allow Mackenzie freedom to act based on his on-site perceptions but were clearly aimed at stopping the comanchero trade. Sheridan approved General Augur's orders to Mackenzie and wrote, "Give him a good swing and ask him for good results." Although Ortíz was not mentioned in the orders, Augur sent him along with the two companies of the Fourth Cavalry from Fort Concho. Ortíz would help make possible one of Mackenzie's most important services. [17]

Mackenzie united most of his force on Duck Creek by the end of June. Shafter's contingent was still absent, halted temporarily by a rumor that Mackenzie and a small escort had been wiped out by Indians. Sparked by no discoverable cause, the story of Mackenzie's death spread quickly. The *Galveston Daily News* reported on June 27 that a rancher had seen Mackenzie and nine troopers killed by about sixty Indians. By July 1, Adjutant General E. D. Townsend in Washington wired Augur asking about a *New York Times* story to the same effect. Augur, of course, denied the validity of the rumor. Shafter paused in his march in order to ascertain the facts and missed the opening of the campaign. [18]

Mackenzie had anticipated marching to the head of the Freshwater Fork and descending that stream while Shafter came upstream to catch any Indians in the area in a pincers movement. Knowing that delaying his movement would allow time for any Indians to move away, Mackenzie displayed his flexibility by dividing his existing force and following the same basic plan. He led four companies of cavalry to the upper reaches of the Brazos, while Major A. E. Latimer marched with two companies of cavalry and one of infantry to carry out Shafter's part in the plan. The expedition left the Duck Creek encampment on June 28 and was reunited on July 1 on the Freshwater Fork. The first day, Mackenzie had seen one small band of Indians, which escaped after a chase of "several miles." No signs of a recent large camp were found, however, and Mackenzie turned his search in other directions. [19]

Mackenzie now believed that "most of the worst bands" were camping to the north and made plans for a sweep in that direction as soon as Shafter arrived. Still not wasting time waiting for Shafter to appear, Mackenzie sent McLaughlin with two companies south to Mucha Que Mountain to ensure that no Indians had slipped into the area since May. Shafter reached the Freshwater Fork on July 6, and Mackenzie shifted his base to that river. From there it was easier to reach the heads of the various tributaries of the Red River, where Mackenzie judged that the Indians located their summer campgrounds. On July 9, four companies followed Mackenzie into the region north of the base camp, taking a line just to the east of the Staked Plain. The expedition covered 208 miles and found very few signs of recent Indian activity, although one promising trail was washed out by a heavy downpour. Mackenzie did see enough to establish that the country along the edge of the Llano provided ample support for the Indians at most seasons of the year. McLaughlin's report that he had found some sign but had made no contact, and Shafter's brief scout of the head of the Brazos, indicated to Mackenzie that he must extend his area of operations.[20]

While Mackenzie was preparing the Fourth for a march to the North Fork of the Red River, where, informants assured him, Indians from the Fort Sill Reservation were living, scouts assisted by Ortíz discovered a broad trail leading out onto the Llano Estacado. It was evidently a main traveled road for comancheros taking wagonloads of trade goods to the Indians and driving stolen herds of cattle to New Mexico. The colonel had not intended to move to the west, "but the trail was so plain that it appeared to me that it should be followed." With five companies of cavalry and one of infantry to guard the wagons, Mackenzie set out across the plains on July 28, 1872. The trail was broad and easy to follow, and there was plenty of water because of recent rains. By August 7 the column camped on Las Canaditas Creek just north of present-day Tolar, New Mexico. After securing supplies from Fort Sumner, Mackenzie continued to follow the trail until it split and then rode into the village of Puerta de Luna. Ortíz had said that three leaders of the comancheros resided there, but Mackenzie was foiled because his quarry had been flushed by a large party of Texas cowboys led by John Hittson, one of the largest ranchers in the Southwest.[21]

Mackenzie halted again at Fort Bascom to resupply before making the return trip by a different route. At Bascom some of his men obtained whiskey and got drunk. Rain that day had turned the ground into a sea of red mud, and many of the men were caked with it the next day, having "wallowed around in the mud like hogs in a mudhole." Mackenzie made no mention of this in his report. Either he thought it not particularly serious, or, just as likely, he thought that his men needed a break. Mackenzie did not approve of drunkenness, but he recognized that the troops benefited from occasional periods of relaxation. His attitude toward discipline had not changed completely, but he seems to have learned that too rigid a discipline could be as bad as no discipline at all. He was concerned about the effects of hard campaigning on men and horses. His second report from New Mexico asserted that the men and horses were still in good shape but that more extended service would begin to wear them down. Mackenzie recommended that if the expedition were to stay out until late fall, the companies in the field and at the posts be rotated.[22]

The return trip followed a more northerly path than the one first used. Another wagon and cattle trail led to Quitaque Creek, which was a common meeting ground for Indians and comancheros. Mackenzie's route led from Puerta de Luna to the Palo Duro Canyon in Texas and from there to Tule Canyon and on to the supply camp below present-day Crosbyton. Only a few Indians were spotted, and no contact was made. By the time the command reached the supply camp, both men and horses were jaded, and two weeks were needed to rest and reshoe the horses. Mackenzie reported that the return route had water available year-round, with no more than thirty miles between water holes. He did not appreciate the significance of what he had done, complained that he had not been "very successful in accomplishing anything useful," and promised more effort for the future.[23]

Mackenzie was thinking like the frontier population of Texas, which saw his main job as killing Indians. Some complaints about his performance so far appeared in the newspapers. The Gainesville, Texas, paper declared that the high hopes that people had in Mackenzie had faded because Indian depredations were worse in 1872 than ever before. Some army officers also failed to grasp the importance of the trek across the Llano. Grierson at Fort Sill suggested that the command had simply gotten lost and had found its way to New Mexico by accident. Nevertheless, Mackenzie's scout had been of great importance. In his annual report, Augur stated that Mackenzie had not only exposed the routes and methods of the comancheros, but also had shown that troops could operate on the Staked Plains. Henceforth, the Llano would no longer be a sanctuary for either comancheros or raiding Indians.[24]

The High Plains had presented a great psychological barrier to white Americans. Accustomed to judging the suitability of land for settlement by the number and size of its trees, the first American explorers had failed to comprehend the true nature of the plains and had labeled them as the Great American Desert. The plains seemed trackless, without any landmarks to guide travelers and without enough rainfall to sustain civilization. Mackenzie had shown that these notions were false. When the Texas rancher Hittson went to New Mexico to recover his stolen cattle, he went by way of Colorado. Now it was clear that the roundabout way was not necessary. The next year, when Colonel John Davidson, who had replaced Grierson at Fort Sill, was ordered to move against the comanchero traffic, he was sent copies of Mackenzie's map to use as a guide. Of equal importance, the expedition had opened up the possibility of white settlement on the Llano. The coming of farmers and ranchers would hasten the day when the Indians of the southern plains would have no place to go from their reservations.[25]

Mackenzie was anxious to resume campaigning and to inflict some damage on the Indians. He waited impatiently while the men and horses recovered from their exertions. The next objective was to check the Salt and North forks of the Red River. At the beginning of the campaign, Matthew Leeper, an interpreter from the Fort Sill Agency, had joined the command. Leeper brought with him Tatum's authorization to "attack and capture" several groups of Indians, Kiowas and Comanches, that had left the reservation. Leeper also provided fairly certain knowledge of the location of these Indians. Sheridan, as head of the Division of the Missouri, had responded by sending out two small columns of troops from Fort Sill. He expected little result, however, and began to consider another winter campaign similar to the one he had led in 1868. Mackenzie chose not to wait. Frustrated by the dearth of measurable results by his campaign so far, and driven by his determination to be the best soldier in the field, he headed north as soon as his regiment was ready.[26]

The new column, consisting of five companies of the Fourth

Cavalry and one of the Eleventh Infantry, pulled out on September 21, leaving Colonel Shafter in command of the supply camp. The Salt Fork was barren of Indians and offered no recent sign of them. Continuing its northward march, the column struck McClellan Creek, a tributary of the North Fork of the Red River, on September 29. After following the creek about two miles, the troops came upon a patch of wild grapes. Mackenzie generously halted to allow his men, who had not eaten all day, to snack on the fruit. While the men attempted take the edge off their hunger, one of the Tonkawa scouts, called McCord, spotted the tracks of two horses and a mule. The mule tracks were judged to be heading in the direction of an Indian encampment, and Mackenzie set the Tonkawas on the trail, with the cavalry following close behind. Moving at a "rapid gait," the army had covered about twelve miles by four o'clock when a large village was spotted in the distance.[27]

A brief pause was all that was necessary for Mackenzie to outline his plan of attack. Companies A, F, and L were to charge the main village in echelon, with the troops in columns of fours. Company D was to cut off the Indians' horse herd while I Company hit a small semidetached village to the right. After making these assignments, Mackenzie ordered the charge, and his first major engagement with hostile Indians was under way. The Indians were unprepared for an attack and delayed moving to meet it, apparently thinking that the dust raised by the cavalry was made by a group of returning buffalo hunters. The leading chief in the encampment at the time was Kai-wotche, who was acting in the place of a greater chief named Mow-way. Kai-wotche discovered the white soldiers and raced to warn his people with the army close on his heels.[28]

The Battle of the North Fork of the Red River lasted only about thirty minutes, but it was furiously fought nevertheless. Mackenzie rode with A Company, which was the base troop for the attack. As the cavalry charged into the center of the village, about seventy-five Comanches rose from behind a ridge only ten or fifteen yards away. Only the fact that the Indians fired high, as they seemed to have had a tendency to do, saved the army from severe casualties. "Like all close Indian fighting," the battle then dissolved into a series of individual contests. The deadliest combat took place on the front attacked by F Company. Three of the four soldiers in the first rank were hit; one was killed instantly, one mortally wounded, and one seriously wounded, although he later recovered. Another hot spot was on the A Company front, where some eighty Indians, trapped in a crescent-shaped ravine, put up strong resistance. There, the warriors twice charged the army, suffering heavy losses in the process. After less than an hour, the Comanches began to break off the fight. The presence of their families explained why they had made such a determined stand.[29]

Mackenzie counted the bodies of twenty-three Indian dead. As was his usual practice, he counted only the bodies actually recovered. A much larger number had been killed, and many of the bodies were dumped into "a deep pool of water" by the Indians to keep them from falling into white hands. One Indian source later admitted that fifty-two warriors had been killed. The fleeing Indians left behind between 120 and 130 women and children. After the main body was gone, the noncombatants who had hidden themselves in thick brush came out and surrendered. To seal the victory, the cavalry captured 262 lodges, with most of the Indians' personal possessions and a large number of horses. The lodges and property were burned before Mackenzie mounted the prisoners and moved away from the battlefield.[30]

The elation of victory was somewhat dampened when the Indian warriors returned the next two nights and recovered most of their horses. Lieutenant Boehm and his Tonkawa scouts were given the task of guarding the herd. They drove the horses into a shallow depression and settled in for the night. On the first night the regrouped Comanches attacked the main cavalry camp in a effort to free the families but failed to accomplish their objective. The second night they turned their attention to the horse herd and were more successful. By circling the detach-

ment, yelling and firing their guns and generally creating confusion, the Indians were able to cut in and free their own horses
and some of the army's as well. Boehm and his scouts were
forced to walk into the main camp the next day and received
the "grand laugh."[31]

In spite of the loss of the Indian ponies, the battle was a major
victory that affected both the Indian wars and Mackenzie's career. The fight was the most severe defeat that the Comanches
had suffered since before the Civil War. Once again it was made
clear to them that the army was in earnest and, when freed from
the restraints of the Peace Policy, could operate effectively against
them. Of special importance was the capture of the women and
children, who were taken to Fort Concho and held as hostages
for the ransom of white captives of the Indians and the general
good behavior of the Indians. Parra-o-coom, one of the major
chiefs of the Quahadas, came into the Fort Sill Agency for the
first time. There he traded four white prisoners for the release of
four of the Indian captives. Moreover, he declared that, having
been soundly whipped, the Indians must now try to do things
the white man's way. For some time thereafter, Indian depredations declined noticeably. The battle did not end the bloody
warfare on the South Plains, but it did foreshadow the final defeat of the plains' hereditary rulers.[32]

Victory on the North Fork greatly enhanced Mackenzie's reputation and fully justified the faith that Sheridan and Sherman
had in him. His ability to accomplish meaningful results made
him one of their main troubleshooters for the future. Wherever
there was a dangerous situation, whether it was Reconstruction
Louisiana, the potentially explosive electoral mess in Washington, the volatile Texas-Mexican border, or elsewhere, Mackenzie's name would be the first to be put forward to deal with it.
Only his relative youth—he was just thirty-two—stood between
him and elevation to the highest ranks offered by the army.

The youthful warrior was generous in sharing the credit of his
exploits. In his report to Augur he specifically praised twelve
officers, including the regimental surgeon, Rufus Choate, who

tended the wounded under fire. Nine enlisted men were also commended for conspicuous bravery; they would eventually receive the Medal of Honor for their actions. Mackenzie as a matter of policy usually commended only those whose conduct he had personally observed, so it is likely that others not cited performed as well as those who got the medals. Mackenzie's habit of citing only those he had actually seen in action caused some bitterness toward him in later years and contributed to his reputation as an unfair martinet.[33]

As the companies of the Fourth Cavalry returned to their proper posts in the late fall of 1872, Ranald Mackenzie could look back on the year with pride. He had gained valuable experience; had become better acquainted with the geography of the Texas Panhandle, where he would again have to campaign; had broadened the area of army operations; and had administered a hard blow to the aspirations of the Indians of the southern plains. The coming years would give him the opportunity to build upon this experience and make himself one of the most successful of all army officers in the Indian Wars.

CHAPTER EIGHT

DOWN ON THE RIO GRANDE

AS the companies of the Fourth Cavalry returned to their posts, Mackenzie was again confronted with the ordinary problems of a regimental commander. He had to maintain scouts for hostile Indians and cattle thieves. He also provided escorts for a variety of activities, from conveying prisoners to safeguarding surveying parties and accompanying the departmental commander on an inspection tour. Discipline again became a problem as the troopers began to settle back into the dull routine of barracks life once more. Company A was a special problem in this regard, and Mackenzie took harsh action to shape up its men. Lieutenant Carter, who had had experience with bounty jumpers during the Civil War, was given temporary command of the company while its captain and first lieutenant were sent on recruiting duty. Carter used tactics such as suspending men by their thumbs and drenching them with cold water to bring order to the ranks quickly.[1]

Another concern was an outbreak among the horses of a mucous membrane infection, which Carter called "Russian influenza" and which was listed in the records as "epizootic catarrh," that disabled the animals and threatened their lives. Prescribed treatment was to put a nosebag partially filled with boiled oats on each infected animal. This seemed to promote the flow of a "thick, yellow secretion" which was washed off with a solution of carbolic acid. The horses were fed "hot bran mashes." Such treatment seemed to work, because only a few horses were lost and the epidemic was over within two months.[2]

Mackenzie, of course, was also concerned about planning a campaign for 1873. Neither he nor any of his superiors believed that the Comanche prisoners would exert a permanent pacifying influence on the warriors of that tribe. In November, Mackenzie met with General Augur to discuss possibilities. They decided to transfer the headquarters of the Fourth from Fort Richardson to Fort Concho but to leave the companies at their present stations. Concho was closer to the center of the scattered companies and was somewhat more convenient for operations on the plains. The transfer began on December 31, 1872, and was completed on January 10, 1873. The headquarters stayed at Fort Concho three months while the Fourth carried out its routine missions and Mackenzie developed his plans for the coming spring. New orders relayed to Mackenzie by Augur in February dramatically changed those plans.[3]

The new orders sent Mackenzie and the Fourth Cavalry to deal with an old trouble spot that seemed to be growing worse. Since the Texas Revolution, the border area along the Rio Grande had seethed with tension that occasionally boiled over into open violence. A variety of Indians, Mexican revolutionaries, and ordinary bandits operated along the banks of the river, taking advantage of the international boundary to avoid the authorities. Comanche and Apache Indian raids into Mexico from the United States complicated the problem, as did the simple racism common to many of the Americans who moved into the area. After the Civil War, problems had increased and had drawn more attention from the U.S. government.[4]

An especially volatile ingredient had been added to the ethnic stew when in 1865 the southern band of Kickapoo Indians migrated from Indian Territory to Mexico. The Kickapoos were invited to settle, and were given land by the Mexican government to serve as a buffer against raids by Indians from the United States. Because they were traveling with their families, the Kickapoos attempted to avoid conflict with Texans by selecting a route across that state that went wide of any settlements. Unfortunately, their trail was discovered, and the word was passed to Texas military authorities that a large band of Indians was loose just beyond the settlements. No attempt was made to discover who the Indians were or what their intentions were. Instead, a large force of combined Texas militia and Confederate cavalry made a surprise attack as the Kickapoos camped on Dove Creek on New Year's Day, 1865. Recovering quickly from their surprise, the Kickapoo warriors rallied and drove off the Texans. The fight ended, but the Indians, fearing a renewed attack, abandoned most of their possessions and resumed the trek to Mexico. It was as if war had been declared. From that day, the Mexican Kickapoos considered Texas and Texans fair game. Residents of the border area became the particular targets of Kickapoo vengeance.[5]

Much of the violence along the border, rightly or wrongly, was blamed on the Mexican Kickapoos, and the U.S. government's efforts to calm the area concentrated on those Indians. By 1871, Kickapoo raids from Mexico extended as far into Texas as Kendall County, only a short distance from San Antonio, and raids along the border had become so common that the residents often did not bother to report them. One newspaper reported that four million dollars' worth of stock had been stolen. Secretary of State Hamilton Fish tried to secure an agreement with Mexico to allow U.S. troops to cross the border in hot pursuit of raiders, but he was unsuccessful. Likewise, an effort to persuade the Kickapoos to return to their reservation in Indian Territory failed in 1871. After a commission designated by Congress to investigate the troubled area reported that much of the traffic in stolen goods took place with the connivance of Mexican officials, Fish increased the pressure. His warnings to Mexico in early 1873 clearly hinted of possible incursions by U.S. troops if the raids did not cease.[6]

Fish's message was given a sharper point by orders from Sherman to Augur in February 1873. After conferring with President Grant, Sherman ordered Augur to shift the Fourth Cavalry to the troubled border to replace the Ninth Cavalry, which had made no progress in halting the raids into Texas.

Sherman's message made it clear that Mackenzie was Grant's personal choice to command along the Rio Grande. The impression created during the Civil War, and sealed by Mackenzie's success in 1872, had moved the colonel to the forefront of those officers who could be relied upon to handle difficult assignments. Augur reflected this confidence by replying with a suggestion that a new military district be created for the border region, with Mackenzie to be placed in "control of all operations against *thieves and Indians depredating* there."[7]

Because of the epizootic, the movement of the Fourth Cavalry to Fort Clark, close to the Rio Grande, was delayed until March. In that month the companies at Fort Richardson began their march to the border, as did Company G from Fort Concho. Company M, which had been operating along the lower Rio Grande, was ordered up to Fort Duncan, which lay about fifty miles to the south of Clark. Company I and the headquarters detachment arrived at Fort Clark on April 22, 1873. By June the remaining companies arrived, and the entire regiment was posted in the general vicinity of Fort Clark. Before the consolidation was complete, however, Mackenzie led six companies on his most famous and most daring campaign, an unauthorized raid across the border into Mexico.[8]

While the troopers were moving toward Clark, Mackenzie traveled to San Antonio to meet with General Augur and Secretary of War William W. Belknap, who was touring Texas for a personal assessment of the situation accompanied by General Philip Sheridan. After conferring a few days in San Antonio, Mackenzie, Belknap, and Sheridan rode to Fort Clark, arriving on April 11. Following army custom, the outgoing officers held a big dance in honor of the new commander and visiting dignitaries. As the officers' wives excitedly dressed themselves in their finest raiment—such a dance with such distinguished guests was a great rarity—they discovered that they were infested with lice. They presumed that the vermin were acquired when the companies had paused at Fort Concho on the southward march. The women had visited the Comanche prisoners taken at the

Red River fight and had played with the children. The resilience of army wives was demonstrated when they calmly agreed to keep quiet about their unwanted guests and to proceed with the dance as if nothing were wrong. Unfortunately, there is no record of whether the gallant Sheridan and Mackenzie were attacked by a new invasion force.[9]

A grand review of the Fourth Cavalry concluded the dignitaries' visit. The regiment, both men and horses, was judged to be in excellent condition. Mackenzie naturally was pleased, because the regiment was largely his handiwork. During this period the Fourth was generally rated by the inspector general as number one in general merit. Its performance in the field from 1872 through Mackenzie's relinquishment of command in 1883 reflected his untiring efforts to secure the best horses and equipment and to train his men to meet his high standards.[10]

Between the dance, or "baille," as Lieutenant Carter called it, and the regimental review, Mackenzie continued to discuss the border situation with his superiors. At some point in the discussions, the impatient and impetuous Sheridan gave vent to his feelings. Stressing that Mackenzie had been especially selected to bring an end to the cross-border raids, Sheridan continued, "I want you to *control* and *hold down* the situation, and *to do it in your own way*. . . . I want you to be bold, enterprising, and at all times *full of energy*, when you begin, let it be a campaign of *annihilation*, *obliteration* and *complete destruction*. . . . I think you understand what I want done, and the way you should employ your force."

Mackenzie had no trouble catching the drift of Sheridan's outburst, but in view of the possible consequences of a border crossing, he pressed for a clear-cut authorization from his commander. Sheridan exploded, "Damn the *orders*! Damn the *authority*. You are to go ahead on your own plan of action, and your authority and backing shall be Gen. Grant and myself. With us behind you in whatever you do to clean up this situation, you can rest assured of the fullest support. You must assume the risk. We will assume the final responsibility should any result."[11]

There it was. Sheridan, without actually saying it, had made it clear that Mackenzie should take his troops into Mexico if he thought it necessary and had implied that such an action had the approval of the president himself. That such approval had been given is far from certain, however. Sheridan's remarks have the earmarks of spontaneity, not planning. True, Grant had personally selected Mackenzie for the border post, but that does not automatically imply that he intended a violation of the international boundary. Sherman, the titular head of the army, was not aware of such a plan, and it is not at all clear that Secretary of War Belknap understood the underlying meaning of Sheridan's speech. Certainly Sheridan's messages to Washington after Mackenzie's raid suggest a worried man appealing for support instead of simply reporting that a previously planned action had been carried out. [12]

Mackenzie had some fears about the possible ramifications of the mission Sheridan had assigned him, but, characteristically, he quickly began to develop plans to carry it out. Because of poor facilities at Fort Clark and the scarcity of grazing for the horses, Mackenzie had scattered most of his companies in isolated camps. This made it easy to establish in relative security a rigid training program to prepare his men for their hazardous expedition. The training included mounted and dismounted drill, target practice, and small-unit tactics. Other preparations included gathering supplies and ammunition, reshoeing the horses, and even sharpening sabers. This last caused a great deal of speculation among the men and officers, as sabers were almost never carried on expeditions against the Indians. [13]

Mackenzie directed extensive efforts to locate the camps of the Kickapoos and associated tribes. He offered a large reward which secured the knowledgeable assistance of a fairly large group of "renegade Mexicans and half-breeds" to find the villages of the Indians responsible for the major incursions into Texas. Mackenzie relied especially on Ike Cox, the post guide, and two half-Mexican ranch owners, Green Van and Art McClain, "both first class men, who knew the country even better than

Cox." Those three were aided in turn by men from a nearby Muscogee village—mixed Negro-Indians—who had been mistreated by the Kickapoos. The scouts ranged deep into Mexico seeking to locate targets and mapping out trails.[14]

Mackenzie grew increasingly nervous and irritable while waiting for his scouts to bring in their reports and for the situation to develop as he wished. He had no doubt that he had correctly interpreted Sheridan's meaning, yet there were no clear orders, oral or written. By acting on his own, the young colonel ran the risk of court-martial and disgrace if the expedition should explode into a major international incident. The extent of Mackenzie's concern was revealed one night when he summoned Lieutenant Carter "with an impatient snap of his finger stubs." He had earlier confided his conversation with Sheridan to Carter, and now he accused his subordinate of telling the secret. Lieutenant Lawton had been acting as if he knew what sort of enterprise was in the offing, or at least knew how to find out. Carter was able to soothe Mackenzie's fears, but the incident showed the stress the colonel was under.[15]

The location of the Indian villages was not all that Mackenzie needed. He also had to have a favorable situation, one that would offer the best chance for success while reducing the possibility that his troops might be caught in Mexico by a superior force, whether Indian or Mexican. As information began to filter in, Mackenzie studied the few, and poor, maps available, working out in his mind the best approaches. About eleven o'clock on May 16, 1873, his scouts brought the news that spurred Mackenzie into action. Most of the warriors in a previously located Kickapoo village near the Mexican town of El Remolino had joined a group of Lipans who were camped close by to go on what appeared to be an extended hunting trip. Their absence offered the chance for Mackenzie to strike the Indians with the greatest chance of success. Resistance would be sharply reduced, and the results of the attack on Mow-Way's village had amply demonstrated that destroying lodges and supplies and taking hostages was as effective a blow to the Indians as killing warriors.[16]

With the situation developed as he desired, Mackenzie moved quickly. He immediately sent couriers to order the companies in the grazing camps to rendezvous on Las Moras Creek about twelve miles from Fort Clark. Mackenzie himself left the fort early in the morning of the seventeenth with I Company and eighteen Seminole-Negro scouts. By one o'clock the command was united and ready to ride. It consisted of six companies of the Fourth Cavalry, the Seminole scouts, now commanded by Lieutenant John L. Bullis of the Twenty-fourth Infantry from Fort Duncan, and a handful of civilians. Mackenzie led the regiment slowly toward the Rio Grande under a sun that already burned with a midsummer intensity. So great was the heat that the men fell back on the technique of putting a wet sponge under their hats to ward off its effects.[17]

The column moved slowly because Mackenzie did not intend to cross the river until after dark, and, once across, there would be little time to rest. The column reached a ford near where Las Moras Creek empties into the Rio Grande shortly before dark, and Mackenzie called a halt. He took advantage of the break to tell the troops what was before them. Without mentioning the lack of official sanction, he explained the object of the expedition and warned of the danger of falling behind or of being captured. The warning of possible summary execution was strong enough that the men did not need to be informed of the added risk of lack of authorization.[18]

Shortly after dark, between eight and nine o'clock, the crossing began. Some delay was incurred while the lead elements cut down the steep bank on the Mexican side, leaving portions of the regiment waiting in the middle of the river, which reached to the saddle girths. Occasional pockets of quicksand also hampered the crossing, but it was completed without loss in less than two hours. Impatient as he was to be on the march—it was important to reach the target villages before light if possible— Mackenzie still allowed a brief rest during which the men smoked, snacked on food carried in their saddlebags, and quietly discussed their chances in the coming action. About ten o'clock, the colonel gave the order to mount and led his regiment out of the relatively dense vegetation along the river into the open, desertlike plains of Mexico.[19]

Mackenzie ordered his guides to set a fast pace, and they led out at a trot, although they would vary the gait from a fast walk to a lope to save the horses as much as possible. A night march was a difficult operation, and soon the men began to string out along the trail. The rear elements were guided by the dust, illuminated by the light of the "blood-red" moon, left hanging in the air by the lead companies. The pounding of the hooves of several hundred animals carried a long distance, and the troopers could see the lights of the few isolated dwellings blink out as they approached. As the column rode on, it became increasingly clear that the pack train would not be able to keep up. Mackenzie, at the head of the column, was unaware of the problem until he was told by Lieutenant Carter. The colonel was now faced with a choice. He could slow the entire movement, lessening the chance of surprise while increasing the danger of being cut off from the border, or he could abandon most of his supplies. After a burst of profanity, he chose the latter and ordered that the pack train be caught up and the packs cut loose after the men had filled their pockets with bread. This was done as quickly as possible, and the regiment was soon on its way again. Freed of their burdens, most of the mules were able to keep up, and only a few were lost. The delay prevented the column from reaching the Indian villages before first light, but it made little substantial difference.[20]

When dawn first began to light up the eastern sky, the regiment was still far from journey's end. The pace set by the guides precluded the possibility of quick naps, and many of the men had been without sleep for twenty-four hours. Dust-covered and bone weary, the troopers must have begun to wonder if the ride would ever end. Then the peaks of the Santa Rosa Mountains appeared in the growing light, and the column began to move into a "lovely valley" with occasional herds of stock that indicated the approach to the hostile villages. It was the valley of the San Rodrigo River, and there Mackenzie called a halt. While the horses drank from the scattered pools formed by the small stream, the men tightened saddle girths and checked their arms, knowing that the villages would be in sight once they left the stream bed.

Having been aware of the general layout of the Indian villages for some time, Mackenzie had already developed a battle plan. He rejected suggestions by his subordinates that the regiment be divided in order to cut off possible escape routes. The potential danger of having separate detachments cut off and annihilated was intensified by being deep into Mexico without legal authority. Undoubtedly, splitting the companies would have caught more of the Lipans in the village adjoining the Kickapoos, but Mackenzie was treading on dangerous ground just by crossing the border. There was no reason to add another level to the danger. Before forming for the charge, Mackenzie took another precaution. He ordered his men to stuff all their spare ammunition into their pockets rather than leave it in their saddlebags. This would ensure that a trooper who got separated from his horse still would be able to defend himself.[21]

Mackenzie ordered the regiment into column of platoons and led them out of the stream bed with McLaughlin's I Company at the front. About a mile of gently sloping land covered with prickly pear, a variety of other cacti, yucca, and mesquite lay between the army and the first village, that of the Kickapoos. As the pace quickened to the charge, a wild cheer from the troops sent the Indians "flying in every direction." The warriors who had remained with the village to defend it reacted quickly, and "a sharp skirmish" ensued that lasted for "a few minutes." Each platoon fired a volley then wheeled to the right and returned to the end of the column to reload. When the regiment had charged the length of the village, the rear companies dismounted to search the grass lodges for stragglers. The Lipan and Mescalero Apaches in the neighboring villages were alerted by the firing, and most of them escaped. McLaughlin's company was sent to round up such refugees as it could find, and Carter was sent with a detachment to corral the Indians' horses. The remaining troops were put to work burning the lodges in the three villages.[22]

When the fighting was over, Mackenzie counted nineteen Indian dead, although probably several more were killed or died of wounds. Mackenzie's report did not specify that all of the dead were warriors. Both Carter and Captain E. B. Beaumont used the term *warriors* to refer to the dead, but Carter also mentions seeing dead or severely wounded children, so it is probable that they were included in the body count. This is not to say that a massacre of innocents had taken place. Clearly the defenders were mostly adult males, and it must be remembered that women and children can shoot as well as men. Forty women and children were taken prisoner along with Costalietos, a principal chief of the Lipans, and about sixty-five ponies. Each village had fifty or sixty lodges, which were burned along with the stores in them. The cavalry suffered only three casualties. One private was mortally wounded; another, Private William Pair, suffered a shattered right arm; and the third received a slight facial wound that did not incapacitate him. Besides the mules that had strayed off after the packs were cut loose, two horses were shot and a few more were lost to exhaustion.[23]

So far, the raid was a smashing success, but the tired men and animals of the Fourth Cavalry were still a long way from the safety of the north bank of the Rio Grande. Despite the possibility that the local population might rise up against him, Mackenzie wisely allowed a lengthy rest period before beginning the homeward march. The horses were not unsaddled but were staked out and allowed to graze while the men not on guard duty got what rest they could. The layover also allowed time for Dr. Donald Jackson, the contract surgeon of the regiment, to treat the wounded; that treatment included the amputation of Private Pair's arm. Travois were improvised to carry the two seriously wounded soldiers. Mackenzie's natural impatience and his awareness of the danger of taking too much time brought the respite to an end after four or five hours. Then the men were mounted, the prisoners were placed on horses, the captured stock was rounded up, and the homeward march was begun.[24]

The return journey was, perhaps, the most harrowing part of the whole expedition. The tired, hungry troopers had to cope with their Indian prisoners and captive horses while fighting to remain alert against possible reprisals. Lieutenant Carter later remembered that "*we did not feel safe.*" As they rode through a nearby Mexican village, the cavalrymen were met with looks of hatred and threatening mutterings not calculated to increase their confidence. It was obvious that word of the American presence was by now widespread, and interception by regular Mexican soldiers or an aroused citizenry seemed likely. By nightfall, the long period in the saddle with only a little sleep began to take its toll. Men went to sleep on their mounts and occasionally fell off. Officers used threats and sometimes force to keep the men moving. As the night deepened, even threats seemed to have little effect, and only the fear of the consequences of being left behind kept the men going. When the Indian children began to fall off their horses, they were tied on. Halts to close up the rear became more frequent. Increasingly, the whole regiment seemed to lose its drive and determination and was carried along only by the sheer will of its commander. Shortly after dawn, the long night of agony came to an end as the Rio Grande was sighted.[25]

Both men and horses were rejuvenated by the sight and sound of the river, and the crossing was begun immediately. Crossing was a slow business, as the ford was deep and narrow and the horses stopped to drink as they entered the water. When they emerged on the Texas side of the river, the men unsaddled their horses for the first time in two days. Most of the men then bathed in the river while waiting for the supply wagons to arrive. Green Van, the guide whose land the regiment stopped on, brought out "several buckets" of mescal, but Mackenzie ordered it poured out. He probably would have allowed a small celebration except that there was a definite threat that a large party of Mexicans and Indians would try to cross the river seeking revenge. This threat was great enough that Mackenzie deployed sharpshooters at the ford to hamper any crossing while the remainder of the men were placed under arms some distance back from the river. Some figures appeared on the south bank shouting abuse, and a few shots were fired at random into the campsite, but no assault was attempted. Tight security was maintained during the night while the men got their first extended rest in three days. The only serious threat to their peace was the numerous ants that attacked many of them.[26]

Mackenzie pulled back the regiment to a more secure position the next day. That night, as recalled by Lieutenant Carter, Mackenzie joined several of his officers sitting around a campfire. These officers, most of them veterans with Civil War experience, were discussing their recent adventure when the question of authority came up. When Mackenzie admitted that he had no official authorization for the raid, Captain Beaumont declared that it had been illegal and that the officers and men would have been justified to refuse to cross the river. McLaughlin then backed Beaumont, asserting that he would not have gone if he had known that there were no orders. "Mackenzie flashed up, and in a very firm, crisp and decisive voice, replied: 'Any officer or man who had refused to follow me across the river I would have shot.'" McLaughlin, who had a reputation as an excellent shot, retorted, "*That would depend, Sir,* upon who *shot first!*" This exchange was followed by a few minutes of uncomfortable silence until, one by one, the officers rose to go to bed.[27]

This episode has many of the earmarks of Carter's fondness for melodrama, and it can be doubted that it took place as described. It seems unlikely that these hardened veterans, who had served with Mackenzie for almost three years and who almost certainly shared the common American contempt for Mexicans, would have seriously challenged their colonel's leadership. The question of a soldier's obligation to follow an illegal order might have arisen, but that any of the officers would have reacted as Beaumont and McLaughlin are said to have done does not fit their characters. Whatever the case, Mackenzie's response, as reported by Carter, rings true to his personality and shows the kind of determination that contributed so much to his success.

The Fourth Cavalry had performed a remarkable feat. Because they had been camped at various sites, the number of miles covered by each company varied. The official monthly reports give total miles covered by a company for the whole month, so calculation for the Mexican venture is difficult, but Carter, who rode with Beaumont's Company A, figured from his diary that he covered 159 miles in thirty-two hours, which is probably a fair estimate for the regiment as a whole. Mackenzie, as usual, was generous in his praise for his regiment. He listed all of the officers who accompanied him and, although he singled out some for special mention, declared that all "acted handsomely and deserve consideration." The men, too, Mackenzie continued, demonstrated "a creditable eagerness to attack." In view of Mackenzie's knowledge that most of the Indians' fighting strength was gone, some commentators have judged his praise of the troops to be overstated. This might be true if the attack were all there was to the operation. What Mackenzie was applauding was the performance of the men in very trying and unpredictable circumstances. That the regiment made a long night march, attacked eagerly and efficiently, and then returned burdened with prisoners and captured horses without breaches of security and organization, was, indeed, remarkable and deserving of praise.[28]

Mackenzie sent a preliminary report by courier to Fort Clark. Major J. K. Mizner then relayed news of the raid to the commander of the Department of Texas. From there the message was sent through channels to Washington. Mackenzie did not at this time, or in his official report of May 23, admit to crossing the border. That he had, in fact, done so was fairly clear from the beginning, and Sheridan wired Secretary of War Belknap to warn him and began to build a case for supporting the incursion. It is clear from Sheridan's tone in this and the flurry of other messages he sent to the capital that he was not at all sure that the government would sustain Mackenzie or himself. By May 31, Sheridan's suspense ended, and with it any fears that Mackenzie might have had regarding possible disciplinary action. Belknap telegraphed that he had talked to the president, the secretary of state, and the attorney general and that "you and Mackenzie will be sustained as thoroughly as possible." Oddly omitted from Belknap's list of consultants was the commanding general of the army, William T. Sherman. Although Sherman, too, thought that Mackenzie's action would be supported, he was clearly piqued at being taken by surprise by news of the raid.[29]

Relieved to be assured of government support, Sheridan wrote a congratulatory letter to Mackenzie. The government has acknowledged, said Sheridan, that Mackenzie had acted on proper principles, and he was free to do the same thing again if circumstances warranted. Sheridan then expressed his hope, fueled by nervousness about his shaky position, that "there may be no such necessity." Sheridan's concern was justified, for Mackenzie, supported at first by Augur, was ready to cross the river again as soon as a suitable target was located. Mackenzie's eagerness was prompted to some extent by the possibility, real or imagined, of retaliatory raids by Mexicans or Indians. The United States' consul at Piedras Negras—just across the border from Eagle Pass, Texas—informed Mackenzie in a congratulatory note that a large mob had formed with the intention of going after the "gringos" but was dissuaded when informed of the expedition's purpose. William Schuhardt, the consul, thought the threat was over but could not promise that there would be no attempt to retaliate. Two days later, Lieutenant Colonel Shafter, in charge at Fort Duncan near Eagle Pass, reported various rumors of large-scale Indian crossings on revenge raids. Although the rumors were probably groundless, Shafter did remind Mackenzie that the Indians could raise a formidable number of warriors. Mackenzie was alert to dangers and reported the rumors and his precautionary measures to Augur.[30]

Mackenzie kept his troops on guard and prepared to repulse an attack. The threat seemed real, and the nervousness of the men resulted in one amusing false alarm. The night of May 26 was very dark, and the difficulty of seeing increased the tension of the men. The situation seemed ideal for an attack, and the guard was doubled. A thunderstorm, accompanied by high winds, then blew in, and the fearful anticipation of the garrison grew. Just at this point, a shot rang out, quickly followed by a fusillade. Excitement took over the fort. Drums were beaten, officers shouted orders, women and children were sent to cover, and the troops turned out to repel an attack. Then a highly embarrassed sentry admitted to having shot in the darkness at a moving figure which turned out to be a wandering hog. His shot had triggered a chain reaction among the other keyed-up sentries and created the resulting confusion.[31]

Public response to Mackenzie's raid was generally favorable, and overwhelmingly so in Texas. The first stories of the border crossing in the *New York Times* had an approving tone, and a later editorial endorsed the action. Likewise, the *New York Tribune* expressed support for the action as a means of solving the Indian problem on the border. In Texas, some disapproval was expressed by newspapers, which were concerned that a general war with Mexico might result. As could be expected, however, most Texans strongly cheered Mackenzie for taking strong measures. An Austin, Texas, paper hailed the raid as "glorious news" and exclaimed, "All honor to the noble and gallant McKenzie." A correspondent of the *San Antonio Express* offered "three cheers" for Mackenzie. The *Galveston Daily News* was somewhat more restrained and approved Mackenzie's course while cautioning that it might lead to war. Perhaps the most extraordinary reaction came from the Texas legislature. That body, which had been considering a resolution thanking Mackenzie for his attack on the Comanche village on the North Fork of the Red River for several months, was electrified by news of El Remolino and quickly voted to change the wording accordingly. The resolution was passed on May 26, 1873, and a copy was sent to

Mackenzie in the mid-1870s. The added weight and full mustache give the appearance of "a noble specimen of the *beau sabreur*." *(Courtesy Western History Collection, University of Oklahoma Library)*

General Augur. This appears to be the only time that the Texas legislature officially thanked a U.S. Army officer for any kind of action.[32]

Mackenzie was not content to remain passive and await possible attack. Instead, he took active measures both to guard against retaliation and to find an opportunity to strike another blow against marauding Indians. The colonel sent word, through Consul Schuhardt as well as through scouts, that he meant no harm either to Mexican citizens or to peaceful Indians, but raiders would be punished. Tired as he and his troops were from the expedition to El Remolino, Mackenzie was back in the saddle leading patrols along the river within a few days. If the Indians did not come across the river, he wrote to his department commander, he would look for the opportunity to "hit them another blow that will hurt them." Augur, who had already ordered the remaining companies of the Fourth to join the regiment at Fort Clark, gave his energetic subordinate leave to make another cross-river sortie as long as he was careful to avoid attacking the Kickapoos, who were now talking peace with United States' commissioners. Lipans and Mescaleros were to be the target unless the Kickapoos broke off talks. Then they, too, wrote Augur, would "be your chickens."[33]

The most enduring result of Mackenzie's foray across the border was to speed up the efforts of the United States to get the Kickapoos to return to their old reservation in the Indian Territory. Before the raid, two commissioners, Henry M. Atkinson and Thomas G. Williams, were sent to Mexico to try to induce the Kickapoos to come home. Mackenzie wasted little time in informing the commissioners of his action and asking them to tell the Kickapoos that the prisoners he had taken would be well cared for. He also asked the commissioners to tell the Indians that they, too, would be protected if they came home. "No citizen," wrote Mackenzie, "will be allowed to say a cuss word to them or claim a pony." The choice lay with the Kickapoos, Mackenzie went on: "I am ready to fight or make peace just as they please."[34]

Mackenzie had, indeed, shown great concern for the prisoners. His willingness to help and protect peaceful Indians would be more fully revealed when he asssumed command of Fort Sill two years later, but his efforts in behalf of the Kickapoo prisoners were an accurate forecast of that attitude. He sent the prisoners to San Antonio because Fort Clark had no facilities for holding them, and the nearness of the river might encourage escape attempts. Yet he urged General Augur to allow them to camp in the open and to prepare their own food "so as to change their mode of living as little as possible, in order to prevent injury to their health." As had been the case with the Comanche prisoners taken the year before, the good care received by the Kickapoos enhanced Mackenzie's standing with the Indians.[35]

The commissioners had mixed reactions to the raid. Williams wrote directly to Mackenzie saying that he was "glad" to hear of the affair and predicted that it would "have a most beneficial effect" on the talks with the Kickapoos and other raiders generally. Atkinson, on the other hand, complained to the Indian commissioner in Washington that Mackenzie's action was an impediment to successful talks. The Indians initially refused to talk until the prisoners should be freed, and Williams and Atkinson tried to convince the army to let them go. Although the commissioners were able to persuade Mackenzie, against his better judgment, to support release of the captives, they found no sympathy in the higher ranks, and the request was rejected. Atkinson, who seems to have fallen into the position of chief negotiator, then decided to do what should have seemed obvious from the beginning. He returned to the Indians and told them that the only way they could see their missing families again would be to agree to return to Indian Territory. This approach had the desired effect, and on July 7, 1873, Commissioner Atkinson informed Mackenzie that some of the Kickapoos, along with a few Potawatomies, had agreed to go back.[36]

On his own initiative, Mackenzie tried to help the commissioners as well as to secure Mexican cooperation for joint military action against hostile Indians. The commissioners had applied to Victoriano Cepeda, governor of the Mexican state of Coahuila, for aid in negotiating with the Kickapoos. Cepeda promised to help and delegated Alfredo Monteros to represent the interests of the Mexican government and also to keep Mexican citizens from interfering with the talks. Prompted by the commissioners, Mackenzie promised to present Monteros with a fine horse if the Kickapoos agreed to return. The idea matched Mackenzie's contempt for Mexicans. In reference to the Mexican leaders, Mackenzie told Augur, "I have for their individual character not the slightest respect." When Williams wrote to tell Mackenzie that the Indians had agreed to return, he began by declaring, "You owe Monteros a horse." Unfortunately for Mackenzie, his order to have the horse turned over to Monteros was judged illegal by the departmental commander. Apparently he was forced to pay for the horse with personal funds.[37]

Mackenzie, at the same time, opened a personal correspondence with Governor Cepeda. He tried to justify his raid into Mexico by pointing out that Mexican forces had done the same many times. He also attempted to persuade the governor to agree to the creation of a joint force to operate against the Indians. For this purpose Mackenzie requested that Colonel Pedro Valdez be assigned to the border area. In a letter to Augur, he stated that the colonel, who Mackenzie referred to as Colonel Winker because of a tic in one eye, was "a very gallant and corrupt" man whose cooperation could be insured by the promise of a large share of any captured horses. Mackenzie also accused the citizens of the village of Santa Rosa of having abetted the Indians by buying their loot stolen from Texas and recommended to Cepeda that the village leaders be arrested because they were hindering the commissioners' efforts. Mackenzie's dealings with Mexican authorities were mildly censured by Augur and Sheridan, who worried that the good done by Mackenzie might be spoiled "by corresponding too much with Tom, Dick and Harry."[38]

Mackenzie sought to deflect criticism by replying that he had told the Mexicans that his letters represented only his personal opinion and had no official sanction. Nevertheless, it is clear that Mackenzie, perhaps inspired by the boldness of the raid itself, was overstepping the limits of his authority. Sheridan's order to cross the river had been vague and the authority doubtful, but Mackenzie, once set on course, let his aggressive instincts take him further than even Sheridan would allow. Mackenzie's correspondence, combined with his continued practice of sending spies into Mexico looking for further opportunities to strike Indians, led his superiors to tighten the reins on him. Augur ordered that Mackenzie not cross the river again without provocation and was supported by Sheridan and Sherman.[39]

Certainly Mackenzie's actions expressed his belief that one raid had not est .olished peace on the Texas border. Sheridan did make such a claim when trying to secure government sanction for the raid. Sheridan was not so naïve as to claim that the raid had solved all of the problems of the border, but he did declare in his annual report that "depredations have diminished very materially" as a result. Lieutenant Carter went further in claiming success for the venture, asserting in his memoirs that the peace brought about by the crossing lasted for years. The truth was that, except for forcing the return of the Kickapoos, the expedition had little discernible influence on border tensions. Not only did Mackenzie keep looking for an opportunity to strike into Mexico again, but the Fourth also was kept busy tracking down marauders on the Texas side of the river. The colonel was compelled to send troops as far into the interior of the state as Bandera County, where a company was posted on the head of the Sabinal River.[40]

By 1874 the situation along the Rio Grande was almost as bad as it had been before Mackenzie arrived at Fort Clark. This continuing activity suggests that the Kickapoos were only a small part of the problem and were, perhaps, unfairly blamed. In late May 1874, Mackenzie led about one hundred men across the Rio Grande after a band of cattle thieves who were, reported the colonel, all Mexicans. The pursuit followed the thieves about sixty miles into Mexico before Mackenzie called it off because the danger of being cut off from the river was too great. In his report of the chase, Mackenzie requested more men and horses and warned that the situation could still lead to war. The situation would be left to fester for years to come, and Mackenzie would again be sent to the border to deal with it. In 1874, however, a danger of greater urgency, war on the South Plains, demanded his services.[41]

Mackenzie paid a heavy personal price for his participation in the El Remolino raid. The pounding he had taken from the long, hard ride into Mexico aggravated his old war wounds and brought on a physical breakdown. Within a few weeks he was so badly crippled by what was diagnosed as rheumatism that he could barely get out of bed. According to the report of the departmental surgeon in September, Mackenzie was suffering from "acute rheumatism" which extended from the right shoulder to the right knee. Swelling and stiffening of the joints rendered the colonel unfit for active service. The surgeon recommended an extended leave of absence outside the state of Texas. In consequence, Mackenzie applied for and was granted a thirty-day leave, which was soon extended to three months. A later leave extension would make it early 1874 before the colonel returned to Fort Clark to resume his duties.[42]

Mackenzie spent his leave visiting his mother and other relatives in Morristown and New York and at least twice went to Washington to see friends. The opportunity to build on his relationship with Grant and Sherman was too great to pass up. The long rest was beneficial, because Mackenzie was able to resume active command upon his return. His return to field service showed again his spirit and determination, because he was never completely well after that time. His long-time adjutant, Joseph Dorst, claimed that "there was hardly a day that he did not suffer." The physical strain that Mackenzie was subjected to makes all the more remarkable a career that still had its greatest challenges in the future.[43]

CHAPTER NINE

THE RED RIVER WAR

THE Red River War was the last great effort of the Indians of the South Plains to retain their sovereignty over their lives and their land. A variety of pressures pushed the southern tribes toward war in 1874. The activities of government surveying parties in the spring of 1873 led many Indians to believe that their land was to be divided and opened to settlement by whites. Although many of the older tribal leaders, such as the Kiowa chief Kicking Bird, saw the futility and danger of continuing hostilities, the younger men, especially those who had yet to win battle honors, chafed at restraint. The main obstacles to resuming the normal raiding patterns had been the Comanche prisoners taken by Mackenzie in 1872 and the continuing imprisonment of Satanta and Big Tree. The hostages were returned to their tribe in June 1873, and although many of the tribe promised never to make war on the whites again, others saw the restoration as the removal of a major check on raiding activity. Satanta and Big Tree were freed in October, and the Kiowas, too, then felt it safe to resume old practices.[1]

The Comanches and Kiowas had never ceased hostile activity, but now they turned their full attention to raiding. In November a mixed force of about thirty Comanches and Kiowas left on an extended raid through Texas into Mexico. All went well for the Indians until they returned to recover their spare horses left near Kickapoo Springs in Edwards County, Texas. There they were intercepted by a detachment of the Fourth

Cavalry led by Lieutenant Charles C. Hudson. In an exemplary small-unit action, Hudson's men routed the Indians, killing at least nine, while suffering no dead themselves. Later, in early 1874, ten Comanches were killed near the Double Mountains in Texas by a force led by Lieutenant Colonel George P. Buell. This number, added to Hudson's score and the results of other, smaller, actions, brought the number of Indians killed during the winter to thirty. These heavy losses by the Indians demanded vengeance and assured that the new year would be a bloody one.[2]

Other developments in 1874 worked to end any illusions that the Indians might be persuaded to remain on the reservations. In the early spring, large numbers of buffalo hunters invaded the Texas Panhandle accompanied by merchants who established a trading post on the Canadian River near the site of Kit Carson's fight at Adobe Walls. The Medicine Lodge Treaty of 1867, which involved Cheyennes and Arapahos as well as Comanches and Kiowas, had seemed to reserve the Panhandle for the exclusive use of the Indians, and the threat of the destruction of their commissary led many of the Indians to believe that they must fight to save it. Another grievance was the continual loss of Indian horses to white thieves operating out of Kansas and Texas. Finally, heavy rains in the spring delayed the arrival of the annuities due the Indians.

In these circumstances it was not surprising that a leader appeared who promised to carry the Indians to victory over the encroaching whites. The prophet in this instance was a Comanche, named Isa-tai, who had lost an uncle in the fight with Lieutenant Hudson. Isa-tai claimed special powers to protect the Indians from the white men's bullets as well as the ability to raise the dead. He was reported also to have spit up "nearly a wagonload of cartridges at one time," a sign that he could supply unlimited ammunition for the warriors. The pressure was so great on the Indians that Isa-tai was able to lead the Comanches into making medicine together as a tribe for the first time. The gathering was climaxed by a sun dance, which had never before been a part of the Comanche tradition. Clearly, Indian affairs on the South Plains had reached a dangerous stage.[3]

Two excursions by the Indians can be said to mark the beginning of the Red River War. One was the famous attack on the trading post at Adobe Walls. On June 27, 1874, a large number of Comanche, Kiowa, and Cheyenne warriors attacked a group of buffalo hunters clustered at the tiny settlement. The fight, intended to drive the whites back to Kansas, resulted in failure for the Indians. It did serve, however, to warn the whites that the Indians were out in mass in an attempt to halt the spread of white civilization. Shortly after the Adobe Walls fight, the Kiowa chief Lone Wolf organized a raid into Texas to revenge the death of his son and nephew killed in the fight with Lieutenant Hudson the previous December. His raid culminated in a famous battle with Texas Rangers led by Major John B. Jones in Lost Valley, Young County, Texas. In that fight the Rangers came out second best. Other incidents also indicated the intensification of hostilities, but these two battles were the major causes of the death of the Peace Policy.[4]

The acceleration of hostile activity brought about what amounted to a declaration of war against the Indians of the South Plains. Pressed by Sheridan and Sherman, Secretary of War Belknap secured the consent of both the secretary of the interior and the commissioner of Indian affairs for the army to follow raiding Indians onto the reservations. The only restraint was that any Indian who came in and registered with the agent would be given the protection of the government. Indians who had not enrolled by a set date would be considered hostile. On July 20, 1874, Sheridan received the word to move against the hostiles, and he wasted no time in ordering the commanders of the two departments—Missouri and Texas—to take action.[5]

Exactly who deserves credit for the ensuing campaign is not entirely clear. Even before getting clearance to launch a major offensive, Sheridan and Sherman had been conferring by telegraph about the proper course to follow and had taken preliminary steps. A general order by Sheridan issued on July 10 allowed units operating against Indians to ignore departmental boundaries. A few days later, Sheridan suggested that cavalry be sent against Indians in the vicinity of Fort Sill after the friendly Indians there were first warned to seek the shelter of the post itself. Both these ideas were implemented once the campaign proper had begun, but beyond overseeing the broad outlines of the campaign, Sheridan left the actual operation to his departmental commanders. When he sent orders to those officers after receiving his instructions, Sheridan made it clear that actual responsibility for troop movements would rest on them. So reluctant was the divisional commander to interfere that he only "suggested" to Augur that Mackenzie and the Fourth Cavalry could be spared from duty on the border.[6]

There was no doubt in Augur's mind that Mackenzie would take a leading role in the upcoming operation. He immediately replied to Sheridan's "suggestion" that, because Mexican officials seemed committed to controlling raiders on the border, Mackenzie and most of his regiment could be sent against the Indians. Augur visualized two columns operating from Forts Griffin and Concho, both under Mackenzie's command, but told Sheridan that he would make no specific plans until he had conferred with his young field commander. He summoned Mackenzie to San Antonio to work out actual plans while the involved companies of the Fourth were to converge on Fort Concho in order to be available when needed. Mackenzie was given discretion to employ whatever medical personnel and Indian scouts he felt necessary as well as some infantry companies. Expressing concern about the lingering effects of Mackenzie's bout with rheumatism, Augur authorized sending Lieutenant Colonel John Hatch with the Fourth, but clearly, his desire was for Mackenzie to lead in the field.[7]

By chance, Mackenzie was already on his way to San Antonio on other business, so he incurred little delay in developing plans for the southern portion of the coming campaign. The wording of Augur's telegram officially transmitting the proposed plan indicates that it was essentially Mackenzie's work. "We have talked the matter over very fully," wired Augur, "and I have agreed with him upon what should be done." Mackenzie's suggestions of 1871 formed the basis of the plan. The forts in Texas were to be stripped of most of their troops, as not many Indians would be able to slip past the converging columns of the army. All available troops would be sent out in three columns: one from Fort Concho under Mackenzie's direct command, one from Fort Richardson nominally under Mackenzie but led by Lieutenant Colonel George P. Buell, and one operating independently from Fort Sill under the leadership of Lieutenant Colonel John W. Davidson. Caught between the Texas regiments and two columns General John Pope was sending from the Department of the Missouri, Indians on the plains would have no escape routes left open and would be severely punished. Most importantly, the columns were to be prepared to stay in the field as long as it took to get the job done. Augur estimated that six months would be required. Mackenzie's early suggestion that large scale forces be sent to operate continuously against the Indians was now the accepted plan of the campaign.[8]

Mackenzie decided to use Fort Griffin as the supply base for his column. It was the easiest place from which to supply his troops because it was more accessible to the railroad than was Fort Concho, and the trail to the Staked Plain used in 1871 and 1872 was well established—was, indeed, beginning to be known as the Mackenzie Trail. While at Fort Griffin arranging for supplies and conferring with Buell, Mackenzie set his troops in motion. Major Thomas M. Anderson, Tenth Infantry, was temporarily in command of what would become known as the Southern Column. It consisted of eight companies of the Fourth Cavalry, four companies of the Tenth Infantry, and one company of the Eleventh Infantry. A contingent of civilian and Tonkawa Indian scouts was also included. Anderson was to move to the old supply camp on the Freshwater Fork of the Brazos, where Mackenzie would join the column and assume command. From there, Mackenzie intended to lead the troops along the eastern edge of the Llano Estacado as far north as necessary. Buell's command, consisting of six companies of cavalry and two of infantry, would operate independently. In general, it was to move between the Pease and the Main Fork (Prairie Dog Town Fork) of the Red River, but both commanders were free to "disregard any general directions if any probability offers of overtaking Indians." The objective was large Indian camps, and small groups of hostiles were not to distract from that mission. Colonel Davidson was expected to move straight west from Fort Sill.[9]

Delayed by difficulties in obtaining adequate forage, Mackenzie did not reach the supply camp until September 19, 1874. A small swarm of newspaper reporters at Fort Griffin clamored for permission to accompany his westward march, but Mackenzie refused to allow any of them to go along. On his arrival at Anderson's Fort, as the supply camp was called, scouts reported that they had found three trails leading in the direction of the Pease River. Recent rains had obscured indications of the sizes of the parties making the trails, but they appeared to be small. Nevertheless, Mackenzie proposed to move immediately in hope that one of these trails might lead to significant numbers of Indians. The cavalry was therefore shifted across the river, and more scouts were sent out with extra horses.[10]

On the next day Mackenzie led the cavalry in the direction the scouts had taken. About two o'clock that afternoon, the scouts limped into camp minus their extra horses, having had a fight with a large group of Indians. Sending more scouts ahead, Mackenzie went looking for the Comanches but did not make contact. For the next few days, the story was similar. Scouts found trails, and Mackenzie sent out detachments, but none of them made contact with the quarry, although Indian sign abounded. The troops' movement was often hampered by rain, and on several days the column covered only a few miles or did not even break camp. The weather was so wet that the Indians later referred to the whole fall conflict as the "wrinkled hand chase."

Mackenzie had divided the regiment into two battalions to

allow for better coverage of the territory. On the evening of September 26, the command was reunited in a camp near Tule Canyon amid increasing indications of large numbers of Indians and a growing expectation that a fight was imminent. About thirty Indians appeared within a thousand yards and tried to entice pursuit. This may have been the bait of a trap, but in any case a running fight on the open plains was not Mackenzie's aim, and the troops stayed in camp.[11]

As night came on, Mackenzie ordered special precautions to guard against surprise attack. He remembered his humiliating experience at Blanco Canyon three years before and had the horses picketed, hobbled, and sidelined. Troops slept in their clothes in a ring outside the horses. There was a full moon, and the light was bright enough to read by. The Indians used feeder canyons of the Tule to come to within 150 yards of the cavalry before making their charge, which struck the front guarded by A Company. Intending primarily to run off the whites' horses, the warriors came yelling, screaming, dragging dried buffalo hides, and in general making as much noise as possible. The troopers were awake and ready before the clamor began and easily turned the assault. They held their fire until the Indians were thirty yards away, then cut loose. Lack of target practice on the part of the soldiers kept the number of Indian casualties low, but the weight of the concentrated fire quickly broke the attack.

Having failed to stampede the cavalry's horses, the Indians retreated to cover and began a sporadic firing into the camp. Many of the Indians who could speak English used obscenities to try to antagonize the troopers and challenged them to come out to fight. This kept up all night, with the only casualties being a few wounded horses. As dawn approached, the firing became hotter, and Mackenzie ordered two companies to saddle up and drive the Indians away. Having in mind the favorite Indian tactic of bait and trap, he placed a two-mile limit on the distance to which the hostiles could be followed. At the end of the two-mile limit the troopers were only 150 yards behind the

Indians, but Lieutenant Boehm, who was in command, wisely broke off the action. The chase generated considerable firing but only one Indian casualty. The cavalry had none.[12]

Mackenzie had good reason for wanting to keep the command intact. Shortly before the Indians attacked on the night of the twenty-sixth, his scouts brought word that they had discovered a large number of Indians camped in Palo Duro Canyon about thirty miles away. Lieutenant Lawton, again doing invaluable service as quartermaster, brought a supply train in during a lull in the firing, and Mackenzie was now in a position to inflict heavy damage on a large camp. Aware of the likelihood that he was being watched by Indian scouts, Mackenzie waited until about one o'clock in the afternoon to move and then led his men in the direction that the Indians had taken that morning: away from Palo Duro. After a few miles, he called a halt and ordered his men to make preparations to settle in for the night. As soon as dark set in, however, he ordered the troopers to mount, and the column moved north towards the canyon "at a great pace."[13]

Mackenzie called another halt about 2:00 A.M. to avoid reaching the canyon too soon. He resumed the movement about four o'clock, and the column reached the canyon's edge just as light began to appear in the east. Kiowas, Comanches, and Cheyennes were in camps that strung out over several miles along the Prairie Dog Town Fork of the Red River where Cita Blanca Canyon cut into Palo Duro Canyon. At that location the canyon was almost one thousand feet deep, and the Indians' horses on the canyon floor appeared no larger than sheep. There was some delay until the scouts located a frequently used trail that led to the bottom of the canyon. Then Mackenzie, as calmly as if he were on the parade ground, approached the company of scouts and said, "Mr. Thompson, take your men down and open the fight!"[14]

This may have been the most daring of all of Mackenzie's combat actions. He sent his men down a narrow trail, so steep that they were forced to lead their horses, against an unknown

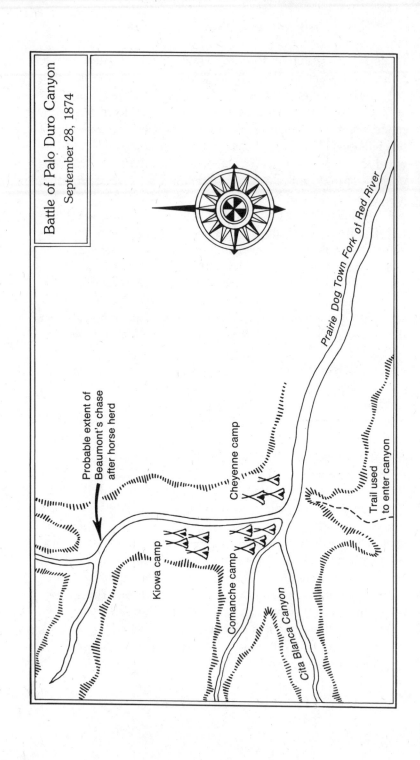

Battle of Palo Duro Canyon
September 28, 1874

Prairie Dog Town Fork of Red River

Probable extent of
Beaumont's chase
after horse herd

Cheyenne camp

Kiowa camp

Comanche camp

Cita Blanca Canyon

Trail used
to enter canyon

but very large number of Indians. There was no advance planning, and there was no way of predicting the Indian reaction to the attack. If the troops were discovered early in the descent and the Indians chose to fight, the result could well have been a disaster for the whites. In his earlier actions, as well as in the Dull Knife fight to come later, Mackenzie had good intelligence and at least some time to outline a plan of attack. It was a measure of Mackenzie's confidence and determination that he acted swiftly in spite of the great uncertainty that faced him. He would take great risks against all hazards when the chance of great success offered itself.

Moving as rapidly as the narrow trail allowed, Thompson and his scouts pushed halfway to the bottom before they were discovered by the Indians. A sentry spotted the descending troops at this point and fired at them, then hastened to alert the camps. The Indian reaction was crucial. If they chose to counterattack with the cavalry still stumbling down the narrow track, the troopers could have been cut to pieces, and Mackenzie's reputation and career would have been destroyed. Instead of attacking, however, the Indians rushed to remove the women, children, and horses from harm's way. "The effect was . . . pandemonium." The tribes in the canyon had been lulled into a sense of security by the Kiowa medicine man Maman-ti. After the appropriate rituals, he had declared that the white soldiers would not disturb the Indians in the canyon. The panicked reaction to the discovery of the attacking forces can be largely explained by Maman-ti's assurances.[15]

Mackenzie went down with the leading elements in the attack, either in company with Thompson's scouts or with the Second Battalion, commanded by Captain E. B. Beaumont. Thompson's men were met by heavy fire when they approached the canyon floor. As soon as all the scouts were down, Thompson mounted a charge that scattered the defenders and gave the Second Battalion room to form up. Mackenzie ordered two of the Second Battalion's companies to join the scouts in a sweep through the scattered encampments, while the remaining two companies followed to guard the flanks. When the First Battalion got down the canyon wall, Mackenzie set it to work destroying the Indian lodges and supplies and trying to suppress a galling fire from warriors who had taken cover among the rocks on the sides of the canyon.

The fight is difficult to piece together from accounts of isolated episodes usually recalled years later, but it is clear that Mackenzie was actively involved and tried to maintain personal control over the action. When Captain Sebastian Gunther, H Company commander, sent a sergeant with a detachment to clear a group of Indians from the canyon wall, the colonel intervened, saying that it was too dangerous and that "none would ever live to see the top." One of the troopers, intimidated by the heavy fire of the Indians, wondered aloud how they would be able to escape. Mackenzie silenced him by stating flatly, "I brought you in and I will bring you out." The colonel's concern with the safety of his men led to one amusing incident. A private McGowan had his horse shot out from under him, but instead of running for cover, he began to rummage around his saddle while Indian bullets splattered around him. Mackenzie yelled at him to seek shelter, "the last time pretty sharp. McGowan responded d——d if I do til I get my ammunition and tobacco and he did not." Mackenzie gave up on Trooper McGowan and turned back to the fight.[16]

Mackenzie was keenly aware of the danger of allowing his command to become scattered and possibly cut off by the Indians. He was especially concerned that Beaumont would lead his battalion into trouble and sent a courier to call him back. Beaumont, just on the verge of overtaking a large herd of Indian ponies, temporarily disregarded the command until he had the horses in hand. Meanwhile, some Indians were sighted apparently attempting to reach the head of the trail to cut off retreat and trap the whites in the canyon. Mackenzie quickly ordered Gunther to take his company and secure the outlet. This was possibly the greatest danger faced by the command, but Gunther beat the Indians to the trailhead, and the fighting was essentially over by midmorning.[17]

Instead of trying to follow the fleeing Indians, which would have dispersed the regiment and created a dangerous situation, Mackenzie kept some troopers working on the destruction of the Indians' property while others began the tedious process of driving the captured horses up the trail to the plains. This work was completed by early afternoon, and Mackenzie prepared to return to the camp on Tule Canyon. Concerned that the Indians might attempt to recover the large herd, Mackenzie ordered his companies to form a hollow square with the captured animals in the middle. The return drive was hard on the troopers, who had had little sleep in the past forty-eight hours. Mackenzie had rested less than most, but he stayed alert, moving among the men, encouraging them, and eliciting the last bit of effort from them. They reached the camp on Tule Canyon shortly after midnight, and the weary soldiers could rest at last. After a late breakfast the next morning, the Indian scouts were allowed to select some of the Indian ponies for their own use, the half-blood Johnson being allowed forty as reward for having found the camp in the Palo Duro. The horses that were serviceable for cavalry use were held out, and the remaining animals, one thousand to fifteen hundred ponies, horses, and mules, were killed by Mackenzie's order. The slaughter was repugnant, but there was little choice.[18]

The Fourth Cavalry had achieved a great victory at very little cost. Only one trooper was wounded, while three horses were killed and ten wounded. In exchange, the Indians lost at least three dead, by Mackenzie's official count, and probably many more. The scout Henry Strong claimed, "I killed seven of the ten Indians known to have been killed in this fight." One veteran claimed that an Indian later told him that fifty or sixty tribesmen had been lost. Another recalled that "we passed over dead Indians everywhere." Even if the highest number were accurate—which is extremely unlikely—it did not encompass the real loss for the Indians. The tepees, food, blankets, pots, saddles, and horses destroyed by Mackenzie's troops comprised the most serious injury the Indians suffered. They had lost much of their mobility and their means to support themselves while off the reservation in the harsh plains winter to come. The significance of the loss of shelter and equipment was apparent immediately. Rain fell the night after the battle, and the Indians were forced to sleep on their horses or "in puddles of mud and water like swine." The Indians might have survived if they had been left alone, but now the most important part of the campaign began. [19]

Mackenzie's suggested plan of campaign in 1871 had emphasized keeping troops in the field to maintain pressure on the smaller groups of Indians scattered by a major confrontation. He began to execute this stage of the plan almost immediately. September 30 was given to rest, but the next day the cavalry moved camp, and on October 2 the search for Indians resumed in earnest. Lieutenant Thompson and his scouts went ahead to the battle site to search for trails showing the direction taken by the Indians, while the main column followed at a steady pace. Most of October was consumed by a constant search for Indians. The expedition was marked mainly by a succession of hard days in the saddle with occasional sightings of Indians and tantalizing signs of recent camps. Mackenzie followed the few Indians that were spotted, hoping to be led to a big camp, but nothing came of the efforts. Two groups of Mexicans, supposed to be comancheros, were taken with their ox carts. The soldiers destroyed the wagons and slaughtered the stock to feed themselves. Two or three of the comancheros agreed to serve as guides, but the first patrol effort accomplished few tangible results. [20]

Before starting on a second search for Indian stragglers, Mackenzie proposed a plan that would enable him to keep part of his regiment in the field throughout the winter. He intended to send three of his companies in the field (out of a total of eight) to Fort Richardson, there to be joined by two companies from Forts McKavett and Concho. Those five companies would then be refitted and remounted and prepared to return to the plains in January 1875. The five companies still with Mackenzie would continue to patrol to maintain pressure on the Indians. When the fresh companies arrived, those in the field would then be rotated back to regular posts. Mackenzie said nothing about himself, apparently taking it for granted that he would stay in command of the field forces for as long as it took to complete the work begun at Palo Duro Canyon. This plan was aborted even while Mackenzie was writing it down. New information was brought in which caused him "to start a command to the Plains to the West." This force included two of the companies he had just designated for rest and refitting.[21]

Marching mainly at night in very cold weather, Mackenzie led his command in a southwesterly direction to the general vicinity of present-day Lubbock, Texas. Indian sign was abundant and sightings frequent. On November 2, fifty to sixty Indians flanked the column all day, staying well out of carbine range. The troopers' horses were too feeble to attempt pursuit, so the standoff continued until nightfall. Mackenzie's luck improved the next day when his detachment surprised a small camp of eight families. Mackenzie's troopers killed two warriors and probably wounded several more. They took nineteen women and children prisoners and captured a sizable herd of horses. Mackenzie dared not chase the Indians who ran—he was pushing his horses up to thirty miles a day on short forage—but he continued to seek other camps. Two days later, the scouts under Thompson killed two more Indians and captured more horses.[22]

These two encounters were encouraging, but Mackenzie was forced to return to the supply camp to rest the horses and secure more fodder. Indeed, the whole campaign had been exceedingly difficult, and both men and horses suffered great hardships. A major problem was securing forage for the animals. Mackenzie complained more than once about the failure of the quartermaster's department to provide the requested amounts of fodder at Fort Griffin. From Fort Griffin, supplies had to be hauled about 250 miles to Anderson's Fort. From there, wagon trains accompanied by infantry struggled up the caprock escarpment and across the plains to reach Mackenzie's troopers. Frequent heavy rains added to the difficulty of transport, and the wagons often had to delay movement a day or two to allow the ground to dry. Mackenzie's hard-pressing tactics ground down horses already weakened by inadequate food, sporadically delivered. In November he reported the loss of forty-four animals during the campaign. Although some of the loss could be made up with captured Indian horses, the colonel still requested the delivery of two hundred more horses.[23]

The troops suffered almost as much as the horses. Many of the men had left their posts "in the lightest marching order possible" and had no extra clothing. Not only was that clothing worn down by hard use, but it also did little to protect the men from the treacherous weather of the South Plains. Some of the men were "half naked" and "nearly barefoot," with but one blanket to cover them at night, but the troops bore the hardship with little complaint, and in late November, Mackenzie judged that both officers and men were "in better health and spirits" than they had been at their posts. In spite of this positive declaration, Mackenzie soon warned that continued hard service would ruin the horses and cause "the men to run down." He constantly pressed plans to rotate troops in the field and have the men's personal gear sent to their new stations.[24]

Mackenzie suffered along with his men. It is remarkable that a man who had been forced by rheumatism to take an extended leave of absence less than a year earlier was able to maintain the pace he set for himself. He appeared to have no regard for his own well-being and never complained about his personal hardship. Henry Strong, the scout from Jacksboro, described a cold December day with rain turning into sleet and snow. Strong and other scouts built a fire and were cooking supper when Mackenzie "came around shaking as though he would fall to pieces." The scouts forced their leader to sit down and warm himself and eat a hot meal. The episode demonstrates Mackenzie's strength and determination, but also hints at the price he would eventually pay for such stubbornness.[25]

Mackenzie was one of the realists who saw that the Indians had to be thoroughly whipped in battle before they would stay on the reservations. He failed to see, however, the effect that the present campaign was having on the hostiles and apologized to Augur for his meager tangible results. He thought the Indians not yet ready to "behave themselves" and was determined to take one more crack at locating a big encampment before he was forced to take his troops in to the shelter of the forts. The question was which direction to look for Indians. He heard conflicting advice from his scouts, and the information from captured Indians suggested still other possibilities. Bad weather prevented him from having to make an immediate decision, and he took advantage of the delay to send three scouting parties to check likely campsites for hostiles. The scouts found no significant sign of Indians to the north, northwest, or west. There was some hint of Indian movement to the south, so Mackenzie determined to make his last scout of the year in that direction.[26]

On December 3, 1874, Mackenzie mounted his regiment, now greatly reduced by loss of horses, and headed south. In spite of the weakened condition of the horses, he pushed his troops hard, covering fifteen miles the first day after a late start. On the second day, he slogged about thirty-four miles, much of it through a driving wet norther. The marches of the next two days were shorter, as Indian signs began to appear and the scouts needed time to check out the trails. On December 7 the scouts killed a lone Indian—Strong and a Private McCabe were commended by Mackenzie—but the encounter did not prevent another long march. Approaching the vicinity of modern-day Lamesa on the next day, the column spotted a party of Indians, and Lieutenant Lewis Warrington went in pursuit with a small detachment. Warrington and his men were able to take one prisoner and, after a chase lasting several miles, killed two more warriors.[27]

Warrington had spotted another twenty Indians riding off in another direction, and Mackenzie led the regiment after them. A hard drive lasting about fourteen hours covered thirty-three miles but did not discover any Indians. Finally, Mackenzie was forced to rest his men and horses, and, realizing that their condition severely limited their abilities, he ordered that they begin the journey back to Anderson's Fort the night of December 9. Mackenzie's command moved slowly, compelled to do so by continuously soggy ground and the poor condition of their horses. Rain and snow forced a two-day halt, so it was not until ten days later that the troops reached the supply camp and Mackenzie began to break up his expedition.[28]

One revealing incident took place on the return march. Mackenzie overheard the sergeant major refuse to hold a mule while a packer unloaded it. The colonel immediately broke the noncom to private, saying, "I will make a man of you." This story may be apocryphal: it is unlikely that Mackenzie would reduce the regimental sergeant major to private. It does illustrate Mackenzie's concern that each man carry his share of the burden.[29]

Varied success greeted the other columns in the campaign. Miles's command, consisting of eight companies of cavalry and four of infantry, plus one field gun and two Gatling guns, left Fort Dodge, Kansas, on August 8. He moved first to Camp Supply, Indian Territory, then out into the Texas Panhandle. His troops and horses suffered from the extreme heat and poor, almost undrinkable, water but Miles pushed them relentlessly. On August 30, Miles's main force made contact with a large number of Cheyenne warriors, which resulted in a running battle for about twenty miles following the line of the caprock escarpment. The Indians finally broke free by climbing the escarpment and dispersing onto the Llano Estacado. Miles, desperately short of supplies, was unable to follow. His troops had killed few, if any, Indians, but the Cheyennes had suffered heavy material losses.

Major Redwood Price, leading the column from Fort Bascom, New Mexico, was less effective. After what Miles judged to be two inept performances on Price's part, he absorbed Price's command into his own. Davidson led two forays from Fort Sill; the first effort had little to show for it, but the second resulted in

Nelson A. Miles, Mackenzie's great rival for a brigadier's star. *(Courtesy Montana Historical Society)*

the capture of sixty-nine warriors with their families and about two thousand horses. Buell, operating from Fort Griffin, struck three villages in October. Although his claims of success were probably greatly exaggerated, his force did help to keep the Indians off balance.

Davidson and Buell then retired their main forces from the field, but Miles, determined to achieve more, pressed his men to greater effort. On November 8 a detachment from his command, led by Lieutenant Frank D. Baldwin, routed a Cheyenne camp with a bold attack and rescued two of four sisters who had recently been kidnaped by the Indians. Efforts by Miles as well as patrols sent out by Davidson caused the surrender of another group with the two remaining sisters. Units from both Miles's and Davidson's commands continued to roam the Panhandle until severe weather drove them to their posts. Miles was the last to quit, keeping some of his men in the field until January 1875.

As Mackenzie dispersed his companies to their regular posts, his role in the main phase of the Red River War came to an end. As early as October 1, 1874, some Indians, already buffeted by the various columns of troops in the field, began to go back to the reservations to surrender. On October 4 the Kiowa leader Satanta, claiming to be innocent of fighting the whites, surrendered to Lieutenant Colonel Thomas H. Neill at the Cheyenne Agency in Oklahoma; 145 other Indians came in with him. About the same time, another 500 Kiowas and Comanches appeared at Fort Sill to give themselves up. Neill took the surrender of another small group, "who were in the fight with Mackenzie," on the twentieth. By the end of October, Sheridan was optimistically predicting an end to all Indian troubles on the South Plains. Sheridan's faith was justified, although it would not be until the summer of 1875 that the war could be said to be definitely over.[30]

Mackenzie played a major role in the successful outcome of the Red River War. The victory at Palo Duro Canyon was crucial in reducing the ability of a significant number of Kiowas and

Comanches to survive on the plains. Mackenzie, in the face of serious logistical problems and intermittent harsh weather, was able to maintain constant pressure on the Indians. Lieutenant Thompson wrote later that "the moral effect, as well as the damage inflicted, was more than any kind of human being could stand." Without Mackenzie, the outcome of the conflict would certainly not have been as conclusive as it was.

Still, Mackenzie did not act in a vacuum. The contributions of Miles, Buell, and Davidson and their troops were just as necessary to victory as those of Mackenzie. Especially important was the continuation of the combined effort into the winter. The Indians were unable to make good their material losses or feel secure in their usual refuges. The relentless pursuit into the heart of winter was vital in the destruction of the Indians' ability and will to resist. It is impossible to ascribe to any one field commander the major credit for the success, and Sheridan has to be considered a major contributor for initiating and supporting the campaign. Perhaps most of all the Red River War shows that the frontier army could, if given adequate numbers and support, defeat the Indians in the field.[31]

CHAPTER TEN

JAILER TO HALF-STARVING CRIMINALS

RANALD Mackenzie's performance in the Red River War fully justified Sheridan's confidence in him. The divisional commander began to search for an appropriate new assignment for his best field commander even before the full measure of the victory was known. His first thought was to create a new post on McClellan Creek in the Texas Panhandle. Sheridan assumed that a major post would be necessary to control the movement of Indians on the South Plains and to protect the whites who were sure to swarm into the region once the war was over. He proposed that Mackenzie shift his base camp to a site on McClellan Creek and, later, that the Fourth Cavalry be used to garrison Forts Sill and Reno (near the Cheyenne Agency) as well. After some negotiations through the mail which included Mackenzie, the decision was made to allow Mackenzie to take his men in to rest at their old stations and let them recover from their hard campaign. The Fourth would then transfer to Fort Sill early in the new year. General Pope, commander of the Department of the Missouri, was to establish a post on Sweetwater Creek in Wheeler County, Texas, as a temporary forward position.[1]

Room for Mackenzie and the Fourth at Fort Sill was created by transferring the Tenth Cavalry and its acting commanding officer, John W. Davidson, to Fort Griffin. Sheridan was dissatisfied with Davidson's performance, although no specific complaints were made against him. Davidson's personality, too, was against him. He was not well liked, and many of his fellow officers believed him to be insane. Sheridan was also bothered by a scandal that had come to light in the summer of 1874. A lieutenant was discovered carrying on an affair with another officer's wife. Sherman blamed the woman and urged that the young officer be allowed to resign rather than be cashiered. Still, Sheridan believed, "the nest at Fort Sill should be broken up. Davidson has never been the proper man for the place." Probably, however, neither Davidson's leadership nor his personality was the main factor in the reassignment. He was, simply, in Mackenzie's way. Sheridan wanted his favorite to have a post that would give him wider experience and greater visibility than he had had previously. Benjamin F. Grierson, the Tenth's permanent commander, also rubbed Sheridan the wrong way, and that made the decision for change even easier for the general.[2]

Mackenzie was fortunate that he was still young to be holding such high rank; he was thirty-five when assigned to Fort Sill. Electoral trouble and threats of violence had broken out in Louisiana, where the federal effort at reconstruction had been especially turbulent. Sheridan, sent by President Grant to investigate in early 1875, was not satisfied with Colonel William H. Emory, who commanded the federal troops in the troubled area. Sheridan at first recommended Mackenzie to be Emory's replacement but then changed his mind because of his protégé's age. In February, Sheridan withdrew the nomination because he feared "great dissatisfaction" among the numerous senior colonels. Such an assignment could have added no luster to Mackenzie's fame, so his relative youth served him well.[3]

In January 1875, Mackenzie reported to Augur in San Antonio. From there he went to Washington on leave. After two months of visiting family and friends, the young Indian fighter returned to the West and assumed command of Fort Sill in March. Fort Sill sat on a rolling prairie broken by wooded creeks and bordered by the Wichita Mountains. Although subject to extremes in temperature, Fort Sill was a relatively attractive post. The living quarters for officers and men were made of stone and quite pleasant. There was abundant game of all sorts, and Mackenzie was able to indulge his passion for hunting. Perhaps the worst thing about the post was the mosquitoes that spread malaria and gave the post a reputation for being unhealthy. "A man has to go through a course of malaria before he is fully qualified to call himself initiated," wrote one newly arrived officer.[4]

The new post brought Mackenzie under a new departmental commander, General John Pope. Pope had a spotty Civil War record; he had done well in the West but had fallen prey to overconfidence and Robert E. Lee in the East. After his ignominious defeat at Second Manassas, Pope was transferred to Minnesota, and he spent the rest of his army career fighting Indians. As commander, Pope showed a strong interest in developing a humane policy for dealing with the red men. Unfortunately, his ego required that his ideas be the only ones followed, a fact that often put him at odds with Sheridan and other superiors and reduced his effectiveness. When Mackenzie took over at Fort Sill, he found that Pope, perhaps influenced by Colonel Nelson Miles, had divided command of the regiment and control of the various Indians between Mackenzie and Miles, Mackenzie's closest rival for preferment, giving command of Fort Reno to Miles and assigning part of the Fourth Cavalry to that post.[5]

Sheridan had already warned Pope to "watch Mackenzie on the matter of his wants," as he is not "bashful about such" and could end up being "much better off than anyone else." Indeed, Mackenzie was not bashful. He got off a long, revealing letter to Sheridan complaining about the situation. The arrangement proposed by Pope was, Mackenzie wrote, "bad." One officer should be in charge of Fort Sill, Fort Reno, and the Cantonment (the post on the Sweetwater, soon to be made permanent and to become known as Camp Elliot). He said he did not want to leave Pope's department and had no desire to go back to Texas, as suggested by that department's new commander, General E. O. C. Ord. Nevertheless, he insisted that he should have full control of all three posts and the Indians associated with them or else any officer could do the job and he should be assigned "some fancy duty North and allowed to have a quiet, comfortable time till such time as I am wanted particularly."[6]

Mackenzie asserted that he "did not do any intriguing" to obtain the post, but he had already made plans for dealing with the remaining Indians off the reservation, and dividing authority between two commanders would undermine his ability to execute those plans. Pope had promised him field command of any major expedition, but Mackenzie was "quite sure" that Miles would resent any such arrangement. The colonel then acknowledged Pope's having full authority within his department and returned to the theme of duty. "I shall," he said, "of course under any circumstances go ahead and do the best I can." Near the end of the letter Mackenzie reiterated his desire to fulfill his duty but said that he wanted to spend as much time as possible in the East when duty did not prevent. Mackenzie's closing, "Very respectfully, your friend," indicated the special relationship he felt he shared with Sheridan.

Mackenzie felt uncomfortable writing to Sheridan as he did, but ambition overrode his essential shyness. He twice said that he preferred a face-to-face conversation rather than writing a letter. He was not at ease pushing his own claims and admitted to having "said more about myself in this letter than I think I have spoken or written previously in all the course of my life." Perhaps Mackenzie also realized that he did not express himself well in writing. The letter is rambling, repetitious, and awkwardly composed. It makes clear that Ranald did not inherit even the modicum of literary talent his father possessed.

Mackenzie won his point. Sheridan responded to his request by suggesting gently but firmly to Pope that his plan would not do. Both the Fourth Cavalry and the Indians should be under the control of one officer—Mackenzie. Sheridan tried to soothe Pope's feelings by saying that he was acting in "the most kindly way & perhaps from a better knowledge of Mackenzie than anyone else."[7]

In the letter, Mackenzie outlined his plan for rounding up the Quahada Comanches, who had still not come in to the reservation. His two-part proposal relied on deception to get within striking distance of this band, which had never signed an agreement with the whites. First, he had arranged for José Piedád Tafoya, a comanchero apparently captured during the recent campaign, to go to New Mexico to outfit a trading venture. Tafoya was then to make contact with the Quahadas and to let Mackenzie know of their location, sending an unnamed associate to guide the army to the place. Second, Mackenzie made a deal with Kicking Bird, the leading Kiowa peace advocate, to stage a fake buffalo hunt. A large group, including women and children to create an air of authenticity, would be escorted by the largest number of troops available with usable horses. Kicking Bird would then communicate with the Quahadas and pinpoint their location. The whole group would move to within seventy miles of the Indians. At that stage the army would go after the Comanches. Mackenzie flatly stated that he could move troops with moderately good horses seventy or eighty miles in twenty-four hours. The Quahadas would presumably surrender or be as badly mauled as their cousins had been in Palo Duro Canyon.[8]

As it turned out, Mackenzie's elaborate campaign was not necessary. The Indians had suffered more than the army suspected, and those that did not come in voluntarily at first were easily persuaded to do so when gently pressured. Colonel Davidson had initiated the policy of sending scouts out onto the plains to convince the off-reservation Indians that only more suffering awaited them if they stayed out. Shortly after Mackenzie took command of Fort Sill, the scouts Jack Kilmartin and Jack Stillwell brought in Mow-way, whose band Mackenzie had punished on McClellan Creek in 1872. With him came chiefs Wild Horse and Kawertzen and about 175 followers plus six hundred to eight hundred horses and mules. Mackenzie credited Davidson for the surrender and adopted the policy for himself.[9]

The most important group still out was the Quahada band of Comanches, and Mackenzie selected Dr. J. J. Sturms to seek

Kicking Bird, the most important Kiowa peace advocate. His cooperation with the army cost him his life. *(Courtesy National Anthropological Archives, Smithsonian Institution; photography no. 1381a)*

them out and convince them to surrender. Sturms was married to a Caddo woman and knew the Indians well. Speaking several Indian languages, he had long served as an interpreter for the government and was well respected by the Indians. Sturms took three of the recently surrendered Comanches with him and headed for the plains. On May 1, Sturms located the biggest remaining group of Quahadas, who were led still by Isa-tai but were best known as Quanah Parker's band. Faced with the choice of surrendering or of being constantly pressed by Mackenzie, the Indians elected to come in. Mackenzie came close to jubilation as he reported Sturms's achievement to Pope: "His success will be much greater than I anticipated when I sent him. It will be a wonderfully rich surrender." On June 2 the last major band of hostile Indians on the South Plains surrendered to Ranald Mackenzie at Fort Sill. About three hundred men, women, and children were in the group. They were "much poorer" than expected, having only about one thousand ponies and mules instead of the four thousand Mackenzie had anticipated. [10]

To some extent Mackenzie had no options in dealing with the defeated Indians. Higher authority had already made two decisions in an effort to punish the Indians and prevent their ever being able to take the warpath again. The most important of the war leaders were to be hustled off to Florida to eliminate their bad influence. Then most of the Indians' horses would be destroyed or sold so that the tribes would have no choice but to remain on the reservation. Beyond these two required steps, Mackenzie made an effort to treat the Indians fairly and ease their transition to reservation life. Like many officers, he felt a genuine sympathy with the Indians in their struggle to retain their traditional way of life and respected them for their prowess as warriors. That his respect for the Indians was closely related to their resistance was shown by Mackenzie's reaction to the Quahadas as they surrendered: "I think better of this band than of any other on the reservation as they have been steadily out and now come in at a most unusual time. I shall let them down as easily as I can." These Indians, who had never used the reservation as cover for their raids and had surrendered at the beginning instead of the end of the raiding season, earned his respect, and Mackenzie did try to make it easy for them. Only ten Comanches were sent to Florida, although a few more were imprisoned at Fort Sill for a short time, and about five hundred of their horses were returned to them. [11]

By a careful mix of benevolence and firmness, Mackenzie was able to establish control over the Indians. As one of his junior officers wrote, "The Indians had faith in Mackenzie" because they knew he was looking out for their interests and because he would act quickly to punish any wrongdoing on their part. Mackenzie appears to be the one most responsible for elevating Quanah Parker to the position of principal chief of the Comanches. Motivated partly by Quanah's mixed parentage, Mackenzie also saw in him a leader who had gained the respect of his peers but who was young enough to adapt to the new dispensation. For his part, Quanah respected Mackenzie as a "brave man, good soldier," and the two worked well together. Their first joint effort was to persuade the remaining off-reservation Indians to come in. Twice in the summer of 1875, Quanah, armed with a document of protection from Mackenzie, rode out in search of stragglers. [12]

Mackenzie, like many army officers, seemed to know instinctively that the Indians loved to talk, often used talks to delay making decisions, and would respect the whites only if their words were backed by force. This understanding was graphically illustrated in the spring of 1877 when a few Quahadas who had jumped the reservation returned. Mackenzie sent for the chiefs to have them arrest the renegades. Typically, the chiefs wanted to talk it over. Mackenzie ordered Lieutenant Parker quietly to arm and mount the cavalry, then sat patiently for half an hour while the Indians droned on. When Parker reported that the troops were ready, the colonel ended the talks by standing up and telling the interpreters to inform the Indians that the talks were over. He gave them twenty minutes to bring in the outlaws, or "I will come to their camps and kill them all." After deliberately repeating the threat, Mackenzie turned and stalked out of the room. The Indians were "thunderstruck" and hastened to bring in the wanted men within the allotted time.[13]

His new position threw Mackenzie into a close relationship with the agent for the Kiowas and Comanches, J. M. Haworth. Mackenzie was prepared for trouble with Haworth, who was not only a devout Quaker but also a strong believer in the defunct Peace Policy. His efforts to rely on persuasion to control the Indians earned the contempt of most military men. Mackenzie was at first no exception. Now that the Indians had been thoroughly whipped, however, the two found themselves working for the same end, ensuring that the Indians received a fair deal. This new perspective led Mackenzie to change his opinion of Haworth. With his usual generosity of spirit, he admitted to General Pope that he had been wrong about the agent. In a letter complaining of the failure of the Interior Department to provide promised annuity goods to the Indians, he said that he had misjudged Haworth based on hearsay evidence. Instead of interfering, Mackenzie wrote, Haworth "is doing what he is able and what is right."[14]

As early as November 1874, Sheridan had suggested that money from the sale of captured horses should be used to purchase livestock for the Indians. This may have been the first suggestion that the Indians would be more amenable to stock raising than to cultivation of the soil. Sheridan was, no doubt, partly influenced by the disdain that soldiers have always felt for farmers and partly by the recognition that running cattle was closer to the Indian way of life than plodding along behind a plow. When Mackenzie sold the horses surrendered by the Kiowas and Comanches, he netted about twenty-two thousand dollars. For reasons that he never officially stated, he decided to purchase sheep instead of cattle at first. It may have been that he was influenced by agent Haworth, who may have perceived sheep raising as being closer to "civilization" than cattle raising. In a later comment, Sheridan noted that the choice was based on the feeling that the Indians would be less likely to kill and eat sheep than cattle. Finally, Mackenzie may have believed that sheep could be handled more easily on foot, and the reduction of the Indian horse herds therefore made the sheep more practical. [15]

In the summer of 1875, Mackenzie sent Lieutenants A. E. Wood and W. H. Wheeler to New Mexico, where they bought thirty-five hundred sheep. Twenty-nine ewes and two rams died on the four-hundred-mile journey back to Fort Sill, but the surviving animals were then distributed to the Indians according to who was judged "most deserving." The experiment seemed to get off to a good start, and in April 1876, Mackenzie requested permission to send men to purchase three hundred goats for the Indians. Nevertheless, the sheep experiment did not end well. The Indians were unfamiliar with sheep and could not or would not adapt their ways to deal with the animals. Only loosely guarded by the Indians, the sheep were easy prey for coyotes, mountain lions, and other predators. Indian boys often used the animals for target practice. Within a few years the sheep and goats were gone, although some survived in the wild for years afterward. [16]

A similar experiment with cattle seemed destined to greater success. Cattle were more like buffalo than sheep, and horses were necessary for herding, which gave the Indians an opportunity to raise horses and ride them. Even better, the Indians would not have to learn completely new skills to benefit from the cattle. Cows did not have to be sheared, and there was no wool to have to dispose of. Unlike mutton, beef tasted much like buffalo meat. Moreover, cattle could be ridden down and killed just like buffalo (one witness observed that the Indians followed the old practice of cutting out the liver and eating it raw), a fact that did nothing to encourage the Indian Bureau to support the stock-raising effort. The Indian herds became the target of white thieves, and inefficiency and corruption in the Indian Bureau did the rest. When promised food supplies did not arrive, the Indians were forced to slaughter their cattle, including their breeding stock. [17]

The problem of inadequate supplies for the Indians engaged much of Mackenzie's time and led him to condemn the Indian Bureau and add his voice to those who urged that the army be given charge of the Indians. In the fall of 1875 he wrote to General Pope describing their plight. For two months in the summer, he wrote, only beef was supplied to the Indians by the bureau. Other items, such as flour and sugar, were supplied out of the post commissary. Mackenzie predicted "very great suffering" if this situation did not dramatically improve. Haworth was absolved of any blame, but Mackenzie wanted "the highest authority" to be aware of the shortcomings of the bureau. He denied any wish "to assail" the Interior Department, but he felt "a heavy responsibility resting on me to try and act rightly for these Indians."[18]

Shortages continued through the winter, and in the spring Mackenzie asked Pope for permission to loan sugar to Haworth for the Indians. Pope replied that he had no authority to sanction the move but would back the colonel if he did it. Mackenzie did so and complained again about the treatment of the Indians in June. "The position of a jailer to a vast band of half-starving criminals can never be very pleasant," he wrote, and he declared that either the Indians should be turned over to the army, or the army to the Indian Bureau. Mackenzie's complaints achieved little, and near the end of his tenure in Indian Territory he was still predicting outbreaks of hostilities if the Indians were not treated fairly. This last effort to obtain supplies was in regard to the Northern Cheyennes who had recently been shifted to Fort Reno, and the tragic effort of those Indians to return to their northern homeland in 1878 fulfilled the prophecy.[19]

White horse thieves preying on the Indians were another serious problem that Mackenzie had to handle. The Indians lost large numbers of horses—as many as one hundred in a night— and the thieves were so bold that they even took officers' horses from the fort. Mackenzie was as zealous in his efforts to stop white depredations as he had been to stop those of the Indians. He put detachments in the field with orders to chase off any whites without authorization to be on the reservation. If the thieves made it across the Red River into Texas, Mackenzie still attempted to bring them to justice. Besides sending scouts over the river, the colonel corresponded with the civil authorities to secure their cooperation. Suspects who were arrested were sent to Fort Smith, Arkansas, to be tried before the famous "hanging judge," Isaac Parker. Convictions were rare, because the distance involved made it difficult to secure witnesses. The problem continued throughout Mackenzie's tenure but was greatly reduced by his efforts.[20]

Whites trailing cattle herds across the reservation also created problems. Mackenzie was faced with the difficult task of protecting the interests of both sides. One incident suggests that he tilted toward the Indians. Julian Gunter, a Texas cowman, rode into Fort Sill seeking the colonel's permission to cross the reservation with his herd. Gunter rode his horse onto the parade ground and "ground hitched" it in front of Mackenzie's headquarters. Mackenzie did not stand as Gunter entered the room and ignored the rancher's proffered handshake. Instead, Mackenzie asked if it were Gunter's horse on the parade ground. When Gunter answered in the affirmative, Mackenzie declared, "It is strictly against the rules for a horse to be on the parade ground. If he is not removed in five minutes, you will be under arrest." Mackenzie then gave reluctant permission for Gunter to cross the reservation, but he refused to provide an escort. Gunter later made contact with Quanah Parker, who helped him in exchange for six cows. On at least one occasion Mackenzie had to warn off whites who attempted to settle on Indian land.[21]

Many other matters also demanded attention from Mackenzie. Maintaining the general health and well-being of the men and horses was an ongoing chore. Post medical records testify to the effort needed to keep up high standards for food and hygiene. Lack of adequate funds sometimes hampered such efforts, as testified to by the fact that almost a year was required to obtain zinc-lined sink boxes for the enlisted men's latrines. To overcome the monotony and deficiencies of the official rations, the men were encouraged to grow their own vegetables. In the summer, Mackenzie allowed the wearing of straw hats to help ward off the effects of the extreme heat.[22]

Another headache for Mackenzie was to provide hospitality to visiting dignitaries. In September of 1875, for example, Prince Starhenburg of Austria and Baron Thielman, chargé d'affaires of the German legation, arrived at Fort Sill. In spite of Mackenzie's love of hunting, he sent Captain Heyl to escort the visitors on a hunt, which suggests that the colonel did not much care for such responsibilities. Another odd job for Mackenzie was to allow a Swiss named Andreas Eisenring to try to communicate with the Indians, as he claimed he could, by speaking Old Latin and Romanish.[23]

Several whites who had been captured as children were living with the Indians when they surrendered. In at least two cases, Mackenzie used his influence to help persuade the captives to return to their white families. Gottlieb Fischer found his son living with the Yamparika Comanches. When the boy seemed unwilling to go back with his father, Mackenzie pressured him to do so and the boy did. Herman Lehmann, another reluctant returnee, stated that it was the effort of Mackenzie and Quanah that persuaded him to go live with his mother. The proper course in such situations is largely a matter of perspective, but Mackenzie clearly accepted the majority white opinion that Indian ways were not suitable for whites.[24]

During his time at Fort Sill, Mackenzie displayed a certain touchiness that would become more noticeable over the years. He complained in December 1875 that the Fifth Cavalry was receiving special treatment. He was especially bothered by the construction work that his own regiment was required to perform at Fort Reno and Camp Elliot. "I do not want to get out of my share of work," he wrote, "but it seems to me not good" that one regiment should get preferential treatment. In reply to earlier complaints by Mackenzie, General Pope wrote soothingly, suggesting that the hard service the Fourth had seen was a compliment to his "intelligence and energy." If Mackenzie continued to be unhappy in the spring, then exchange of station with the Fifth might be possible. After a bit more rumbling, Mackenzie let the matter drop.[25]

Mackenzie was especially provoked by an article that appeared in the *New York Times* in April 1876. The newspaper printed excerpts from the letters "of an agent of the Board of Indian Commissioners" which criticized the army for not protecting the Indians and for being a corrupting influence on them. The anonymous writer asserted that "Fort Sill is a sort of young Sodom, and the garrison is mostly made up men who neither fear God nor regard men." The troops were depicted as drunkards and gamblers led by officers who were not much better. The writer went on to claim that the Kiowas and Comanches lived in dread of being turned over to the army, which gave them little protection from cattle thieves from Texas. The excerpts ended with hints of corruption in the procurement of supplies.[26]

Mackenzie rushed to defend his reputation and that of his men. He was dissuaded from sending a reply directly to the *Times* but instead went through channels with his letter of protest. The outraged officer charged that the letter in the newspaper was the work of civilians who wanted to discredit the army and ensure that responsibility for the Indians would not be transfered to the War Department. He did not blame the Indian Bureau or agent Haworth, he said, but he did feel slandered and declared that the author should be punished for writing the letter. Mackenzie requested an investigation by someone selected by the secretary of state, who would presumably be neutral between the army and the Indian Bureau. "Someone ought to be punished," Mackenzie concluded, "for, either I am a very poor officer, or these people are bad men."[27]

Mackenzie's superiors were somewhat embarrassed by his sensitivity but dutifully endorsed his letter as it passed through channels. Pope saw no need for an investigation but endorsed the letter "in deference" to Mackenzie. Sheridan concurred with Pope, and Sherman believed the article should be ignored.

"General Mackenzie is too good an officer," wrote the commanding general, "to be damaged in reputation by anonymous flings." Still, he sent Mackenzie's complaint on to the secretary of war with the recommendation that it be sent to the House Committee on Military Affairs. There the letter met the common fate of being printed in a report, then forgotten.[28]

The intensity of Mackenzie's reaction to the *Times* article was tied in with his response to a congressional investigation into corruption in the military. The House Committee on Expenditures, chaired by Heister Clymer, learned from the testimony of Lieutenant Colonel Alexander McCook and Lieutenant Robert G. Carter of the possible malfeasance of General J. J. Reynolds when he commanded the Department of Texas. These were essentially the same charges brought up by Mackenzie during his feud with Reynolds. Mackenzie was disturbed by a statement made by General Sherman that he was sure Reynolds "can make a satisfactory explanation of the allegations." To Mackenzie this mild defense of Reynolds was an attack on himself. He wrote to Sherman saying he felt that he had been done an "injustice." He said Sherman was so influential that he should not speak until fully informed of the facts. The colonel claimed to be reluctant to pursue the matter except to say, "I have nothing in the world to care for except the respect of respectable people." Reynolds, Mackenzie concluded, "was a bad officer."[29]

The *New York Times* reported on April 8, 1876, that the Clymer committee had requested documents relating to the Mackenzie-Reynolds feud from the secretary of war. The charges against Mackenzie could not be found, but McCook's report on the practice of "greasing" to secure army contracts did appear. The resurrection of the court-martial charges prompted Mackenzie to get off another letter to Sherman. Denying any desire to "press Reynolds," Mackenzie asserted that Reynolds's friends were trying to defend him by smearing Mackenzie. The colonel denied wanting to carry on a dispute through the mail or press, but commented that "there is such a thing as allowing too much to pass unnoticed." Sheridan at this point tried to mediate between his subordinate and his superior. He assured Mackenzie that Sherman's remarks relating to Reynolds's defense were "not much." Sheridan strongly cautioned Mackenzie against testifying before the congressional committee as Custer had done. The charges Reynolds brought against Mackenzie were trivial and were a dead issue anyway, Sheridan concluded.[30]

Mackenzie was not quite ready to let the matter drop. He mailed copies of the papers relating to his charges against Reynolds to Sheridan. He again stated his belief that friends of Reynolds and the suspect contracting firm, Adams and Wicks, were trying to create a smoke screen to hide their own crimes. Denying any wish to disregard Sheridan's advice, Mackenzie reiterated his belief that the conflict should be fully aired. Next, Mackenzie sent copies of the documents to Sherman with the assurance that he would do no more unless Reynolds pushed the issue. Mackenzie had learned that President Grant supported him, and he expressed his pleasure about this to Sherman. That was the end of the episode. The Clymer committee dropped the investigation of Reynolds in its effort to pile up evidence for the impeachment of Secretary of War Belknap. Reynolds was preoccupied with another serious problem: court-martial charges growing out of his mishandled attack on the village of the Northern Cheyenne leader, Two Moon. Mackenzie's name did not come up again.[31]

Mackenzie's behavior in these two situations bordered on paranoia. Even he recognized that his course might appear "irrational" to some, but protecting his reputation was uppermost in his mind. His driving ambition combined with the stress of his demanding position led him to press both issues much farther than either warranted. It was clear that he would be a top candidate for the next brigadier general's slot to come open. Anxious that no stain on his record might hinder his advancement, Mackenzie ran the risk of antagonizing his superiors with his complaints.[32]

In spite of his intemperate reaction to these minor provocations, Mackenzie continued to remain on good terms with his superiors. He felt a special regard for Sheridan, considering him to be a friend and protector. When Mackenzie felt that high-level officers in Washington were working to limit his opportunities, it was to Sheridan that he turned for help. "I write to you," he said, "because I regard myself as under more obligations to you than to any other officer in the army." Sheridan returned Mackenzie's regard and took pains to smooth the relations between his subordinate and the high command. When Mackenzie complained about the modification of an endorsement by a subordinate instead of General Sherman, which he felt was a slight, Sheridan prevailed on the commanding general to send an explanation. Sheridan admitted that Mackenzie was worked up over a trifle, "but a little gentle treatment will heal the wound."[33]

Mackenzie cultivated friendship with Sherman as well, but his peculiar temper prevented the relationship from being a smooth one. Evidence of the growing friendliness of the association between the highest-ranking officer in the army and its most promising young colonel can be found in their correspondence. As early as May 1875, Mackenzie was writing to Sherman as much as a friend as a subordinate, ending a letter with a wish to be remembered to the general's wife and daughter. At Sherman's request, Mackenzie selected some surrendered Indian ponies for him. He offered to find a special one for "Mrs. Fitch," Sherman's recently married daughter, who, Mackenzie wrote, "I have always regarded . . . as a special ally." When Sherman proposed a visit to Fort Sill to view the reservation situation for himself, Mackenzie suggested that he travel with some officers returning to duty from Saint Louis, because "they are pleasant young men" and would entertain "Miss Lizzie," one of Sherman's unmarried daughters. Mackenzie, also with typical humor, warned Sherman to bring boards for tent flooring, because lumber was scarce "except for coffins. The quartermaster dept[.] always seems rather tender toward the dead soldiers, though sometimes rather tough with the living."[34]

Sherman's tour was a success. The general was strong in his approval of the condition of the post and of Mackenzie's leadership. He supported the younger man's claim for sole authority over the Indians, writing to Sheridan that "if McKenzie can have the entire control, we will have no more trouble with these Indians." Sherman's good opinion of Mackenzie held in spite of the latter's occasional fits of temper. Considering the value of Sherman's friendship to his ambitions, it is surprising that he challenged his superior at all. Fortunately, Sherman's maturity, and Sheridan's intercession, prevented these occasions from becoming major confrontations.[35]

Mackenzie did not enjoy his tour of duty at Fort Sill. Although he claimed to admire General Pope, he did not approve of the way Pope divided command or posted troops. Particularly, Mackenzie was put off by the duty of supervising Indians who were forced to suffer shortages of food and supplies because of the derelictions of Congress and corruption in the Indian Bureau. Fort Sill was a sickly place, and Mackenzie had at least one bout with malaria. Even so, when there was a threat of trouble in the Indian Territory, he wrote from another troublesome post that he wanted to be there even if it meant commanding only two companies under another officer. The experience at Fort Sill had obviously left a deep mark on the young colonel.[36]

CHAPTER ELEVEN

THE VERY MAN FOR THE JOB

AFTER two years of growing tension, the last great Indian war broke out on the northern plains. To some extent the war was forced by army officers, especially Generals Sherman and Sheridan, who were fed up with the conflicts in Indian policy and desired to get matters straight once and for all. In the spring of 1876, Sheridan put the forces in his northern departments into the field in an effort to drive the Sioux who had not signed a peace treaty with the United States, along with a large number of warriors who had abandoned their pledges of peace, onto the reservations. For the most part the campaign was a series of blunders and disasters. General J. J. Reynolds gained and lost a victory in March and was court-martialed by his superior, General George Crook. Crook himself was beaten by Sioux led by Crazy Horse at the Battle of the Rosebud on June 17. Just six days later, Lieutenant Colonel George Armstrong Custer was killed along with more than 250 troopers of the Seventh Cavalry by a large combined force of northern Indians.[1]

Driven by a desire to revenge Custer's death, to vindicate his own reputation as an Indian fighter, and finally to bring the northern plains under control, Sheridan brought in reinforcements from other departments and pressed the campaign. The magnitude of the Custer debacle gave the army temporary ascendancy over Indian affairs, including control of the reservations. To prevent Indians presently on the reservations from slipping off to join their fellows in the field, Sheridan developed a plan to disarm and dismount them. Sheridan specifically selected Mackenzie for this duty and ordered Pope to transfer elements of the Fourth Cavalry to Camp Robinson near the Red Cloud Agency. Mackenzie was to command that post if he could be spared, as "he is the very man" needed in the situation. The order went out in July, and in early August, Mackenzie began to shift his regiment northward. He also called Lieutenant H. W. Lawton back from leave to serve as quartermaster and requested that Sheridan secure Winchester rifles for his troops. The repeating rifles were not forthcoming, but having Lawton as quartermaster went a long way toward making up the deficiency.[2]

The government had not given up hope of settling the troubles peacefully. On August 15, 1876, President Grant signed a new appropriations bill that provided funds to purchase the Black Hills from the Sioux. He then appointed a seven-man commission to attempt to persuade the Indians to grant land cessions and to accept reservations closer to the Missouri River or in the Indian Territory (either of which locations would presumably have simplified the task of getting annuity goods to the Indians). The military men had little faith in the mission of the civilians. Mackenzie complained that the presence of the commission "unsettles the minds of these Indians." The officers' objections to the commissioners' efforts were based on their knowledge that the Indians were expert at prolonging negotiations to gain more time. Their years of experience in dealing with the red men had also led them to believe that a thorough thrashing was necessary to bring the Indians in line with white men's desires.[3]

After a meeting with Sheridan and Crook, Mackenzie wrote a letter expressing doubts about the good faith of the Indians in the talks. He had failed in his efforts to get the Indians on the Red Cloud and Spotted Tail agencies to surrender renegades who had been raiding off the reservation, and Mackenzie believed that most of the Indians had no intention of cooperating with the civilian representatives of the government. He proposed that all dealings with the Indians be handled by the military and that Grant suspend any agreements already made. Mackenzie said that he "had no clash" with the commissioners and had endeavored to work with them in their efforts. He simply did not believe that the Indians were sincere. This letter to General Crook, who was now Mackenzie's immediate superior, was endorsed up the line by Crook, Sheridan, and Sherman. One of the commissioners, George W. Manypenny, later claimed that the letter was the product of a conference among Mackenzie, Crook, and Sheridan and was intended to negate the influence of the civilians. Manypenny's charge was basically true. The officers simply believed that force would have to be used sooner or later and that sooner was better than later.[4]

When Mackenzie first arrived at the Red Cloud Agency, he found the Sioux in an unsettled condition. He estimated that half the warriors assigned to the agency had gone north to join the hostiles. Some of these men had returned, but their fellow tribesmen refused to cooperate by revealing their names. More ominous was the fact that Red Cloud, a leading Sioux chief, and several lesser leaders had taken their followers to campsites along Chadron Creek about thirty miles from the agency. Red Cloud was apparently trying to avoid any involvement in the hostilities, but he picked a poor time to assert his independence of mind. The whites feared that he might lead his whole band to the north or, at the least, that his young warriors would be free to ride out on raids and return without detection.

After his conference with Crook and Sheridan, Mackenzie returned to Camp Robinson under orders to bring the recalcitrant Indians back to the agency. Mackenzie first sent a messenger to tell the Indians that their conduct greatly distressed "the Great Father and all that sort of thing that is customary with Indians, and about as efficient as the plan which is sometimes recommended of catching birds by the use of salt." The Indians would not come in unless "strong power" were applied. When the appeals to Red Cloud brought no response, Mackenzie collected a force to go out and compel the Indians to return to the agency.[5]

Mackenzie made his move on October 23, 1876. He combined two companies of the Fifth Cavalry with six of his own Fourth and moved out to bring in the Sioux. En route he was joined by the North brothers, Frank and Luther, and fifty Indians from their famous battalion of Pawnee scouts. The detachment rode hard through the night to reach the Sioux encampments before daylight. The cavalry was alerted to the nearness of Red Cloud's village by roosters crowing. The old Sioux had a fondness for chickens and always kept a flock with him. Mackenzie divided his forces, sending Major George Gordon of the Fifth Cavalry with half the troops to bring in the village of Swift Bear and Red Leaf, while he took the other half to secure Red Cloud's people. At both villages the same basic procedure was followed. The villages were surrounded, and messengers were sent in to call upon the Indians to submit peacefully. The Pawnee scouts were used to round up the Sioux horses. No shots were fired, and both operations were accomplished without violence.[6]

After the roundup was complete, Mackenzie ordered the women to take down the tepees and load the Indians' belongings on pack horses. At first the women made no move to comply with the order, and Mackenzie repeated it, adding that he would burn the lodges unless his command was obeyed. Still, no one moved to obey the white officer until the troops actually began to fire the lodges. Once begun, the loading went quickly, and soon the Sioux—120 men with their families and horses—were on their way back to the agency. Mackenzie allowed the old and feeble to ride, but the young warriors were forced to walk.

Mackenzie's deft handling of Red Cloud cleared the way for Crook to mount a major expedition toward the Powder River, and he began to gather his forces in early November. Crook brought together eleven companies of cavalry, eleven of infantry, and four of artillery. Mackenzie was made commander of the cavalry, which was composed of companies from the Second, Third, Fourth, and Fifth regiments. Colonel Richard I.

Dodge commanded the infantry and artillery. All told, the troops numbered some eleven hundred men. Almost four hundred Indian auxiliaries, representing the Sioux, Arapaho, Shoshone, Bannock, Pawnee, and Cheyenne tribes, accompanied Crook's force. The Indian scouts were largely responsible for Mackenzie's smashing success in the campaign.[7]

Mackenzie presented a marked contrast to his immediate superior. Crook was widely known for his eccentricities of dress and manner. He sported a full beard with pointed ends, often wore canvas clothes and a pith helmet, and preferred riding a mule to a horse. Mackenzie, on the other hand, was viewed as "a noble specimen of the *beau sabreur.*" Compared to Crook, the younger officer was considered to be "impetuous, headstrong, perhaps a trifle rash." Rather than affect oddities of dress, Mackenzie wore the regulation officer's undress uniform, varying its appearance only during very cold weather by wearing a fur cap, blue overcoat, and overshoes.[8]

During the campaign, Mackenzie maintained the same strict discipline for which he was noted. Two privates who addressed their commander informally were put to saluting a tree stump for an hour and a half in very cold weather. Men who appeared late for guard duty were forced to walk carrying bundles of forage as punishment. At the same time, Mackenzie revealed his basic human decency in his treatment of his men. When an Indian scout brought the colonel half an antelope, he shared it with his orderlies. On another occasion, an orderly had a run-in with a sergeant, who complained to Mackenzie. Mackenzie called the orderly in and told him to bring any complaints directly to him and to bypass the noncommissioned officer. Yet Mackenzie failed to properly discipline a drunken Lieutenant Lawton when the lieutenant physically attacked an enlisted man. Mackenzie needed Lawton too much to risk losing him by pressing charges.[9]

Crook had his army ready to march on November 14, 1876, and that day he led it north toward the Powder River country. It was, perhaps, the best prepared and best equipped force ever to be sent against the Indians. The troops were mainly veterans accustomed to hardship and wise to the ways of Indian warfare. They were supported by a large supply train consisting of wagons and a large number of pack mules to allow maximum mobility for the cavalry. Each man was provided with the best available cold weather gear to help deal with the harsh winter weather to be expected on the northern plains. [10]

When the movement first began, there was a spirited competition between the infantry and the cavalry to get on the road first. At stake in the race was the best camping spot for the evening and first access to the limited supply of firewood available. Mackenzie and Dodge apparently were unacquainted before the campaign, and the rivalry for good campgrounds could have turned bitter. After two days on the march, however, Dodge visited Mackenzie in his tent. He found Mackenzie to be friendly and helpful. The cavalry commander supplied Dodge with two orderlies and offered to help out in other matters if he could. The two officers also agreed to alternate days taking the lead in order to eliminate the competition for good camping. Dodge felt some grievance at the way he was treated by Crook, and the two probably shared their complaints, although there is no record of specific ones by Mackenzie. [11]

Crook sent scouts ranging far out ahead of the column to look for indications of Indian activity. Some of the scouts were assigned to the cavalry and reported directly to Mackenzie. One of them was a well-known figure named Frank Grouard who had lived at the Red Cloud agency. The relationship between colonel and scout can be seen in a dialogue reported by a rookie private assigned to duty with Grouard:

"Well Frank, what have you seen?" asked Mackenzie after shaking hands with the frontiersman.

"Seen heaps," he replied.

"And how did our new man do?" inquired the General alluding to me.

"Him heap good Indian."

"Where are the reds?"

"Over in the mountains," replied the scout.
"Well come to my tent in about an hour," said the Gen. and left us.[12]

On November 22, an Indian scout named Sitting Bear brought Mackenzie a report of a large village of Northern Cheyennes in the Big Horn Mountains. Mackenzie took Sitting Bear to Crook, who, after listening to the scout's story, ordered Mackenzie to take the cavalry and go after the village. If possible, Mackenzie was to avoid a fight and to bring the Indians in peacefully. Mackenzie immediately issued orders for his troops to prepare for movement. The men were to pack ten days' rations and have them ready to load on the pack mules the next morning. Troopers on sick call were detailed to stay behind and guard the wagons. The men moving with the column were to have two blankets, one of which was to be placed over the saddle blanket to help protect the horses from the intense cold. A shelter half and overcoat completed the protection the soldiers were afforded. Each man was to carry one hundred rounds of carbine ammunition and twenty-five rounds for the pistol. Mackenzie ordered the officers to "*mess with their companies.*"[13]

Mackenzie led his troops out on November 23 and camped that night on a creek that emptied into the Crazy Woman Fork of the Powder River. They had already begun the next days' march when Indian scouts rode in and reported that they had pinpointed the location of the Cheyennes about fifteen miles to the southwest. Mackenzie hoped to catch the village by surprise and ordered the troopers to make a fireless camp and rest until night. As darkness approached, the column moved out, led by the Indian scouts. Captain Luther North remembered the march as "about the hardest" he had experienced. The trail was extremely rough, going up steep slopes then dropping sharply into narrow ravines. At times the column was forced to march single file, and the troops would become strung out over several miles. Mackenzie had ordered no smoking, but many lit up anyway, seeking even that small relief from cold and boredom.

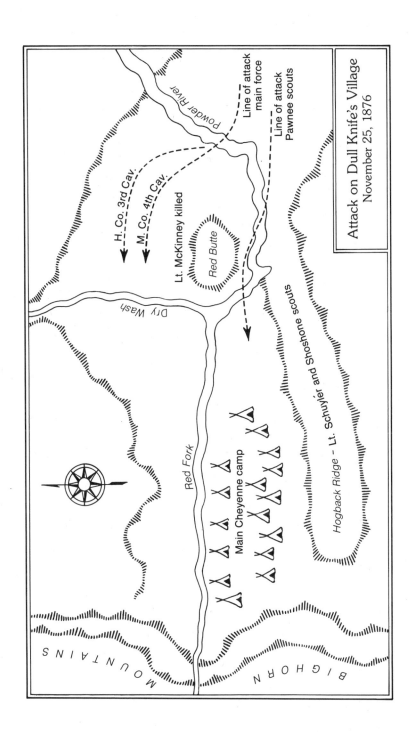

Attack on Dull Knife's Village
November 25, 1876

Line of attack main force

Line of attack Pawnee scouts

Powder River

H. Co. 3rd Cav.

M. Co. 4th Cav.

Lt. McKinney killed

Red Butte

Dry Wash

Hogback Ridge – Lt. Schuyler and Shoshone scouts

Red Fork

Main Cheyenne camp

BIGHORN MOUNTAINS

Many of the horses gave out, and some of the men were so tired that, in spite of below-zero temperatures, they laid on the ground to sleep during rest halts.[14]

As the cavalry neared the camp, the men began to hear the sound of drums pounding for a dance in the Cheyenne village. The dance, along with the fact that the Indians made no effort to prepare to defend the village, led some observers to believe that Mackenzie had caught the Cheyennes by surprise. Such was not the case. The Indians were well aware of Mackenzie's coming, but for reasons that seem unfathomable from a white perspective, they allowed themselves to be bullied by Last Bull, a leader of the Fox soldier society, into staying in place without preparation for defense.[15]

The drums stopped and the Indians retired to their lodges as the cavalry got within striking distance of the village. It was just first light when Mackenzie ordered his men to tighten their cinches and prepare for a charge. The Indian auxiliaries quickly stripped for battle and painted their faces. There was a pause of ten or fifteen minutes while Mackenzie went ahead to scout the village. When he returned, he quickly outlined his plan. He hoped to catch the village in a kind of pincers movement by sending the Pawnees and Shoshones to the left to cut off the Cheyennes' retreat while the rest of the auxiliaries led the cavalry in a charge against the center and right. One of Mackenzie's orderlies recorded that the Indians were placed at the head of the charge so that if a trap were waiting "they will catch it first." The entrance to the valley where the Cheyenne camp lay was just wide enough for a column of fours, but as the ground opened up, the cavalry shifted to a broad front for the final assault. Mackenzie, at about that point, signaled for the North brothers and their Pawnees to cross the creek separating them from the main force and to join the general charge. Although Luther North thought this delay might have allowed enough time for many of the Cheyennes to reach the rocks and escape the full fury of the attack, Mackenzie's move added the weight of the Pawnees to the main charge.[16]

As Mackenzie's force neared the village, the lead Indian auxiliaries veered to one side, leaving Mackenzie and a small group
almost alone. A Cheyenne warrior suddenly appeared and
fired at the colonel from just ten steps away. The shot was hurried and missed, and the daring man was cut down by Mackenzie's orderlies. One of the orderlies, Private Earl Smith, was
sent rushing back to hurry up the companies. Thoroughly
alarmed now, some of the Cheyennes hustled to get the wom-
en and children into the relative safety of the rocks. Other warriors provided covering fire. One small group tried to sneak
back into the village to retrieve the horses. Mackenzie spotted
their movement and ordered Lieutenant John A. McKinney
with M Company to drive them back. The charge carried the
company past a deep ravine, where a large group of Cheyennes was hiding. As the troopers drew abreast of them, the
warriors rose up and delivered a "murderous fire" which cut
down McKinney—who was probably dead before he hit the
ground—and wounded six of the troopers. This deadly trap
spurred a retreat by M Company that threatened to spread
panic among the other soldiers. Lieutenant Lawton, temporarily relieved of his quartermaster duties and assigned to a combat
company, was instrumental in regrouping the troopers and sav-
ing the situation.[17]

The fighting now became general, with all elements of Mackenzie's command hotly engaged. Perhaps the decisive action
was provided by Captains Wirt Davis of the Fourth Cavalry and
John Hamilton of the Fifth. Their troops cleared the last of the
Cheyennes who tried to defend the village and forced them to
retreat to the rocks on the mountainside. They, in their turn,
were aided by accurate fire provided by the Shoshone scouts
under Lieutenant Walter Schuyler, who had gained a ridge
from which they could command the battlefield. Throughout
this phase of the fight, Mackenzie rode from one portion of the
field to another, exposing himself to the bullets of Indians still
fighting on the flats as well as the increasing sniper fire from the
Cheyennes who had reached cover on the slopes behind the

village. The shooting was so heavy that Mackenzie sent his orderlies to cover while he continued to direct the battle.[18]

The first part of the fight, which Mackenzie described as "brisk," lasted about an hour. Then it settled down into minor skirmishing and sniping back and forth. At one point, a Cheyenne began to shoot into the wounded gathered at the aid station. Half a dozen Pawnees were sent by Frank North to silence him. Luther North and a single Pawnee managed to round up a hundred or so Cheyenne horses while under a heavy fire. The Cheyennes put on their own show of daring, some of them recklessly exposing themselves to the cavalry. Lieutenant J. G. Bourke was particularly struck by the bravery of one warrior, who died in a vain attempt to recover the body of a fallen comrade.[19]

Mackenzie took advantage of a lull in the fighting to send a scout to try to persuade the Cheyennes to surrender. What followed is not clear, but apparently Dull Knife, one of the principal chiefs, was willing to surrender, although most of the others were not. The Cheyennes chided the Indian auxiliaries, saying they could handle the bluecoats but not other Indians as well. Possibly Mackenzie offered surrender as a way for the Cheyennes to save their tepees and other worldly goods. When it became clear that the hostiles would not give up, Mackenzie ordered the village to be destroyed. The colonel had already sent back word for Crook to have the infantry brought up to help finish the battle, but he knew from experience that the real victory came from ending the Indians' ability to stay off the reservation. As the troops went about their work of destruction, they discovered a large quantity of relics from Custer's last fight, clear evidence that warriors from this village had participated in the Battle of the Little Big Horn and that, in the minds of the white soldiers, their attack was justified.[20]

The temperature dropped as the early winter darkness set in. All along, the weather had been bitter, and this night was no exception. Mackenzie set out guards while the rest of the command huddled under its blankets and tried to sleep among the rocks. The moans of the wounded soldiers kept some troopers awake a large part of the night. Mackenzie's orderly, Private Smith, troubled by his sprained knee and the cries of the wounded, woke frequently during the night, always to see his commander pacing restlessly. When Smith awoke early to make breakfast, Mackenzie sat down with him and drank a cup of coffee while talking over the battle and worrying about the dead and wounded. Mackenzie had been especially fond of McKinney—he had helped the young lieutenant straighten out his finances—and was reported to have cried when he saw the body.[21]

In the mountains without most of their buffalo robes and with but little food, the Cheyennes suffered more than the whites, and many of them froze to death during the night. Before first light, the Indians had begun to retreat further into the mountains. Early in the morning Mackenzie's scouts discovered that the Indians had withdrawn about six miles and were in even stronger defensive positions than before. Dislodging the Cheyennes now would take a heavy toll, even if the Infantry came up, so Mackenzie decided to break off contact. The decision was really made the evening before at an officers' conference, at which Mackenzie discussed with his subordinates the practicality of attacking the Cheyennes among the rocks. After some discussion, the decision was made that the effort to inflict more damage on the Cheyennes would cost more than the result would warrant. The situation that greeted Mackenzie on the morning of November 26 merely confirmed the choice. He issued orders to complete the destruction of the Indians' property and to mount up for the difficult trek back to the main column.[22]

Mackenzie ordered travois to be made to carry the wounded and assigned Lieutenant Homer Wheeler the responsibility for managing them. Considering the difficulty that the command had encountered in reaching the Cheyenne camp, it was a formidable task, but Wheeler carried it off successfully. The dead were merely thrown over the backs of mules, where the bodies froze into grotesque positions. At the rest stop that night, the stone-hard corpses were taken off the mules and stood on their hands and feet like hoops for some ghoulish game of croquet.[23]

That night, also, some of the Indian auxiliaries held a scalp dance for the fascinated soldiers. The antics of the friendly Indians probably did little to calm the nerves of the soldiers. Mackenzie was concerned that the Cheyennes might follow and seek revenge or that other bands of hostile Indians might be near. This worry led him to keep scouts out at all times as well as to set up a strong guard for night camp. Scouts shooting at buffalo generated a momentary panic among the troopers on the night of November 27. Some of the men saw the danger of Indian attacks as less of a threat than the cold, and Private Smith refused to extinguish his fire even though more nervous men demanded that he do so.[24]

Mackenzie rejoined Crook's main force a few days later. The unpleasant business of burying the dead could now be carried out. About noon on November 30, 1876, services were held, and the dead enlisted men were buried (Lieutenant McKinney's body was sent back east for burial). After the scriptures, bugles, and rifle salutes, the command was paraded over the graves to obliterate them so that Indians might not dig up the corpses and mutilate them. Lieutenant John G. Bourke found the service "tenderly imposing," but the enlisted men were only reminded of the harshness of the country and the hard fate of the soldier.[25]

Mackenzie's fight with the Northern Cheyennes was the only combat action of Crook's winter campaign, but it was enough to label the effort a success. Mackenzie's official report counted twenty-five Indians killed, 173 lodges with their contents destroyed, and five hundred horses captured. The cavalry command lost one officer and five enlisted men killed, twenty-five troopers and one Shoshone scout wounded, and a few horses killed. Crook acknowledged the significance of the battle in his report to headquarters, saying that it was a "terrible blow" to the Cheyennes. Certainly the increasing number of Indian surrenders in the spring of 1877 was largely a result of the fight against Dull Knife's band. The chief himself surrendered to Mackenzie in April of that year, saying, "You are the one I was afraid of when you came here last summer." Sheridan's annual report also stressed the effect of Mackenzie's victory while very correctly lavishing praise on Colonel Miles for maintaining pressure on the Indians throughout much of the winter.[26]

Some thought the victory not as complete as it could have been. Colonel Dodge, for one, believed that his infantry would have killed or captured all of the Cheyennes. Even Mackenzie succumbed to momentary depression about his early withdrawal from the battlefield. Dodge recorded in his diary that Mackenzie considered the fight to be "an utter failure." The cavalry commander was concerned not only that most of the Cheyennes had gotten away, but also that his refusal to press the fight the next day might be seen as cowardice. Another officer told Dodge that Mackenzie was so downcast that he had contemplated suicide.[27]

The full meaning of this fit of depression is hard to measure. Taken with the displays of sensitivity to slights that bordered on paranoia, hindsight might suggest early signs of the mental derangement that would force Mackenzie's retirement in a few years. Viewed without knowledge of what was to come, a different judgment seems obvious. The intensely ambitious and competitive young officer was fearful that he would not gain as much credit for the Dull Knife fight as he would have had all of the Indians been forced to surrender. In the close rivalry for preferment, any little slip or slight bit more success might make the difference in winning or losing. Quite likely Mackenzie's despondency was caused by his feeling that he had not taken full advantage of his opportunity. Dodge was able to improve Mackenzie's spirits by emphasizing his success. Mackenzie's spirits were further elevated by telegrams of congratulations from Sherman and Sheridan. Dodge wrote in his diary that Mackenzie was "very like himself" and "quite jolly" after reading his superiors' praise.[28]

Ironically, Mackenzie soon became General Crook's comforter as the Powder River campaign fizzled into a fruitless series of marches and countermarches. Crook, ordinarily one of the most capable of officers in the Indian-fighting army, seemed to lose direction. He sent out scouts and marched his army this way and that, usually in extremely bitter conditions, but accomplished nothing. When Dodge told Mackenzie that Crook was feeling low, the cavalry commander suggested that they should try to cheer their leader.[29]

When Crook broke up the expedition, Mackenzie and the Fourth Cavalry were ordered back to Camp Robinson. On the way, Mackenzie was intercepted by orders to report to Washington to place himself under the orders of the secretary of war. Many people thought that the nation was on the verge of another civil war. As a result of disputed election returns from three southern states, the outcome of the presidential election of 1876 was still in doubt. Some of the more rabid Democrats were threatening to raise armies to ensure that their candidate was seated in the nation's highest office. President Grant was determined to preserve order and began to call troops in from the western frontier to be ready if necessary, and he personally selected Mackenzie to come to the capital to take command of all the forces concentrated there. As it turned out, the troops were not needed, and the so-called Compromise of 1877 ended the crisis. The summons was, nevertheless, a remarkable testimony to the president's faith in the abilities of Ranald Mackenzie.[30]

Sheridan was impatient to have Mackenzie back in the West and ordered his return as soon as the compromise was settled. The commander of the Division of the Missouri had developed a plan for further campaigns against the northern plains Indians in which Mackenzie and his arch-rival, Nelson Miles, were to play the leading parts. Sheridan's plans were not put into effect, however, as the off-reservation Indians began to come in in large numbers. By May 1877, most of the once hostile Indians had surrendered, and there was no longer a need for a large-scale campaign on the northern plains. Mackenzie returned to Camp Robinson to await a new assignment.[31]

As usual, Mackenzie was not content simply to bide his time

while decisions regarding his and the Fourth Cavalry's future were being made. He got off a long letter to Sheridan expressing his concern about his regiment and himself. For the regiment, Mackenzie asked for a station other than Fort Sill and enclosed letters from two officers indicating how unhealthy that place was. The Fourth, Mackenzie continued, was in a worse place now (Camp Robinson) than any of the other regiments in the department and deserved assignment to a post along the railroads. For himself, Mackenzie expressed concern that his achievements were not fully appreciated by General Sherman and Adjutant General E. D. Townsend. While willing to accept any assignment, Mackenzie went on, he was "not engaged in anything of the nature of a race" with anyone and desired a quiet post until he was needed and assured of full support from Washington.[32]

Sheridan sent the letter on to Sherman, who responded with an offer of appointment as commandant of the Military Academy at West Point. Mackenzie turned it down on the grounds that the post did not call for a full colonel and he did not "wish to go east to such an extent as to desire a position which belongs to a lower rank." Although he said that he would go east to serve on a significant commission or board, it is clear that Mackenzie was stepping cautiously to avoid losing position in the maneuvering for the next brigadier general's appointment. With no eastern assignment in view, Mackenzie and his regiment returned to Fort Sill once again.[33]

A growing clamor on the Rio Grande ensured that Mackenzie's second stay at Fort Sill would be short-lived. Whatever calming effect his actions in 1873–74 had had on the border region had worn off rapidly. As early as the summer of 1875, the commander of the Department of Texas, General E. O. C. Ord, had asked that Mackenzie be transferred back to the troubled region with authority to cross the border. General Sherman had turned down the request, correctly judging that increasing the number of troops on the border would not alone solve the problem. But as the troubles grew, the pressure for

Mackenzie's return also grew. In 1876 the adjutant general of Texas, with the endorsement of the governor, asked one of the state's U.S. senators, Samuel B. Maxey, to use his influence to have the Fourth Cavalry brought back. He pointed out that Mackenzie was experienced in the region and highly popular with the people of the state. Sherman again quashed the move, but it became increasingly clear that the existing forces in Texas were not up to handling the job. Even after Ord received permission to send troops across the border in hot pursuit, incidents of robbery and murder continued to take place. The commanding general then gave up and told a congressional committee that Mackenzie should be assigned to the Rio Grande.[34]

Sheridan and Sherman had reached the conclusion to send Mackenzie and the Fourth back to the border after an exchange of telegrams in November. Accordingly, on December 3, Sheridan issued orders which sent Mackenzie and six of his companies on the overland march to Texas. Mackenzie began preparations immediately, although weather conditions made quick movement difficult. Heavy rains turned the trails into quagmires, and it took the regiment thirteen days to move forty miles to the Red River and another three days to cross that swollen stream. Mackenzie was "furious" at the delay, the more so because nothing could be done about it. Nor could he do much more to prevent the delay caused when the citizens or Henrietta, Texas, insisted on honoring him with a banquet. "This bored Mackenzie greatly" and put him in the uncomfortable position of having to respond to the fulsome praise heaped upon him by local dignitaries and having to avoid the liquor proffered to him. The troopers of the Fourth had no problem as far as accepting alcohol was concerned, and a large number got drunk. Mackenzie punished the worst cases by spread-eagling them on the ground and then forcing them to walk the next day's march.[35]

Once in Texas, Mackenzie was made commander of the District of the Nueces in order to give him control of all of the troops in the troubled region. His command included elements of the Fourth and Eighth Cavalry regiments, the Tenth, Twentieth, Twenty-fourth, and Twenty-fifth Infantry regiments, three batteries of artillery, and the usual contingent of Seminole-Negro scouts. Mackenzie went to San Antonio to confer with Ord, then arrived at Fort Clark in February 1877. There he took several initiatives. He made an attempt to secure joint action with Mexican General A. R. Falcón, and he established several subposts in an effort to speed reporting of and response to incidents and enhance chances of successful pursuit of raiders. Neither effort had much success. Falcón would make no agreement, and raiders into Texas continued to escape unpunished. Frustrated, Mackenzie began to plan for a major incursion into Mexico, which he believed was the only way to effectively halt the raids. He saw, too, that war with Mexico would be a probable result of such a move and urged that preparations be made if it came to that.[36]

By the end of May, Mackenzie had completed his plan for the movement into Mexico. He intended to send a cavalry column to the Santa Rosa Mountains after Indians who had raided San Diego, Texas, in early May. The cavalry would be commanded by Captain Samuel B. M. Young, Eighth Cavalry, although Mackenzie would accompany it, because, he wrote, someone must bear the responsibility. The cavalry would be supported by another column consisting mainly of infantry and artillery commanded by Mackenzie's old comrade Colonel William R. Shafter. All that was lacking, Mackenzie reported, were a few details of the route, which his scouts were checking out, and clear instructions from Ord to undertake the expedition. Mackenzie made it clear that he did not intend to run the risk of being made a scapegoat or being accused of acting "from purely ambitious motives." A circular letter sent out by Ord on May 16 failed to satisfy Mackenzie's need for authority, and he again asked for precise orders "telling me to go or relieving me, one of the two." Rethinking Ord's circular letter, Mackenzie decided that it did, after all, register "a complete approval of my proposed action," although he still wished for an explicit statement "for the moral support it will give me." He decided that he would go ahead with his campaign.[37]

On June 11, 1878, Mackenzie issued the orders setting his two columns moving toward the river. The purpose of the campaign was "to punish the Indians and thieves, who committed the raid on the lower Nueces and others more recent." The cavalry column commanded by Young would consist of six companies of the Fourth and Eighth regiments plus the Seminole-Negro scouts. Shafter's column was to be made up of ten companies of infantry and three of cavalry divided into four battalions, plus an artillery detachment of three-inch guns and Gatling guns. Both columns were plentifully supplied with ammunition. If they were to encounter Mexican forces, they were to invite them to cooperate with the expedition. If the Mexicans refused, the U.S. forces would attack if "the Senior Officer" deemed his force to be strong enough.[38]

For a change, Mackenzie submitted an unusually full account of this expedition across the Rio Grande, and that report can be followed in detail from his point of view. The first attempt to cross the river, on June 11, was foiled by high water, but on the afternoon of the next day Mackenzie and Young's command splashed through the shallow water into Mexico. The force moved ten miles the first day and thirty-one the next. On the third day, the guide became sick and confused, and Mackenzie almost called off the project when no water was found where it was expected. When the column backtracked, it found water, and Mackenzie decided to reduce the scope of the expedition. Instead of moving on to the Santa Rosas, the flying column would hook up with Shafter's support group and scout for thieves in the area around El Remolino. The reunion was effected on June 17, and two days later the column encountered Mexican troops near the site of Mackenzie's 1873 fight.

The Mexican troops were led by Colonel Pedro Valdez, the "Colonel Winker" of Mackenzie's earlier acquaintance. Valdez declared that although he agreed with Mackenzie's purpose, he was under orders to "repel the Americans." Valdez's force was smaller than Mackenzie's, so the Mexican colonel did not attack, and both forces went into noon camp on opposite sides of Remolino. After lunch, Mackenzie sent Shafter and Lieutenant H. H. Crews to tell Valdez that the Americans intended no hostility toward any Mexicans "except thieves and Indians" but that the Mexican force was obstructing the path and Mackenzie would move at 3:00 P.M. Colonel Jesús Nuncio had by this time arrived with reinforcements for the Mexicans and had assumed command. Nuncio sent Mackenzie a rather insulting note declaring that if the American officer promised "to give satisfaction," the Mexican army would escort his force to the Rio Grande. Mackenzie rejected this offer and moved his command forward at the stated time. Nuncio, still outnumbered, gave way, and the Americans proceeded without molestation.

Nuncio shadowed the American force for two days as it moved toward the border. Near the river, Nuncio placed his troops on a hill overlooking the trail as if he intended to contest passage. Negotiations between the two armies were inconclusive, so Mackenzie sent out a skirmish line of six companies of cavalry. The Mexicans, appearances served, fell back, and Mackenzie elected to cross the river at the nearest point instead of pressing on to Piedras Negras and inflicting further humiliation on them.[39]

The confrontation with Mexican troops worried Mackenzie. For a brief period war between the United States and Mexico seemed to hang in the balance. Only the caution and good sense of the Mexican commanders prevented a clash with Mackenzie's force that very probably would have led to war. Mackenzie did not want to accept that sort of responsibility, so he sought authorization for future border crossing from the highest level, the president of the United States. Sheridan was not impressed with the results of Mackenzie's latest effort and suggested to Sherman that future expeditions be sent only under "the most distinct and positive orders from the highest authority." The views of Mackenzie and Sheridan found their way to President Rutherford B. Hayes, who responded by having Secretary of War George W. McCrary issue instructions that Mexican troops should not be fought unless they attacked first.[40]

Mackenzie may have expected to receive authority to continue making major thrusts into Mexico as opposed to limited hot pursuit. He expressed his opinion on July 1 that only a long, sustained campaign similar to that used against the Kiowas and Comanches would be successful in halting border depredations. Such an expedition would almost certainly bring war with Mexico, and Mackenzie was ready. He believed that Mexico could be defeated with about 150,000 troops, and then the border should be occupied by Americans until indemnities were paid for damages done by marauders from south of the Rio Grande. On July 4 he had even begun crossing another major force before a courier with orders from the War Department stopped him.[41]

Mackenzie did send several small detachments into Mexico and kept scouts busy looking for thieves and raiders throughout the summer of 1878. Nevertheless, his attitude turned toward moderation by September. In that month he began negotiations with Lieutenant Colonel Felipe Vega, who had orders to cooperate with the American troops in suppressing border crime. Mackenzie told Vega that he was happy to cooperate and sent Captain Samuel Young to work out procedures. While Young talked, Mackenzie suspended scouting operations across the river. On September 22, Young reported that he and Vega had worked out an agreement for cooperation in patrolling the river and chasing outlaws. Mackenzie's efforts through Young went a long way toward easing tensions on the lower Rio Grande. The possibility of war still existed for several months, but with the government of both countries seeking peace, the potential for an inflammatory incident was sharply reduced.[42]

Assessing the significance of Mackenzie's second tour of the border is difficult. It is tempting to accept Sheridan's judgment that "this whole Rio Grande business . . . has produced no good news and I doubt it ever will." Certainly no victories of even the dubious magnitude of the one in 1873 were achieved, and each small-scale crossing ran the very real risk of provoking war between the United States and Mexico. Yet Mackenzie's activities did reduce the number of raids into Texas. More importantly, the working out of the border problem appears to have allowed the Mexican president, Porfirio Díaz, to consolidate his authority and move the United States in the direction of *de jure* recognition of his government. At any rate, Mackenzie was relieved when he was ordered to Washington to serve on a special board to consider new equipment for the army.[43]

CHAPTER TWELVE

LAST CAMPAIGNS

WHILE serving his second tour of duty on the border, Mackenzie took advantage of an opportunity to purchase land in Texas. Several factors combined to motivate the acquisition. The price of the land was a significant factor. Apparently one or more of Mackenzie's admirers helped to set up a deal whereby he could obtain a substantial holding for small cost. Over a period of a year and a half, the young officer gained title to about 3,900 acres of land. He purchased 1,340 acres from two parties for the total consideration of $2,000. Next, he picked up 640 acres at a tax auction—probably as the only bidder—for $7.85. In June and December 1880, he bought rights to State of Texas land patents totaling 1,920 acres for $1,495. All together, then, Mackenzie obtained his land for about $0.90 an acre.[1]

What made this land such a bargain was its location in Kendall County, Texas, close to the town of Boerne and about twenty miles from San Antonio. That area contains some of the most attractive country in Texas. One settler's description of the Boerne area from 1882 could, with only slight modification serve today:

The mountains are cedar bedeckt, the valleys contain delightful prairies with occasional groves of trees of ten or twelve varieties of oaks. The whole valley resembles a park, whose diversity and variety can not be easily duplicated elsewhere. Cactus, yucca, and mimosa give the valley a subtropical appearance especially notable during the spring when the snow white blossoms of the yucca lighten the valley.

The banks of the streams or bottoms contain poplars, mulberries, walnuts, and pecans, also acorns.

Game was still abundant and the rivers and streams were "fish laden." A wide variety of crops were cultivated, and the plentiful mustang grape produced a flavorful wine.[2]

In addition to its natural beauty and resources, the area around Boerne was known for its healthful atmosphere. The local springs were said to possess "very superior medicinal qualities," and the air was reported to be especially beneficial for consumptives. Mackenzie's constant pain from rheumatism offered a strong argument for settling where nature itself offered relief.[3]

There is no doubt that Mackenzie intended to settle and establish a ranch on at least part of his new land. As young as he was, he still had to consider the future. His health might force early retirement, or it might be that reductions in the size of the army as the Indian wars wound down might bring a forced end to the soldier's occupation. Even if he stayed in the army, Mackenzie could look forward to increasingly easy assignments. When his promotion to brigadier general came—as it must in time—the Department of Texas with its headquarters in San Antonio was a likely post. Boerne and San Antonio were already connected by stagecoach, and plans for a railroad connection were in the offing. It would be possible then for Mackenzie to attend to his duties at headquarters and retreat frequently to his ranch. In anticipation of better accommodations in future posts, Mackenzie had for the first time brought his mother and sister to stay with him. Fort Clark, with its heat and dust, was not ideal, but better things could be expected.[4]

Mackenzie's land was in two clusters a few miles apart. Possibly he thought to hold part for speculation and develop the other, or he might have expected to fill in the gap for his own use. After his forced retirement from the army, he talked of returning to Texas to look after his "interests" and never gave up the idea of returning to develop his ranch. His heirs retained parts of his land until 1950, when the last of it was sold.[5]

Whatever Mackenzie's exact plans were for developing his land, they had to be put off. Warfare broke out between the whites and the Ute Indians of western Colorado. The Ute troubles were the product of the usual series of evasions, broken treaties, encroachments, and insensitive agents that figured in most Indian wars. Compounding the problem was the fact that Ute lands were believed to hide vast mineral wealth. By 1879 the Utes had had enough. Nathan C. Meeker, agent for the White River Utes, despaired of persuading the Indians to take up farming and, following instructions from the Indian Bureau, sent for troops to add the threat of force to his efforts. The Utes responded to the coming of troops by ambushing them, and then, having broken tradition by killing whites, they slaughtered Meeker and nine others. They also took several women captives.[6]

While the army moved to relieve the trapped soldiers led by Major Thomas T. Thornburgh, General Sherman issued orders to concentrate more soldiers in Colorado to suppress the uprising. At the same time, the most powerful of the Ute leaders, Ouray, was trying to end the fighting and to work out a permanent settlement. The Interior Department, headed by the noted reformer Carl Schurz, accepted Ouray's efforts as genuine and refused to yield control to the army, which was forced to restrain its thirst for vengeance. A peace commission was appointed which included Colonel Edward Hatch of the Ninth Cavalry. While the commissioners renegotiated—successfully, as it turned out—troops were funneled into Colorado to be available if they were needed.[7]

Sherman's call for Mackenzie and six companies of the Fourth Cavalry to hurry to Colorado amounted to a reflex action. The order went out on October 3, 1879, just four days after the outbreak of violence. Predictably, neither General Ord nor most Texans were happy about the move. Ord had tried to stave off Mackenzie's reassignment in the summer by warning that war with Mexico was still likely and claiming that he couldn't spare Mackenzie. (Both Sherman and Sheridan must have been relieved by the necessity of breaking up the Ord-Mackenzie combination, which seemed as apt to provoke war as to soothe the troubled border.) One Texas congressman protested against sending Mackenzie away and then urged that if Mackenzie had to be sent, public assurances should be given that he would return quickly. This promise would help hold down trouble in the colonel's absence.[8]

Mackenzie moved quickly. Aided by the ever-expanding railroads, the first elements of the Fourth reached Fort Garland, Colorado, on October 23 and were followed two days later by the rest of the designated companies. Mackenzie himself arrived on October 22. He brought with him Lieutenant Joseph Dorst, who served as adjutant, and Henry Lawton, who again was to serve faithfully as acting quartermaster. Fort Garland was situated in the San Luis Valley, a great flatland surrounded by mountains. The Fourth would have to march overland to reach the troubled area. No marching orders were forthcoming, however, while the peace commission did its work, and Mackenzie chafed at the delay.[9]

Mackenzie had no more faith in the Ute Commission than he had had in the one to the Sioux in 1876. He commiserated with his friend Hatch because of the latter's selection to the commission, which he believed could accomplish nothing. In spite of his doubts and impatience, Mackenzie recommended to Pope that the army make no move until the Interior Department was ready to admit failure and give the military full control over the matter to finally completely subdue the Utes. If the negotiations were to break down during the winter, Mackenzie felt he could move his force to the Uncompahgre Agency in spite of the snow. To be ready for such an eventuality, Mackenzie requested reinforcements, more horses, and "a couple of those new breech loading Hotchiss [sic] guns," which were light enough to keep up with the cavalry. Mackenzie complained of renewed suffering from rheumatism, which might keep him from going with his troops, but they would be ready to go regardless of his condition.[10]

In the event the commission did not admit failure, Mackenzie concluded acidly, two things could happen: "Either everything will be remarkably happy and we can all go home with a picture in our mind's eye of the Bad Jack [one of the leaders of the uprising] hanging from a cottonwood, while the good Ouray, in a swallow tailed coat, flanked on the right by Ned Hatch and on the left by Adams [another of the commissioners], pronounces a benediction on the faithful," or there would be "serious trouble in the spring." So, he would just stay put and keep his troops busy making improvements on Fort Garland. [11]

Perhaps Mackenzie had too much time on his hands. By December he was nagging for a permanent post. He claimed that Pope had promised him command of Fort Riley, Kansas. Disclaiming either "begging or demanding," he wanted to know what to expect. He was "aggrieved" that he did not receive the respect accorded others of his rank, and he wanted satisfaction. By February 1880, Mackenzie was attacking the adjutant general for "obstructing my views." He complained of being disliked in Washington and of unfair treatment at department headquarters that caused him to "want to give up." Mackenzie, and his superiors as well, were relieved when spring came and he could march his troops over the mountains. [12]

Mackenzie was ordered to take a combined force of cavalry and infantry with two "mountain guns" west of the divide to back up the peace commissioners and protect the Indians from whites anxious to stake claims on their land. The movement began on May 17, 1880, and, by June 1 all the troops were in camp at the Uncompahgre Agency near the present-day town of Montrose, Colorado. Mackenzie used Cochetopa Pass, and the Fourth moved among rugged mountains that one observer noted made the mountains of Europe seem small. Once on site, there was little for the troops to do. A new commission was negotiating with the Utes to trade their Colorado land for some in Utah, and the Indians seemed to want to avoid trouble. Mackenzie found the Utes to be admirable and expected no resistance from them. [13]

The troops were kept busy scouting the country, and Mackenzie led a hundred-mile march trying to locate a suitable place to build a permanent post. Even in the field Mackenzie maintained his reputation for being a stickler for proper dress and discipline. Troops not on patrol were drilled regularly for hours at a time, and Mackenzie inspired a competition between companies to encourage them to do well. The company officers, at least, caught the spirit and urged their men on. It can be guessed that the troopers were less enthusiastic. If highly drilled troops were not necessary to deal with hostile Utes, they were useful in putting on a fine show for General Sheridan when he arrived in August to get a first hand impression of the situation. After the review of the troops, Mackenzie left with two companies to escort Sheridan to Gunnison City. Sheridan, who one observer called "a great friend of Mackenzie," and his protégé hunted and fished along the way. [14]

Mackenzie did not return to his regiment in the field but went on to Garland and then to Fort Riley, Kansas, where most of his command was to spend the winter. The peace commissioners had secured an agreement from the Utes that the tribe would move to Utah the next summer, and with winter coming on there was no need to keep a large body of troops in the field. Leaving about 250 infantrymen to survive as best they could, the rest of Mackenzie's force returned to Fort Garland in October, and the Fourth went on to Fort Riley. During the winter Mackenzie prepared for a return to Colorado to oversee the Utes' move. Besides the usual concern with horses and mules, he again requested magazine rifles, pointing out that the Utes he might have to fight were mostly armed with Winchester repeaters. [15]

In the spring of 1881, Mackenzie and the Fourth Cavalry, minus the requested additional men and still without repeating carbines, were back in Colorado heading for the Uncompahgre country. Joined by detachments of the Sixth and Twenty-third Infantry regiments, the Fourth returned to patrolling to keep whites away from the Ute land until the Indians had moved to Utah. Mackenzie reported that he did not expect trouble from the Indians, but he prudently assigned a unit from the Twenty-third to string telegraph wire to speed up his communication with his superiors in event of an emergency.[16]

Not surprisingly, the Utes balked at the last minute, and Mackenzie used his telegraph to secure orders to use force if requested by the commissioners or the agent to the Utes. Stymied by the reluctant Indians, the civilian officials asked Mackenzie to intervene, and he moved quickly. First, he prepared his force for action by issuing extra ammunition and field rations. Then he sent for the major Indian leaders to come in for a parley. About twenty armed Utes responded, and as the meeting started, they began to make elaborate speeches, apparently intending to ask for delay or to refuse to move at all. Mackenzie cut them short by standing and telling the Indians that there was no time left for talking. All he wanted to know was whether they would go or not. If they refused, he declared, he would use force to drive them to their new land. He then left the room, leaving the chiefs to decide among themselves. The Utes, stunned by Mackenzie's refusal to negotiate, agreed to move the next day.[17]

The next day, September 1, 1881, the Utes began to move toward their new reservation. It was, thought Lieutenant James Parker, "a thrilling and pitiful sight." Mackenzie, too, felt sympathy for the Indians but knew that nothing could be done for them. A few of the Utes made a last show of resistance when an old, fat chief named Colorow led about fifty warriors in a charge. When he saw Mackenzie's full force drawn up in battle formation, Colorow halted and slowly rode back to join the main body on the western trail. Keeping gold-hungry whites off the Indian land before the Utes were fairly gone required more force than Mackenzie used against the Indians.[18]

Mackenzie had again vindicated his superiors' trust in him and received their highest praise. Pope wrote in sparkling terms and stated that Mackenzie's service should be rewarded by "proper and sufficient acknowledgment," apparently meaning promotion to brigadier general. Sheridan was no less fulsome in his praise, declaring that the Utes would not have moved at all "had it not been for Mackenzie."[19]

Even as Mackenzie was seeing the Utes off to their Utah reservation, orders were being sent for him to move the Fourth Cavalry to Arizona as quickly as possible. There had been an outbreak of trouble with the Apaches, and the first reports were so alarming that General Sherman acted to crush the Indians decisively even if the whole army had to be sent to Arizona. Although Arizona was in the Division of the Pacific, General Pope was ordered to send troops from his Department of the Missouri. Sherman specifically indicated that Mackenzie should be sent, even though he outranked both Colonel Orlando B. Wilcox, the district commander, and Colonel Eugene A. Carr, the operations commander. Wilcox's protest against this arrangement resulted in Mackenzie's being placed in charge of troops in the field while Wilcox retained his official position. Colonel Carr, aware of Mackenzie's reputation, made no official objection.[20]

The situation in Arizona had grown out of the appearance of a medicine man named Nocadecklinny among the White Mountain Apaches. Nocadecklinny claimed the power to raise the dead and preached a religion that seemed to presage the Ghost Dance religion that would cause so much misery a few years later. A personality conflict between Wilcox and Carr complicated the affair; they barely communicated with each other. Carr, on the scene, was not particularly concerned, but the local Indian agent, J. C. Tiffany, feared that the spirit leader's ideas would inspire a general uprising and urged his arrest. When Carr declined to move, Tiffany appealed to Wilcox, with the result that Carr was ordered to bring in Nocadecklinny. Carr carried out his assignment in spite of his doubts about the loyalty of his scouts. Nocadecklinny agreed to return with Carr, but that evening Apaches, including most of the scouts, attacked the column at Cibecue Creek, killing seven whites. Carr abandoned the field under the cover of darkness and brought the rest of his command to Fort Apache safely. The first reports out of Arizona asserted that Carr and all of his men had been killed. Those reports were the main stimulus for Sherman to order Mackenzie to the scene.[21]

Mackenzie got news of Carr's fight and his orders to take his command to Arizona on August 31, 1881. Moving as rapidly as possible, Mackenzie marched the Fourth Cavalry to Gunnison, Colorado. The regiment then traveled by rail to Billings, Arizona, by way of Pueblo, Colorado, and Albuquerque, New Mexico. A march of 138 miles from Billings brought Mackenzie and his troops to Fort Apache on September 26. By the time he arrived, there was little for Mackenzie to do. Carr worked well with Mackenzie and under his orders was able to secure the arrest of many Apaches who had jumped the reservation. Wilcox's changing and contradictory orders, however, limited the good that could have been accomplished.[22]

Mackenzie was distinctly uncomfortable in his temporary assignment. He expressed his concern in a letter to General Pope. First, he reported on the generally peaceful demeanor of the Apaches except for the Chiricahuas, who he believed could be conquered only by joint action with Mexican troops. He wrote that he wished to go to New Mexico to assume command there as had previously been promised. He would stay in Arizona as long as General Sherman wanted him to, but his position was "very delicate," and he much preferred to serve under Pope and Sheridan. He concluded with the usual complaints about troop shortages and the poor condition of the horses. Things would be better all around if he and the Fourth were at their permanent station. He got his wish in November and left Arizona and the simmering feud between Carr and Wilcox.[23]

The new post was the District of New Mexico, with headquarters in Santa Fe. It was an important assignment and marked a definite upward move for Mackenzie. It was both a reward for past service and a promise of promotion in the future. Mackenzie had been using what influence he possessed to secure promotion and easier assignments. When the chief signal officer of the army died in August 1880, two of Mackenzie's supporters recommended him for the position. One of them was Gouverneur, K. Warren, Mackenzie's mathematics instructor at West Point and his commander while in the Corps of Engineers. Warren claimed not to have talked to Mackenzie about the post. The two men had recently met, however, in Washington, where the cavalry officer had gone to testify in an inquiry about Warren's role in the Battle of Five Forks. It seems certain that the younger officer must have impressed his ambition on Warren. General Pope wrote the other letter supporting Mackenzie's appointment, and he stated that Mackenzie "would like to receive the appointment." Neither supporting letter was exactly unsolicited.[24]

Another opportunity for promotion eluded Mackenzie in 1880 when President Hayes, in a controversial action, forced the retirement of General Ord, creating an opening for a new brigadier general. Mackenzie was able to muster some fairly important support for his selection to fill the rank. The full congressional delegations for Texas and New Jersey signed appeals to the president calling for Mackenzie's appointment. Generals Crook, Augur, and Pope, with favorable endorsements from Sheridan and Sherman, also supported Mackenzie's quest. In spite of such endorsements, Mackenzie lost out to Nelson A. Miles, who had married into the Sherman family and was an able self-promoter.[25]

Partly to compensate Mackenzie for missing the promotion, the Department of Arkansas was created for him in the spring of 1881 to allow him to exercise his brevet rank of brigadier general, but the position was short-lived. Mackenzie was needed to lead the Fourth Cavalry back to Colorado to oversee the Ute exodus. Besides, a Department of Arkansas had no real justification, and Mackenzie spent most of his brief time there making preparations for the summer's work in Colorado. The appointment as commander of the District of New Mexico, prestigious because it was more of an administrative post than a field command, was in the works before the Apache outbreak. As the situation eased in Arizona, Mackenzie moved northeast to take up his duties in Santa Fe.[26]

In Santa Fe, Mackenzie immediately had a run-in with Colonel George P. Buell of the Fifteenth Infantry. On November 1, 1881, just one day after assuming command of the district, Mackenzie arrested Buell for "wilfully" neglecting to report upon bringing his command into Santa Fe. Mackenzie blamed Buell's conduct on unspecified old grievances and reported that he took the action in order to ensure the respect of his subordinate officers. Buell was released from arrest by order of General Pope, but Mackenzie never trusted Buell in his command at Fort Lewis. The Fifteenth's commander was, Mackenzie believed, "so peculiar and his mind so lacking in balance" that he should be replaced. Mackenzie also found time to reprimand young officers for incorrectly endorsing communications and failure to use adequate postage on letters. These kinds of actions probably contributed to the growth of Mackenzie's reputation as being excessively strict, although they were a necessary part of maintaining control over a widespread command.[27]

An important concern was the condition of men, horses, and housing. Mackenzie sent Lawton on an inspection tour soon after assuming command. His response to Lawton's report is revealing. Mackenzie wrote to the commanding officer at Fort Craig, New Mexico, stating that while he did "not insist" on full dress uniforms for the troops, their undress uniforms should be "good, neat and but little worn." Mackenzie also noted that the lack of shined boots and brass indicated lack of discipline, which should be corrected. Precautions should be taken to ensure that food was of good quality, and reports that Captain Callahan used abusive language to his troops should be investigated. Finally, Mackenzie ordered that work around the post be done mainly by infantry in order for the cavalry to be ready for field duties. This is not the letter of a martinet but of a commander who is concerned to maintain his troops in the best possible condition.[28]

Troop housing was a special concern of Mackenzie's, and within days of assuming his new duties he was complaining of the "lamentable" condition of barracks in the southern posts.

He asserted that money available for construction at New Mexico forts was not in proportion to the number of troops in the district. When no money was forthcoming to pay civilian workers, Mackenzie ordered that fatigue parties be used in the construction of housing for men and horses.[29]

Mackenzie's main responsibility was, of courses, controlling the Indians, which included the Navajos and various groups of Apaches. In early 1882 the district commander began to make plans in the event he had to move against the Navajos in the north at the same time he was fighting Apaches in the south. He thought the Navajos to be restless and likely to stage a major uprising and asked General Pope for more troops to prepare for such an eventuality. As it turned out, the Navajos remained peaceful except for a few isolated individuals. One problem was the selling of whiskey to the Indians by whites. In one incident, the drunken Navajos ran off the white vendors and stole their whiskey. Mackenzie's response was to call upon the civil authorities to arrest the whites, who were in violation of federal law.[30]

In the south of his district, Mackenzie was faced with a more dangerous situation. In the southeast the Mescalero Apaches were troublesome, while to the southwest and on into Arizona and Mexico the Chiricahuas roamed pretty much as they pleased. Among the Mescaleros the trouble came from individuals or small groups. The agent for the Indians, William H. H. Llewellyn, was having difficulty keeping all his charges in hand. Mackenzie had a conference with Llewellyn soon after taking command of the district and was able to persuade the agent to accept the policy that promises of leniency should not be used to lure renegades back onto the reservation but that all who came in should be arrested by the troops at nearby Fort Stanton and be disarmed and confined. Mackenzie also advised the commanding officer at Fort Stanton to use Indian police to make the arrests, if possible, in order to antagonize the peaceful Indians as little as possible.[31]

The working arrangement with Llewellyn was threatened in

March when the commissioner of Indian affairs, Hiram Price, sent instructions that conflicted with the understanding reached between the army and the agent. Mackenzie complained to his superiors that Price had "complicated matters." He felt compelled to visit the agency in person to oversee the surrender of some off-reservation Mescaleros. Some of the Indians were not punished when they returned because of promises made by Price. Mackenzie let it go because he believed that it was more important to keep promises made to the Indians than to punish them. Some of the Apaches who were to be punished were turned over to the army without food, forcing Mackenzie to appeal to Pope for supplementary rations. Just as had been the case when the Indian Bureau had shorted the Kiowas and Comanches, Mackenzie rejected the idea of making prisoners of the Indians only to starve them.[32]

The most serious concern in the district was the Chiricahua Apaches. Various bands of these desert raiders, under such famous leaders as Juh, Naiche, Chatto, and Geronimo, continued to make life hazardous for white settlers in the Southwest. These Indians respected neither departmental limits nor international boundaries, and Mackenzie worked to coordinate his forces with those of the Department of the Pacific, which included Arizona, and Mexican forces in the states of Chihuahua and Sonora. Mackenzie did not take the field himself but left operations to Lieutenant Colonel George A. Forsyth, who had recently been assigned to the Fourth Cavalry.

Significantly, Mackenzie showed considerably more respect for Mexican officials than he had done earlier. His less than successful incursions across the border in 1878 had tempered his readiness for that kind of action. He recognized, too, that the Díaz regime was taking hold and was serious about controlling the border situation. Precipitate crossings by American troops would make difficulties for the governments of both countries. The report of a scout, Van Smith, who Mackenzie sent into Mexico soon after taking command of the district, strongly influenced him. Smith reported that Mexican troops were adequate to deal with hostiles south of the border, and Mackenzie told headquarters that he believed it "unwise" to send American forces across the border. Instead, he believed, cooperation with the Mexicans would quickly settle the Apache problem.[33]

Mackenzie's forbearance received an early test in January 1882 when Lieutenant David N. McDonald led his group of civilian and Indian scouts into Mexico. McDonald was arrested by Mexican authorities, although he was quickly released. It is easy to imagine Mackenzie's raging against Mexican officials had such an incident taken place a few years earlier. Now, however, Mackenzie ordered an investigation of McDonald's action even before he heard of the arrest. After learning that the lieutenant had been captured and released, he moved quickly to assure the commander of the Mexican army in Chihuahua, General Carlos Fuero, that McDonald had acted without authority. He told Fuero that McDonald's orders were to cross only in close pursuit of hostiles and then to seek the cooperation of the nearest Mexican authorities. Mackenzie thanked the Mexican general for McDonald's quick release and urged united action in the future. To show his displeasure with McDonald, Mackenzie recommended that he be court-martialed even though he was a "brave and energetic officer."[34]

A potentially more explosive violation of the border took place in April 1882. Forsyth combined five companies of the Fourth Cavalry with two companies of the Sixth Cavalry under Captain T. C. Tupper to follow a trail of marauding Chiricahuas deep into Mexican territory. The fleeing Apaches, preoccupied with the American pursuit, failed to scout ahead and ran into a deadly ambush set by Colonel Lorenzo García of the Mexican army. After punishing the Indians severely—about 111 were killed or taken prisoner—García confronted the U.S. troops. The Mexican officer formally protested to Forsyth, who responded as calmly as possible. García, flushed with success, did not take the incursion seriously and seems not to have reported the incident after the Americans returned to home soil.[35]

Forsyth wrote a full report for Mackenzie, claiming a total of ninety-eight Indians killed by American and Mexican troops. He declared that the troops of the two countries parted on good terms after a rather touchy first meeting. Mackenzie wrote quickly to Pope to warn him of Forsyth's crossing, again asserting his belief that such incidents worked against the stability of the Díaz government and that the Mexicans were determined to stop the Indians on their side of the border. Mackenzie had no trouble understanding Forsyth's feeling but knew that the crossings should stop. Having warned Pope that the incident had occurred, Mackenzie decided that the affair was not likely to be reported to the Mexican government and withheld Forsyth's report. He saw no point in stirring up trouble if the Mexicans made no complaint. Mackenzie's decision proved to be the correct one, as nothing come of the episode.[36]

Even as Mackenzie was dealing with the Forsyth crossing, he was negotiating with General Fuero to work out a mode of cooperation that would preserve cordial relations. The talks led to an agreement under which there would be no crossing of the international boundary by either side. In place of the hot pursuit doctrine, a system of information exchange was worked out by which commanders on one side warned their counterparts on the other of movements by the Indians. Mackenzie issued stern orders to his field commanders to avoid crossing and kept Fuero informed of American plans. He was careful to thank Fuero for his aid and to congratulate the Mexican officer when he was successful against the Indians. Both Pope and Sheridan credited Mackenzie for the relative peace on the border by the fall of 1882.[37]

Mackenzie's smooth handling of relations with Mexican officials added to his claim for the next general's spot to come open. Both Sherman and Sheridan, disturbed by what they considered to be injustice to Ord, tried to influence the president's office to retire General Irwin McDowell as well. This retirement would create a vacancy for the "young vigorous colonels" who were clamoring for opportunity. Sheridan, in particular, promoted Mackenzie's claim. In a letter to Secretary of War Robert T. Lincoln, he urged that promotion should be based on service since the Civil War. Mackenzie's record in that period, Sheridan asserted, gave him the clear edge in the scramble for the star soon to become available.[38]

The opening for a new brigadier came in October 1882 when General McDowell stepped down. Immediately Mackenzie's friends launched a campaign to secure the appointment for him. Sheridan wrote again to Lincoln, citing Mackenzie's "handsome record" and urging the secretary to keep the young colonel's name before the president. In addition to the earlier recommendations, Mackenzie enlisted the support of the congressional delegations of Colorado and New Mexico. More importantly, Ulysses S. Grant intervened with President Arthur. Grant pressed for the selection on the basis of Mackenzie's long service and brilliant record and as a personal favor to himself. The word of the great Union war hero provided the needed weight in Mackenzie's behalf, and he received the telegram notifying him of his appointment on October 26, 1882.[39]

Promotion to general meant an end to regimental command for Mackenzie. He had commanded the Fourth Cavalry since 1871 and had forged it into the weapon he had used to become one of the greatest of the Indian fighters. Mackenzie did not record his feelings on giving up his association with the Fourth, but his official order of resignation hints of strong emotion. He began by acknowledging that his promotion was "greatly due" to the "good conduct" of the officers and men of the regiment. He especially thanked the officers for their loyalty and the way they cooperated with one another. Without saying so, Mackenzie was recognizing the absence of the bickering among officers that was common in many other units, most notably Custer's Seventh Cavalry. Mackenzie concluded by thanking the whole regiment for "very much kindly consideration, running through years." The order was not overly sentimental, but it shows that Mackenzie was deeply moved by the moment.[40]

As happy as he was to have his ambition fulfilled, Mackenzie

As brigadier general again in 1883, Mackenzie seems to have gained weight as a result of his increasingly administrative duties. *(Courtesy National Archives and Record Service)*

needed a rest and took an extended leave, spending most of his time in New York with his brother Morris. The elevation in rank created a bit of a problem, as brigadier general was too high a rank to command a district. Sheridan's first inclination was that Mackenzie should take over the Department of the South, which would allow him time to relax and recover from his exertions in the West. Sherman and Secretary Lincoln disagreed, however. They were concerned about the feelings of the present commander of the department, who had been passed over for promotion and had less than a year until retirement. They felt, also, that a relatively unimportant post like the Department of the South was "inconsistent" with the manner in which Mackenzie had earned his reputation. The upshot was that the new general would return to New Mexico when his leave expired. Mackenzie was not displeased with this solution, and if the newspapers are a true indication, the people of New Mexico were very happy about it.[41]

Mackenzie had much the same feeling for New Mexico that he had for Texas. He brought his family to Santa Fe, and a mutual affection quickly grew between them and the citizens of the ancient capital. When the family returned at the end of Mackenzie's leave, they received "a very warm reception from the public as well as the military establishment." Mrs. Mackenzie, in particular, involved herself in community affairs and became noted for her acts of charity and general benevolence. When she died in April 1883, the local newspaper offered a long obituary full of praise for her life and character. After a simple Episcopal service, Catherine Mackenzie's body was placed on a train and returned to New York City. Ranald Mackenzie accompanied his mother's remains on the journey but quickly returned to his duties.[42]

In the fall of 1883, General Sherman resigned as commanding general of the army. Sheridan was more or less automatically boosted to the top spot. His elevation made room for a reshuffling of departments and a new assignment for Mackenzie. In thinking about the job shifts, Sheridan left Mackenzie,

In civilian clothes in 1883, Mackenzie could easily have passed for a prosperous businessman. *(Courtesy National Archives and Record Service)*

who had no seniority among the brigadiers, no choice, but the commanding general clearly angled for a choice spot for his longtime favorite. At first Sheridan indicated that Miles should get Texas while Mackenzie took the Department of the Columbia vacated by Miles. As the event approached, however, Sheridan seemed more inclined to hold Miles where he was and to send Mackenzie to Texas, "which will be satisfactory to Texas and Mackenzie."[43]

Whether Miles rejected Texas or was not given a choice is not clear, but Mackenzie got the post. When the news leaked out, Texans were eager to resume their relationship with the officer who had done so much to relieve the Indian problems of the state. One San Antonio newspaper deplored the loss of General Augur, who had been briefly reassigned to Texas, but was happy that Mackenzie, "a courteous and social gentleman," was to succeed him. Another local paper praised Mackenzie for his services on the frontier and declared that "our people have a sort of 'tomahawk claim' on Mackenzie as a citizen." The paper cited the fact that Mackenzie owned a residence in San Antonio as well as the ranch in Kendall County as evidence of the special relationship between the general and the state. In a sense, Mackenzie was heading home.[44]

CHAPTER THIRTEEN

PERFECT PEACE

RANALD Mackenzie's tour of duty in Texas was doomed to be short and unhappy. Accompanied by his longtime adjutant, Joseph G. Dorst, and his cousin, Lieutenant Alexander Rodgers, whom he had named as aides, he arrived in San Antonio on November 1, 1883. Initially, he seemed to be settling into the ordinary routine without difficulty. He conducted inspections and inventories of his new department and made recommendations for changes and improvements. Private Frank J. Strobel, his old hunting companion who was serving his third enlistment, was offered a position in civilian life, and Mackenzie interceded to secure an early discharge for him. Housing for the new chief of ordnance for the department, Isaac Arnold, was inadequate, and the young general took steps to solve the problem.[1]

Things were not as normal as they seemed to be. Close associates of Mackenzie began to note distressing changes in him. One former subordinate visited San Antonio in November and noted that the general had deteriorated physically. "He had lost flesh and erectness of carriage," wrote Colonel Charles W. Crane. Crane also recorded that Mackenzie's behavior was erratic. By early December, Mackenzie's staff began to become convinced that he was suffering from mental aberration. In a later report on his condition, the medical director of the department wrote that "eccentricity was apparent" by December 15 and that friends thought the general "either drunk or crazy."[2]

A crisis occurred on the night of December 18. Mackenzie

went into San Antonio accompanied by Chief Paymaster Charles M. Terrell and the chief ordnance officer. They were separated, and Mackenzie became involved in an affray with some local people and was beaten up. Exactly what happened is not clear, and there is no explanation in the official records. One version of what happened holds that Mackenzie entered a saloon and became violent, whereupon the owner and "some Mexicans" beat him and tied him to a cartwheel outside. A slightly different telling has Mackenzie trying to force two brothers to open their store to sell him a watch. The storekeepers, aided again by a group of Mexicans, attacked the general when he began to shout and pound on the sides of the store. They beat him and tied him to the wheel. Whatever the exact details, Mackenzie was found and recognized by the local police, who took him to his quarters.[3]

The episode was so uncharacteristic of Mackenzie that the medical director decided that the general was unfit for command and would be for some time to come. Even though Mackenzie had been carrying out daily business in a rational manner, the departmental adjutant general supported the medical conclusion. General John Pope, who had recently assumed command of the Division of the Missouri, then took over command of the Department of Texas, acting through Lieutenant Colonel Thomas M. Vincent, the adjutant general. Vincent's daily reports showed Mackenzie's condition to vary from day to day, although his mind still seemed unbalanced. After a few days, the officers in Texas were beginning to consider the possibility of committing Mackenzie to an asylum, and Vincent inquired about the availability of a Pullman car if the need arose to send him east.[4]

On December 24, 1883, Vincent informed his superiors that Mackenzie was talking of joining with Sheridan to reorganize the army. Convinced that Mackenzie needed specialized care, he suggested that Sheridan send a wire to Mackenzie ordering him to report to Washington with his staff to consult on reorganization. This ruse, Vincent believed, would persuade

Mackenzie to accept a return to the east without trying to resist. Vincent also sent a message to an official of the Missouri-Pacific Railroad asking that a special car be provided for the general. Sheridan's orders arrived the next day, and preparations were made so that Mackenzie could leave on the day after Christmas. Vincent reported that Sheridan's summons had the desired effect, and Mackenzie left without causing difficulties. He was accompanied by the post surgeon, Dr. Passmore Middleton; his two aides; and his sister Harriet. Vincent sent along two enlisted orderlies to alternate with the officers in watching after the general.[5]

The original plan was to conduct Mackenzie to the government asylum in Washington. After consulting with Mackenzie's uncle by marriage, Admiral C. R. P. Rodgers, and army medical personnel, however, Sheridan decreed that the troubled officer be taken to New York instead. There, arrangements had been made to receive Mackenzie at the Bloomingdale Asylum. Rodgers cited "publicity and disturbing influences" as well as the fact that Harriet would not be able to stay at the government facility as reasons for the switch. Rodgers was affected, too, by the relative luxury of Bloomingdale compared to the government asylum. One of Mackenzie's friends visited him and described the institution as being "very desirable." Harriet for some reason protested the change but was overborne by the arguments of her uncle and Sheridan.[6]

Either the prospect of working with Sheridan on an important project or the journey itself brought temporary improvement in Mackenzie's condition. In fact, he was so improved that Surgeon Middleton wired the adjutant general to ask if the general should be taken to the asylum or put in the hands of friends. The decision was for the asylum, and Mackenzie was admitted there on December 29, 1883. While the doctors examined him and studied his condition, Mackenzie's friends waited for news. Sheridan was especially concerned, not only for his friend's sake, but also because of the need to have someone in charge in Texas. He pressed Dr. C. H. Nichols, director of the asylum, for word about Mackenzie's prospects. In February Nichols concluded that the prognosis was "very unfavorable" and so informed Sheridan. Armed with this opinion, Sheridan then asked Secretary of War Lincoln to convene a retiring board to clear the way for the appointment of Mackenzie's successor.[7]

Accordingly, a retiring board headed by Major General Winfield S. Hancock met at the Bloomingdale Asylum on March 5, 1884. The two surgeons on the board agreed with Dr. Nichols that Mackenzie was suffering from "general paresis of the insane," which rendered him incapable of active service and from which he was not likely to recover. The other members of the board voiced no dissent in spite of Mackenzie's pathetic plea to be allowed to stay in the army. He contested the idea that he was insane and argued that his long, hard, and valuable service entitled him to more consideration than he was receiving. "I would rather die," he declared, "than go on the retired list. The army is all I have got to care for." As a way of easing the blow, the board did conclude that Mackenzie's breakdown was the result of wounds and exposure incurred in twenty years of service, entitling him to a full pension.[8]

There is no way to tell for sure at this late date exactly what brought on Mackenzie's malady. A strong possibility is that his problem was the result of syphilis. Since around the beginning of this century, the condition known as paresis or paralysis of the insane has been associated with venereal infection. Such an affliction seems out of character for Mackenzie at first notice. Yet it would have been unusual had he abstained from all sexual contacts during his life. That he might have resorted to prostitutes or conducted an illicit love affair during one or more of his many leaves should not surprise, nor should it detract from his character and reputation. Certainly the development of his condition accords with the classic descriptions of the onset of paresis. He gave increasing signs of instability in his correspondence and suffered an "attack of cerebral trouble" while in New Mexico. This corresponds well with the tiered development of the disease. The physical deterioration that accompanied his collapse also tends to confirm the diagnosis of paresis caused by syphilis.[9]

There are other possible explanations for Mackenzie's decline, and lack of an autopsy prevents a definitive conclusion. Medical consultants have offered several alternate possibilities. Other possible causes of Mackenzie's illness include a hereditary degenerative disease, a dementia, a collagen vascular disease, a metabolic derangement, and peripheral vascular disease accompanied by stroke. It was common at the time to attribute Mackenzie's problem to his supposed sunstroke when a child, a fall on his head while at Fort Sill, or the combined effects of his wounds, long exposure to the elements, and grief over the death of his mother. None of these last suggestions seems to offer a medically sound explanation for Mackenzie's trouble, although the years of subjection to danger and stress might have contributed to a kind of combat fatigue that hastened the collapse. No fully satisfactory explanation for the breakdown is likely to appear.[10]

For contemporaries, Mackenzie's tragedy seemed to be doubled because it appeared that he was about to be married. Soon after assuming command of the Department of Texas, Mackenzie resumed his relationship with Florida Tunstall Sharpe, whom he had known years before. In 1868, while serving on court-martial duty in San Antonio, he had met the nineteen-year-old Florida and possibly even stayed as a guest in the home of her father, a well-known lawyer named Warwick Tunstall. Some sort of romantic attachment developed, but apparently it was not very strong. One historian states that after Mackenzie returned to his post on the border, he made frequent trips to see Florida, driving relays of mules over the 280-mile round trip, but this story seems scarcely creditable. In any event, Florida married an army contract surgeon, some years her senior, named Redford Sharpe. By accident or design, Sharpe was assigned to Fort McKavett while Mackenzie commanded there. There is no record of what Mackenzie's and Mrs. Sharpe's relations might have been at that time.[11]

After Mackenzie left Fort McKavett in 1870, the only recorded contacts between himself and Florida Sharpe were two messages conveyed by Lieutenant Colonel Shafter shortly after Redford Sharpe died. In May and again in June 1873, Shafter passed on greetings from Mrs. Sharpe to Mackenzie. There is so little evidence of an ongoing relationship that the newspaper reports of the impending marriage ten years later come almost as a shock. Mackenzie had been back in San Antonio less than two months. Given that Mrs. Sharpe was a widow and that Mackenzie's mother had recently died, the couple seemed to have decided on a small ceremony with little fanfare. Some confusion prevailed in the papers about the date of the wedding. The first report indicated that Christmas day was the appointed time. Later stories suggested either the twentieth or the twenty-seventh of December as the day. That confusion was of little moment, because on the eighteenth, the day the first item appeared in print, Mackenzie suffered his crisis and the possibility of marriage was shattered.[12]

For the romantically inclined, the wrecked marriage plans only heightened the tragedy. At least one historian has even suggested that it was Mackenzie's newfound happiness that finally pushed him over the edge of sanity. Yet there is another telling of the Mackenzie–Tunstall Sharpe affair that offers less fodder to the romantic imagination. This version of the story makes the romance all on Florida's side, with Mackenzie a reluctant participant. This rendition might be called the army wives' story, and although it reads like gossip, it has a large degree of plausibility.

The basic idea of the army wives' version is that the first relationship was only a flirtation taken much more seriously by Florida than by Mackenzie. When Mackenzie's ambition led him to the frontier, she married Dr. Sharpe expressly because she knew the doctor was to be stationed at Fort McKavett, where Mackenzie was commanding. When her husband died, Florida tried to kindle Mackenzie's interest through Shafter. That attempt failed, but the woman nursed her interest in the young officer until the day he reappeared in San Antonio as the new commander of the Department of Texas. Then the Widow Sharpe called upon Mackenzie and invited him to visit. In her home, she offered brandy and took advantage of Mackenzie's declining mental condition to maneuver him into an engagement. The prospective marriage was not viewed as suitable by Harriet Mackenzie or any of the general's staff. The newspaper leak prompted them to try to pressure Mrs. Sharpe to end the arrangement on her own. When she refused, Mackenzie himself, accompanied by two of his staff, undertook to break the engagement. After the confrontation, which left the widow in a rage, Mackenzie was followed by some of her kinsmen. When the general slipped away from his escort, the relations followed him and beat him up to avenge the insult they felt Mrs. Sharpe had received. This episode took place on December 18, and it was the strain of breaking off with his erstwhile fiancée plus the attack that stimulated Mackenzie's final collapse.[13]

The army wives' version of Mackenzie's romance has a few problems. Some of its "facts" are definitely wrong, and it has a snobbish tone that suggests that class difference played a role in its growth. Nevertheless, it does offer an explanation for some of the curious parts of the accepted story. It makes understandable the haste of the second courtship as well as the facts that no formal announcement was made or invitations sent out. More to the point, it explains why Joseph Dorst makes no mention of Florida Tunstall Sharpe in his memoir of the general. In fact, Mrs. Sharpe herself did not mention Mackenzie in her written recollections. The army wives' story also supports the point made earlier that Mackenzie acquired his Kendall County land independent of any thought of marriage. It might also explain the legacy that Harriet Mackenzie left for Mrs. Sharpe in her will. The will provided that the younger brother, Morris R. S. Mackenzie, would inherit Harriet's whole estate, but when he died one thousand dollars was to be paid to Mrs. Sharpe. The will is a hint that Mackenzie's sister felt some obligation to the widow, but not a very strong one. Finally, Mackenzie's breakdown on December 18 becomes more understandable if the army wives' version approximates the truth. [14]

Even while committed to the Bloomingdale Asylum, Mackenzie acted as if he would recover and be restored to his old position in the army. Following the prescribed pattern for officers on leave, he kept the adjutant general informed of his address and plans. He was well enough at first to receive visitors and to be escorted to activities outside of the institution. In June 1884 he was released from the asylum and, with his sister, rented a summer place in Morristown. At the end of the summer he again reported to army headquarters, stating that he intended to stay in Morristown for a few more months then journey to San Antonio "to look after my interests there." [15]

Mackenzie never returned to Texas. His deteriorating condition prompted his sister to move him to the home of a relative on Staten Island. By 1887 he had difficulty speaking clearly and had to be assisted in walking. His mind was reported to be "very weak." On January 19, 1889, not yet forty-nine years old, Ranald Mackenzie died. The official cause of death was "progressive paresis." [16]

Although he had faded from public view, the New York newspapers provided obituaries with brief biographies of Mackenzie. His fame as an Indian fighter was still relatively fresh, and that part of his career received the most emphasis. One paper said he "was very efficient" in his frontier service. Another described his career as "very brilliant." Brilliant was, indeed, an appropriate word to use to characterize Mackenzie's military service. His rapid rise during the Civil War was all the more impressive in that he only began to serve in the second year of the war and obtained a combat command only in June 1864. Daring exploits and rapid promotion were rather common during the war, however. It was a different case on the frontier. Service in the West offered little opportunity for brilliance. Only those officers with determination, intelligence, support from higher command, and good luck could achieve much fame fighting Indians. Mackenzie was one of the few to approach brilliance in the Indian-fighting army. [17]

The idea for using large bodies of troops in the field, while not entirely original to Mackenzie, was pushed by him and demonstrated its worth on the Llano Estacado and in the war on the northern plains. His border crossings were less than completely successful, but they demonstrated the daring that was necessary for success against an unorthodox foe. Mackenzie had a good instinct for dealing with Indians and was effective in negotiations with them. His strong stance with the Utes probably prevented violence when they moved to Utah. His similar approach to relations with Indians on reservations likewise kept those tribes under control. Mackenzie made strenuous efforts to protect and help peaceful Indians, which helped to insure peace once peace was established.

Personally, Mackenzie had a great influence on the men he served with. His superiors came to depend on him in any difficult situation, and he rarely failed them. His subordinates were strongly affected by him, and some almost came to worship him. His longtime adjutant, Joseph Dorst, wrote that Mackenzie combined all the qualities to make a great soldier and a noble gentleman and was a continual force in his own life for years to come. Mackenzie was, declared one newspaper, "a favorite of all who knew him." Henry Lawton, when a general in the Spanish-American War, asked himself what Mackenzie would do whenever he found himself in a difficult situation. Samuel B. M. Young, also a general in the war against Spain, sometimes referred to Lawton, his superior officer, as Mackenzie.[18]

Among the leaders of the post–Civil War army Mackenzie stands with the best. The most obvious comparison is to George Armstrong Custer. Both men had outstanding records in the Civil War, each was intensely ambitious, and each was brave to the point of foolhardiness. Mackenzie's western career must be judged the more successful, however, partly because Mackenzie had more opportunity for independent action and partly because he avoided the controversy that attended Custer's progress.

Mackenzie could be more aptly compared with George Crook and Nelson Miles. Both of those men had outstanding

Joseph H. Dorst as a captain. Mackenzie's longtime adjutant provided one of the most dependable sources of information about him. *(Courtesy United States Army Military History Institute)*

Robert G. Carter, in a photograph probably taken in the 1890s. Although his service with Mackenzie was relatively short, his writings provide an important if not completely reliable source for Mackenzie's Indian-fighting career. *(Courtesy United States Army Military History Institute).*

post–Civil War records, although each had his less than glorious moments. Of the three, Crook was probably the most effective. He was the most willing to deviate from accepted theory and try innovative approaches to Indian warfare. In spite of the blue funk that seems to have gripped him throughout most of 1876, he was generally successful. Miles was less imaginative than Crook but still achieved an outstanding record. He had many opportunities and took advantage of them. He was not brilliant, but his determination and drive usually brought success.

Mackenzie's record approaches theirs but falls somewhat short. His early retirement and death prevented him from playing any role in the last acts of the Indian wars. Crook died in 1890, while Miles stayed on to become the last commanding general of the army. As had been the case earlier, Miles would have stood in Mackenzie's path to promotion. Still, Mackenzie would most likely have stayed in the army also and played an important part in the Spanish-American War. Whatever the exact ranking of army leaders of the period, Mackenzie was in the top group.

Ranald Slidell Mackenzie was buried in the cemetery at West Point on January 22, 1889. Sheridan and Grant had died earlier, and Sherman was too old to attend. Still, three generals were among the pallbearers, along with other officers who had served with the general. The crowd at the service was unusually large, testifying to Mackenzie's widespread popularity. A simple marble cross marked the grave. The inscription on Mackenzie's marker read simply, "Thou wilt keep him in perfect peace."[19]

NOTES

Chapter 1. A Bright Looking Child

1. Joseph A. Scoville [Walter Barret], *The Old Merchants of New York City*, 2:213; 5:45, 250. See also Philip McFarland, *Sea Dangers: The Affair of the Somers*, 10-11.

2. Louis Martin Sears, *John Slidell;* McFarland, *Sea Dangers,* 11.

3. Catherine Mackenzie, "Biographical Sketch of Alexander Slidell Mackenzie," Duyckinck Papers, Rare Books and Manuscripts Division, New York Public Library; Samuel Eliot Morison, *"Old Bruin": Commodore Matthew C. Perry, 1794-1858,* 54-55.

4. Mackenzie, "Biographical Sketch"; Letter of Marie Rosine Slidell quoted in Sears, *John Slidell,* 21; Burton J. Hendrick, *Statesmen of the Lost Cause,* 287; Petition in Historical Society of Pennsylvania quoted in McFarland, *Sea Dangers,* 293; Scoville, *Old Merchants,* 2:213, 260; Frederick F. Van de Water, *The Captain Called It Mutiny,* 15.

5. James Parker to mother, Oct. 8, 1878, James Parker Papers, U.S. Military Academy Archives, West Point, N.Y.

6. McFarland, *Sea Dangers,* 14-16; Mackenzie, "Biographical Sketch."

7. Mackenzie, "Biographical Sketch"; McFarland, *Sea Dangers,* 23-24.

8. McFarland, *Sea Dangers,* 40-47; Andrew Hilen, *The Letters of Henry Wadsworth Longfellow,* 2:232-33.

9. Mackenzie, "Biographical Sketch"; Morison, *"Old Bruin,"* 132, 134, 144-45.

10. For this account I have relied mainly upon McFarland, *Sea Dangers,* which shows great sympathy and understanding for Mackenzie while maintaining impartiality in presenting the case. I have also used Van de Water, *The Captain Called It Mutiny;* Edward L. Beach, *The United States Navy: 200 Years;* and A. J. Liebling, "The Navy's Only Mutiny," *New Yorker,* Feb. 18, 1939, pp. 35-38. The mutiny partly inspired Herman Melville to write *Billy Budd.*

11. Liebling, "The Navy's Only Mutiny," 191; McFarland, *Sea Dangers,* 204-205; Ernest Freeland Griffin, ed., *Westchester County and Its People: A Record,* 349; Florence Leary Reynolds, comp., *Reminiscences of Ossining,* 29; Philip Hone, *The Diary of Philip Hone, 1828-1851,* ed. Allan Nevins, 655-56; Hilen, *Letters of Longfellow,* 2:546-47.

12. Alfred Hoyt Bill, *Rehearsal for Conflict: The War with Mexico, 1846-48,* 108-109; Van de Water, *Captain Called It Mutiny,* 215; Sears,

John Slidell, 74–75; Edward Wagenknecht, ed., *Mrs. Longfellow: Selected Letters and Journals of Fanny Appleton Longfellow, 1817–1861,* 123.

13. Van de Water, *Captain Called It Mutiny,* 217; Mackenzie, "Biographical Sketch"; Griffin, *Westchester County,* 349; Joseph H. Dorst, "Ranald Slidell Mackenzie," *Twentieth Annual Reunion of the Association of Graduates of the United States Military Academy at West Point, New York, June 12th, 1889,* 1. The last is identical to Dorst's article on Mackenzie in *Journal of the United States Cavalry Association* 10 (Dec. 1897).

14. Mackenzie, "Biographical Sketch"; Morison, *"Old Bruin,"* 51; Scoville, *Old Merchants,* 2:260; 3:143.

15. Irving and Mackenzie's letter quoted in McFarland, *Sea Dangers,* 28, 30; *Seventh Census of the United States, Original Returns of the Assistant Marshalls,* first series; Griffin, *Westchester County,* 349; Mackenzie, "Biographical Sketch"; Van de Water, *Captain Called It Mutiny,* 22; Ruth Neuendorfer, librarian of the Historical Society of the Tarrytowns, to Michael Pierce June 11, 1986.

16. Dorst, "Mackenzie," 1; Mackenzie, "Biographical Sketch"; Irving quoted in McFarland, *Sea Dangers,* 31.

17. Irving quoted in McFarland, *Sea Dangers,* 31; Dorst, "Mackenzie," 1. Dorst is probably the most reliable of Mackenzie's earlier chroniclers, as he obviously had access to family papers.

18. Dates of birth are based on ages given in the seventh census. The description of activities popular in the area of Tarrytown is drawn from Howard Hinton, *My Comrades; or, School Days at Mt. Pleasant,* 41–43, 129–36, 150–56, 196, 255. Hinton wrote of the period following the Civil War, but there is no reason to suppose that there was much change from the earlier period.

19. *Catalog of Mount Pleasant Academy: A Department of the University of the State of New York,* 13–15.

20. "Obituary Record," Williamsiana Collection, Williams College Library, Williamstown, Mass.; James S. Knowlson et al., comps., *A Biographical Record of the Kappa Alpha Society in Williams College, Williamstown, Mass., from Its Foundation to the Present Time, 1833–1881,* 210; obituary of Mackenzie in *The Jerseyman,* January 25, 1889.

21. *Catalog of Mount Pleasant Academy,* 14; Greta Cornell, "Mount Pleasant Academy, 1814–1925" (unpublished research paper), Ossining Historical Society, Ossining, N.Y., 4–5; Hinton, *My Comrades,* 12, 27; M. L. Crimmins, "General Mackenzie and Fort Concho," *West Texas Historical Association Yearbook* 10 (Oct. 1934): 17; Dorst, "Mackenzie," 2–3.

22. Dorst, "Mackenzie," 2; George W. Cullum, *Biographical Register of the Officers and Graduates of the U.S. Military Academy,* 2:842. George D. Wolfe, "The Indians Named Him Bad Hand," *True West,* Nov.–Dec. 1961, 16, makes the assertion that Ranald "was quick with his tongue and even quicker with his fists" but offers no documentation.

23. *Twentieth Annual Reunion,* 73. This is a reprint of Mackenzie's obituary which appeared in *The Army and Navy Journal;* Joseph Mills Hanson, "Ranald Slidell Mackenzie," *Cavalry Journal,* Jan.–Feb. 1934, 25.

24. George D. Albee to Parker, Aug. 5, 1916, Parker Papers. Referring to Ranald's reaction to his brother's death, Albee wrote, "It hurt him pretty badly"; Dorst, "Mackenzie," 1. See also Tully McCrea to Belle, July 7, 1862, Tully McCrea Papers, U.S. Military Academy Archives, West Point, N.Y., for a description of the family which McCrea described as "the happiest family that I ever saw." Longfellow to Catherine Mackenzie, October 30, 1848, in Hilen, *Letters of Longfellow,* 3:184.

25. Mackenzie, "Biographical Sketch"; Dorst, "Mackenzie," 2; *Santa Fe Daily New Mexican,* Dec. 22, 1882; Allison Albee, "The Case of the Missing Castle," *Westchester Historical Journal* 45, no. 4 (Fall 1969): 80.

Chapter 2. All That Is Good and Noble

1. Ralph A. Cutler and Carl B. Scherzer, eds., *Morristown and Morris Township: A Guide to Historical Sites,* 4–5; John Brasher, "Morristown, New Jersey, 1850–1860" (unpublished research paper, 1969), Joint Free Public Library of Morristown and Morris Township, 8–9.

2. Brasher, "Morristown," 32–33, 36–37.

3. Philip Hone, *The Diary of Philip Hone,* 64, 571–72.

4. Cutler and Scherzer, *Morristown,* 27; John Brett Langstaff, *New Jersey Generations: Macculloch Hall, Morristown,* 62; *Ossining Citizen-Register,* Feb. 21, 1939; "Historical Notes," bulletin of Saint Mary's Church, Scarborough, New York, in the collection of the Ossining Historical Society, Ossining, N.Y.; *Morristown Jerseyman,* Apr. 2, 1864; *Santa Fe Daily New Mexican,* Apr. 29, 1883.

5. Seventh Census; *Population Schedules of the Eighth Census of the United States,* New Jersey, vol. 14; Langstaff, *New Jersey Generations,* 140; Tully McCrea to Belle, July 7, 1862, Tully McCrea Papers, U.S. Military Academy Archives, West Point, N.Y.

6. *Morristown Jerseyman,* Jan. 25, 1889; July 6, 1906; Langstaff, *New Jersey Generations,* 117.

7. Brasher, "Morristown," 3, 26–27; *Morristown Jerseyman,* Jan. 25, 1889.

8. Joseph H. Dorst, "Ranald Slidell Mackenzie," *Twentieth Annual Reunion of the Association of Graduates of the United States Military Academy at West Point, New York, June 12th, 1889,* 3.

9. Ibid.

10. Ibid., 2; James S. Knowlson et al., comps., *A Biographical Record of the Kappa Alpha Society in Williams College, Williamstown, Mass., from Its Foundation to the Present Time, 1833–1881,* 199.

11. James R. McDonald, "Social Life of Williams," *Lippincott's Magazine,* Oct. 1887, 572.

12. Alan Johnson and Dumas Malone, eds., *Dictionary of American Biography* (20 vols.; New York: Charles Scribner's Sons, 1928–1936), 9:215–17; *Catalog,* Williams College, 1850–1859, Williamstown, Mass., n.p., 1859; "Oath Register for 1845–46" (memo book), Williamsiana Collection, Williams College Library, Williamstown, Mass.

13. Washington Gladden, *Recollections*, 68–71; Arthur Latham Perry, "Recollections and Diaries" (unpublished typescript), ed. Bliss Perry Williamsiana Collection, Williams College Library, Williamstown, Mass.

14. Alan Peskin, *Garfield*, 36.

15. Leslie George Loomis, "The Non-Fraternity Man at Williams College, 1868–1943" (unpublished seminar paper), and William A. H. Birnie, "The Social Organization of Williams College" (unpublished typescript), Williamsiana Collection, Williams College Library, Williamstown, Mass.

16. Leverett Wilson Spring, *A History of Williams College*, 205; Dorst, "Mackenzie," 2. Dorst also comments on Mackenzie's diffident manner and speech impediment. For examples of Mackenzie's aloofness, see James Parker, *The Old Army*, 30, and Parker to Frances Parker, Apr. 2, 1878, James Parker Papers, U.S. Military Academy Archives, West Point, N.Y.

17. Knowlson, *Biographical Record of Kappa Alpha*, 210–11; Lessing H. Nohl, Jr., "Bad Hand: The Military Career of Ranald Slidell Mackenzie, 1877–1889" (Ph.D. diss., University of New Mexico, 1962), 8. The Kappa Alpha Society should not be confused with the Kappa Alpha Order, which was founded after the Civil War at Washington University under the sponsorship of Robert E. Lee.

18. Gladden, *Recollections*, 79; McDonald, "Social Life of Williams," 575–55. See Perry, "Recollections and Diaries," 223, for "chip day." McDonald, "Social Life of Williams," 577–78, describes other optional activities.

19. "Obituary Record," Williamsiana Collection, Williams College Library, Williamstown, Mass., 96; Gladden, *Recollections*, 79; Knowlson, *Biographical Record of Kappa Alpha*, 211; Nohl, "Bad Hand," 8.

20. Nohl, "Bad Hand," 8; Dorst, "Mackenzie," 2.

21. Stephen A. Ambrose, *Duty, Honor, Country: A History of West Point*, 128; Morris Schaff, *The Spirit of Old West Point*, 1858–1862, 2; Catherine R. Mackenzie to John B. Floyd, Jan. 23, 1858, Cadet Application Papers, 1858, File no. 186, U.S. Military Academy Archives, West Point, N.Y.; Mrs. S. F. duPont to H. A. duPont, Mar. 24, 1858, Henry A. duPont Papers, Hagley Museum and Library, Wilmington, Del.; and John Slidell to J. B. Floyd, Jan. 16, 1858; Slidell to Floyd, Jan. 18, 1858; and J. Appleton to J. Buchanan, Feb. 10, 1858, all in Cadet Application Papers, U.S. Military Academy Archives, West Point, N.Y.

22. Mary Elizabeth Sergent, *They Lie Forgotten: The United States Military Academy, 1856–1861, together with a Class Album for the Class of May, 1861*, 73–73; Mrs. S. F. duPont to Henry, March 24, 1858, and H. A. duPont to Mrs. S. F. duPont, March 27, 1858, duPont Papers.

23. Ambrose, *Duty, Honor, Country*, 158; E. W. Anderson to Mother, July 6, 1860, in Francis Sullivan, ed., "Letters of a West Pointer," *American Historical Review* 33 (Mar. 1928): 605; H. A. duPont to Mrs. S. F. duPont, September 12, 1858, duPont Papers.

24. Ambrose, *Duty, Honor, Country*, 147–48.

25. Henry A. duPont declared that the academic competition was "very exciting" and thought high rank "well worth studying for." DuPont to Mrs.

S. F. duPont, May 8, 1857, duPont Papers; class standings in *Official Register of the United States Military Academy,* copies supplied by the Association of Graduates, U.S. Military Academy, West Point, N.Y.; Dorst, "Mackenzie," 3–4. For the effect of the sectional split on cadets at the academy, see Ambrose, *Duty, Honor, Country,* 168–72, and Sergent, *They Lie Forgotten,* 82 and *passim.*

26. Dorst, "Mackenzie," 4; *Official Register,* 1862, 9.

27. E. W. Anderson to uncle, June 17, 1860, in Sullivan, "Letters of a West Pointer," 600; *Official Register,* 1859, 14; 1860, 13; 1861, 13; 1862, 9.

28. "Register of Delinquencies," U.S. Military Academy Archives, West Point, N.Y.; Schaff, *Spirit of Old West Point,* 267.

29. Cullen Bryant to father, Aug. 30, 1860, quoted in Ambrose, *Duty, Honor, Country,* 159; E. W. Anderson to mother, Feb. 28, 1861, in Sullivan, "Letters of a West Point Cadet," 607–608; Schaff, *Spirit of Old West Point,* 99.

30. Vivid pictures of West Point life can be found in Ambrose, *Duty, Honor, Country;* Sergent, *They Lie Forgotten,* which concentrates on the period when Ranald was at the academy; and Schaff, *Spirit of Old West Point.* Schaff was in Mackenzie's class. See also the letter collections cited.

31. Tully McCrea to Belle, Dec. 8, 1861, July 7, 1862, Tully McCrea Papers, U.S. Military Academy Archives, West Point, N.Y.; Sergent, *They Lie Forgotten,* 73–74; Schaff, *Spirit of Old West Point,* 42.

32. Dorst, "Mackenzie," 1, 3; N. A. Miles to *Oregonian,* Jan. 5, 1884, reprinted in *Army and Navy Journal,* Feb. 9, 1884, 564.

Chapter 3. The Most Promising Young Officer

1. Joseph H. Dorst, "Ranald Slidell Mackenzie," *Twentieth Annual Reunion of the Association of Graduates of the United States Military Academy at West Point, New York, June 12th, 1889,* 4. See also Tully McCrea to Belle, September 8, 1862, Tully McCrea Papers, U.S. Military Academy Archives, West Point, N.Y.

2. See the comment of a Virginia private at the Battle of Sharpsburg quoted in Stephen W. Sears, *Landscape Turned Red: The Battle of Antietam* (New Haven and New York: Ticknor and Fields, 1983), 284; "Military Service Record of Ranald S. Mackenzie," cited in Ernest Wallace, ed., *Ranald S. Mackenzie's Official Correspondence Relating to Texas, 1871–1879,* 1:11–12.

3. Tully McCrea to Belle, September 8, 1862, McCrea Papers; "Military Service Record," in Wallace, *Mackenzie's Correspondence,* 1:12.

4. Fred C. Ainsworth and Joseph Kirkley, comps., *The War of the Rebellion: A Compilation of the Official Records of the Union and Confederate Armies,* first series, 21:218–19; 51, pt. 1:952 (hereafter cited as *Official Records*).

5. Tully McCrea to Belle, Jan. 14, 1863, McCrea Papers; C. C. Augur to R. S. Mackenzie, June 24, 1873, Ranald Slidell Mackenzie Letterbook, U.S. Army Military History Institute, Carlisle Barracks.

6. For Mackenzie on marriage, see James Parker to Frances, Apr. 2, 1878, James Parker Papers, U.S. Military Academy Archives, West Point, N.Y.

7. Tully McCrea to Belle, Jan. 26, 1863, McCrea Papers; C. B. Comstock to Mackenzie, Feb. 15, 1863, *Official Records*, first series, 51, pt. 1:987-86.

8. "Military Service Record," in Wallace, *Mackenzie's Correspondence*, 12. See John Bigelow, Jr., *The Campaign of Chancellorsville: A Strategic and Tactical Study*, 300-302 and *passim*.

9. Emerson Gifford Taylor, *Gouverneur Kemble Warren: The Life and Letters of an American Soldier, 1830-1882*, 126-27; Oliver Wilcox Norton, *The Attack and Defense of Little Round Top, Gettysburg, July 2, 1863*, 20, 292-93; Mackenzie to General Meade, Mar. 22, 1864, *Official Records*, first series, 27, pt. 1:138; Joseph Mills Hanson, "Ranald Slidell Mackenzie," *Cavalry Journal*, Jan.-Feb. 1934, 26. The *Washington Sunday Herald*, quoted in the *Army and Navy Journal*, Jan. 5, 1884, 461, credited him with discovering the weakness in the Union line, but there is no support for this.

10. Hanson, "Mackenzie," 26; *Official Records*, first series 36, pt. 3:713-14.

11. *Official Record*, first series, 27, pt. 3:555, 819; Gilbert Thompson, *The Engineer Battalion in the Civil War*, Occasional Papers of the Engineer School No. 44, 43; Dale E. Floyd, ed., *"Dear Friends at Home . . .": The Letters and Diary of Thomas James Owen, Fiftieth New York Volunteer Engineer Regiment, during the Civil War*, 19; *Official Records*, first series, 29, pt. 2:525, 528.

12. Tully McCrea to Belle, Nov. 27, 1862, Jan. 24, Aug. 16, 1863, McCrea Papers.

13. G. K. Warren to G. G. Meade, June 9, 1864, *Official Records*, first series, 36, pt. 3:713-14; Dorst, "Mackenzie," 4-5. Dorst had apparently seen Mackenzie's letters.

14. Report of Captain George H. Mendell, Aug. 5, 1864; *Official Records*, first series, 26, pt. 1:295-97, 317; Report of Major Nathaniel Michler, October 20, 1864, Thompson, *Engineer Battalion*, 56.

15. Thompson, *Engineer Battalion*, 58; Report of Major Michler, 297; Peter S. Michie, *The Life and Letters of Emory Upton*, 95; Floyd, *"Dear Friends,"* 38.

16. *Official Records*, first series, 36, pt. 1:122-47, 305, 574; Floyd, *"Dear Friends,"* 40-43.

17. Dudley Landon Vail, *The County Regiment: A Sketch of the Second Regiment of Connecticut Volunteer Heavy Artillery*, 8-11, 16, 17.

18. Vail, *County Regiment*, 39-40; Theodore F. Vail, *History of the Second Connecticut Volunteer Heavy Artillery*, 68; *Official Records*, first series, 36, pt. 3:713-14.

19. Special Order No. 158, Army of the Potomac, June 10, 1864, *Official Records*, first series, 36, pt. 3:72. Vail, *County Regiment*, 39, says that Mackenzie actually took command on June 6.

20. Vail, *History of the Second Connecticut*, 331.

21. Isaac O. Best, *History of the 121st New York State Infantry*, 168; Vail, *History of the Second Connecticut*, 331.

22. Vail, *History of the Second Connecticut*, 333.

23. Ibid.; Vail, *County Regiment*, 41.

24. Vail, *History of the Second Connecticut*, 69–76. See also Report of Brigadier General Emory Upton, *Official Records*, first series, 40, pt. 1:492–93.

25. Report of General Upton, *Official Records*, first series, 40, pt. 1:493; Vail, *History of the Second Connecticut*, 77–78.

26. "Military Service Record," in Wallace, *Mackenzie's Correspondence*, 1:12; Tully McCrea to Belle, June 3, 1864, McCrea Papers; Sergent, *They Lie Forgotten*, 92.

27. Vail, *History of the Second Connecticut*, 80–82. A good brief account of Early's raid can be found in Shelby Foote, *The Civil War: A Narrative*, 3:446–61. A more detailed picture can be found in Frank E. Vandiver, *Jubal's Raid: General Early's Famous Attack on Washington in 1864*.

28. Vail, *History of the Second Connecticut*, 83.

29. Ibid., 84–85, 331–32.

30. Ibid., 85–86; Jeffery D. Wert, *From Winchester to Cedar Creek: The Shenandoah Campaign of 1864*, chaps. 1 and 2, *passim;* Edward J. Stackpole, *Sheridan in the Shenandoah: Jubal Early's Nemesis,* 22–23, 103–105.

31. See Wert, *Winchester to Cedar Creek*, v–vi, on the importance of the campaign.

32. Ibid., chap. 3, describes Sheridan's situation and the maneuvers of this phase of the campaign. Vail, *History of the Second Connecticut*, 88–92, tells what this was like for Mackenzie's regiment.

33. Wert, *Winchester to Cedar Creek*, 56–70; Stackpole, *Sheridan in the Shenandoah*, 211–12. Henry A. duPont, *The Campaign of 1864 in the Valley of Virginia and the Expedition to Lynchburg*, 114–15, quotes Upton's account of his brigade's charge. Mackenzie's own report is in *Official Records*, first series, 43, pt. 2:179–80.

34. Vail, *History of the Second Connecticut*, 95.

35. Ibid., 96–96, 334.

36. Ibid., 97; Wertz, *Winchester to Cedar Creek*, 80–97.

37. Vail, *History of the Second Connecticut*, 332.

38. Report of General Upton, *Official Records*, first series, 47, pt. 1:162–63; Report of General H. G. Wright, ibid., pt. 2:199–200; U. S. Grant, *Personal Memoirs of U. S. Grant*, 2:541.

39. Stackpole, *Sheridan in the Shenandoah*, 240–60; Wert, *Winchester to Cedar Creek*, 111–19.

40. Vail, *History of the Second Connecticut*, 104–107. See Wert, *Winchester to Cedar Creek*, 124–26, for others who claim to have reached the summit first and 120–28 for a good description of the fight.

41. Wert, *Winchester to Cedar Creek*, 157–74.

42. For this and the preceding paragraph, as well as the general description of the Battle of Cedar Creek, see ibid., 174–238, and Stackpole, *Sheridan in the Shenandoah*, 281–82, 290–334.

43. Vail, *History of the Second Connecticut*, 121; Best, *History of the 121st New York*, 190–94.

44. Best, *History of the 121st New York*, 194–201; Vail, *History of the Second Connecticut*, 121–26; Tully McCrea to Belle, Oct. 30, 1864, McCrea Papers.

45. Report of H. G. Wright, and Report of P. H. Sheridan, *Official Records*, first series, 43, pt. 1:33, 159.

46. Mackenzie's remark is in Vail, *History of the Second Connecticut*, 332; Tully McCrea wrote of Mackenzie's recklessness to Belle, Oct. 30, 1864, McCrea Papers.

47. Hanson, "Mackenzie," 27; J. H. Wilson to General R. W. Johnson, Oct. 24, 1864, and Wilson to General J. A. Rawlins, Oct. 26, 1864, *Official Records*, first series, 39, pt. 3: 424, 444; Wilson to Rawlins, Oct. 27, 1864, ibid., 52, pt. 1:649.

48. Best, *History of 121st New York*, 202-205; Vail, *History of the Second Connecticut*, 132-35.

49. Grant to Meade, Mar. 13, 1865; Meade to Grant, Mar. 13, 1865; Wright to Meade, Mar. 13, 1865; Special Orders no. 79, Mar. 20, 1865; General Orders no. 25, Mar. 20, 1865; all in *Official Records*, first series, 46, pt. 2:947, 950, 967; pt. 3:55, 66.

50. G. W. Coles, John L. Roper, and Henry C. Archibald, *History of the Eleventh Pennsylvania Volunteer Cavalry, Together with a Complete Roster of the Regiment and Regimental Officers*, 147.

51. Ibid., 147-48; Horace Porter, "Five Forks and the Pursuit of Lee," in Robert U. Johnson and Clarence C. Buel, eds., *Battles and Leaders of the Civil War* (4 vols; New York: Thomas Yoseloff, 1956), 4:710-11; Ranald Mackenzie to P. H. Sheridan, Aug. 7, 1880, Ranald Slidell Mackenzie, Letterbook, typescript in the Thomas Gilcrease Museum, Tulsa, Okla. (hereafter referred to as Gilcrease Letterbook).

52. Mackenzie to Sheridan, Aug. 7, 1880, Gilcrease Letterbook; Porter, "Five Forks," 713; Coles, Roper, and Archibald, *History of the Eleventh Pennsylvania*, 148.

53. Report of General Ranald Slidell Mackenzie, n.d., in Philip H. Sheridan Papers, Manuscript Division, Library of Congress, Washington, D.C.; Mackenzie to Sheridan, Aug. 7, 1880, Gilcrease Letterbook. Burke Davis, *To Appomattox: Nine April Days, 1865*, 45-48, says that Mackenzie closed off Pickett's path to rejoin Lee.

54. Sherman's report on the Battle of Five Forks, *Official Records*, first series, 46, pt. 1:1106; Coles, Roper, and Archibald, *History of the Eleventh Pennsylvania*, 148.

55. Coles, Roper, and Archibald, *History of the Eleventh Pennsylvania*, 152; Report of Mackenzie, Sheridan Papers; Report of Wesley Merritt, *Official Records*, first series, 46, pt. 1:1118-20; Davis, *To Appomattox*, 294.

56. Davis, *To Appomattox*, 374-75; Report of Mackenzie, Sheridan Papers; Coles, Roper, and Archibald, *History of the Eleventh Pennsylvania*, 156-57.

57. Grant, *Personal Memoirs*, 2:541.

Chapter 4. Gone to Texas

1. *Official Records*, first series, 46, pt. 1:58; pt. 3:694, 696.

2. G.W. Coles, John L. Roper, and Henry C. Archibald, *History of the*

Eleventh Pennsylvania Volunteer Cavalry, Together with a Complete Register of the Regiment and Regimental Officers, 161; Grant to Gibbon, and General Orders No. 28, Cavalry Command, Apr. 10, 1865, *Official Records,* first series, 46, pt. 3:694, 748.

3. Thomas Little to Thomas Munford, Apr. 13, 1865, Munford to Mackenzie, Apr. 17, 1865; Gibbon to Munford, Apr. 21, 1865; Gregg to Gibbon, Apr. 21, 1865, all in *Official Records,* first series, 46, pt. 3:735, 813–14, 880–81, 882.

4. Gibbon's Orders, April 16, 1865, ibid., 796.

5. Orders of General E. O. C. Ord, May 31, 1865, ibid., 1184; "Military Service Record," in Ernest Wallace, ed., *Ranald S. Mackenzie's Official Correspondence Relating to Texas, 1873–1879,* 1:12; Mackenzie to Adjutant General, Oct. 15, Nov. 6, 1865, Records of the U.S. Adjutant General's Office, Record Group 94, National Archives and Records Service, Washington, D.C. (hereafter cited as AGO, RG 94, NA)

6. Annual *Report of the United States Secretary of War,* 39th Cong., 2d sess., 1866–67, H. Exec. Doc. 1285, 3:418, 432. Catherine Mackenzie's address is given as Portsmouth on a deed in the Morris County Clerk's Office. Aline Dempsey to Michael Pierce, July 8, 1988.

7. The account of Mackenzie's visit to Washington appeared in the *Washington Sunday Herald,* Jan. 1, 1884, and was reprinted in the *Army and Navy Journal,* Jan. 5, 1884, 461.

8. For the reputation of the black regiments, see William H. Leckie, *The Buffalo Soldiers: A Narrative of the Negro Cavalry in the West,* 9.

9. Reports of examining boards, Mar. 13, 1867; Mackenzie to Adjutant General, Mar. 13, 16, 1867, AGO, RG 94, NA.

10. Joseph H. Dorst, "Ranald Slidell Mackenzie," *Twentieth Annual Reunion of the Association of Graduates of the United States Military Academy at West Point, New York,* 8–9; *New Orleans Times-Picayune,* June 26, 1867; William M. Notson, *Fort Concho Medical History, January 1869 to July 1872,* 11; Jerry M. Sullivan, "Fort McKavett, 1852–1883," *West Texas Historical Association Yearbook* 45 (1969):144.

11. *New Orleans Times Picayune,* June 22, 1867; "Military Service Record," in Wallace, *Mackenzie's Official Correspondence,* 1:13; Dorst, "Mackenzie," 9.

12. James Parker, *The Old Army,* 100; Paul H. Carlson, "William R. Shafter Commanding Black Troops in West Texas," *West Texas Historical Association Yearbook* 50 (1974):104, 116; William G. Muller, *The Twenty Fourth Infantry: Past and Present.*

13. Sullivan, "Fort McKavett," 138; Notson, *Fort Concho Medical History,* 18, refers to Mackenzie as commander of the Subdistrict of the Pecos. The title is not listed in "Military Service Record," Wallace, *Mackenzie's Official Correspondence.*

14. Clayton Williams, *Texas' Last Frontier: Fort Stockton and the Trans-Pecos, 1861–1895* (College Station: Texas A&M University Press, 1982), 115.

15. Notson, *Fort Concho Medical History,* 20; J'Nell LaVerne Pate, "Colo-

nel Ranald Slidell Mackenzie's First Four Years with the Fourth Cavalry in Texas, 1871–1874," (master's thesis, Texas Christian University, 1960), 20–21. These engagements are listed in *Winners of the West* 14, no. 4 (Mar. 1937).

16. Margaret Bierschwale, *Fort McKavett, Texas: Post on the San Saba*, 57; Pate, "Mackenzie's First Four Years," 18–19; M. L. Crimmins, "Fort McKavett, Texas," *Southwestern Historical Quarterly* 38 (July 1934): 29–31.

17. Bierschwale, *Fort McKavett*, 59.

18. Ibid., 60–62; Sullivan, "Fort McKavett," 145–46.

19. Bierschwale, *Fort McKavett*, 59.

20. Slightly differing versions of this episode can be found in ibid., 62–63; Sullivan, "Fort McKavett," 144–45; and J. Evetts Haley, *Fort Concho and the Texas Frontier*, 265–70. Haley's is the most detailed and accurately reflects white prejudices of the period. Although Haley expressed great admiration for Mackenzie, he was sympathetic to Jackson in this case.

21. Kimble County Historical Survey Committee, *Recorded Landmarks of Kimble County*, 110–11.

22. *San Antonio Daily Herald*, Nov. 26, 1869, quoted in Pate, "Mackenzie's First Four Years," 21.

23. Assistant Adjutant General, Department of Texas, to Mackenzie, April 23, July 7, 1870, Letters Sent, Department of Texas, Records of United States Army Commands, Record Group 393, National Archives and Records Service, Washington, D.C. (hereafter cited as Letters Sent, DT, RG 393, NA); Muller, *Twenty Fourth Infantry*. On the reductions in the service, see Robert M. Utley, *Frontier Regulars: The United States Army and the Indian, 1866–1891*, 15.

24. Dorst, "Mackenzie," 9.

25. On the support of Grant and Sheridan, see Paul Andrew Hutton, *Phil Sheridan and His Army*, 353; for the Sherman quote, see p. 135. Parker, *Old Army*, 48, is likely the original source for the stargazing story, which has many variations. See, for example, Charles Judson Crane, *The Experiences of a Colonel of Infantry*, 113, and John Chapman, "Fort Concho," *Southwest Review* 25 (Apr. 1940): 272.

26. Mackenzie to Sheridan, Apr. 17, 1875, Gilcrease Letterbook.

Chapter 5. A New Start

1. "Military Service Record," in Ernest Wallace, ed., *Ranald S. Mackenzie's Official Correspondence Relating to Texas, 1873–1879*, 1:13; John K. Herr and Edward S. Wallace, *The Story of the U.S. Cavalry*, 73; Lessing H. Nohl, Jr., "Bad Hand: The Military Career of Ranald Slidell Mackenzie, 1877–1889" (Ph.D. diss., University of New Mexico, 1962), 15–16; quote from Joseph H. Dorst, "Ranald Slidell Mackenzie," *Twentieth Annual Reunion of the Association of Graduates of the United States Military Academy at West Point, New York*, 9.

2. Robert G. Carter, *On the Border with Mackenzie; or, Winning West Texas from the Comanches*, 58. See also Nohl, "Bad Hand," 15–16, and

Robert M. Utley, *Frontier Regulars: The United States Army and the Indian, 1866–1891*, 25. Carter is one of the most important sources for Mackenzie during this period but must be used with some caution. By the time he began to write, he was somewhat embittered about the army and the changes taking place in it. Although most of his facts seem accurate, they are shaped by his opinions. See J. C. Dykes's introduction to *On the Border* and Byron Price's introduction to Robert G. Carter, *The Old Sergeant's Story: Fighting Indians and Bad Men in Texas from 1870 to 1876*.

3. "R. G. Carter Diary for 1871," entry for Feb. 24, 1871, typescript of original in possession of B. Byron Price, executive director of the Cowboy Hall of Fame and Western Heritage Center, Oklahoma City. I wish to express my deep appreciation to Mr. Price for allowing me to use this diary before its publication. The freshness of Carter's diary makes it an important check to some to the excesses of his later writing.

4. Ibid., entry for Feb. 25, 1871.

5. Ibid.; Carter, *On the Border*, 218–19, 396.

6. Carter, *On the Border*, 468–69; "R. G. Carter Diary," entries for Feb. 26, May 14, 1871.

7. Carter, *On the Border*, 116; "R. G. Carter Diary," entry for July 8, 1871.

8. Carter, *On the Border*, 126.

9. Ibid., 134–35.

10. Ibid., xiii; "R. G. Carter Diary," entries for Apr. 20, 25, 1871; Parker to sister, Apr. 2, 1878, James Parker Papers, U.S. Military Academy Archives, West Point, N.Y.

11. Carter, *On the Border*, 63.

12. James Parker, *The Old Army*, 47, 95; Carter, *On the Border*, 338–39; Parker to father, Oct. 21, 1878, Parker Papers; Chalres Judson Crane, *The Experiences of a Colonel of Infantry*, 66.

13. Mackenzie to Lt. Donovan (Adjutant General's Office), Nov. 3, 1873, AGO, RG-94; Mackenzie to H. C. Bankhead, June 17, 1874; Mackenzie to O. W. Budd, July 9, 1874, both in Gilcrease Letterbook; Mackenzie to Sherman, Dec. 27, 1870, William Tecumseh Sherman Papers, Library of Congress, Washington, D.C.

14. Carter, *On the Border*, 341; Crane, *Colonel of Infantry*, 79–80.

15. Carter, *On the Border*, xiii; Mackenzie to Parker, n.d., Parker Papers; Mackenzie to Pope, Sept. 21, 1881, Gilcrease Letterbook.

16. John Chapman, "Fort Concho," *Southwest Review* 25 (Apr. 1940): 272, cites an unnamed sergeant as the source for "Mad" Mackenzie. The other quotes are by Sergeant James S. McClellan, quoted in Fred H. Werner, *The Dull Knife Battle*, 58; John Charlton to Carter, Feb. 14, Oct. 13, 1921, in Carter, *Old Sergeant's Story*, 52, 59, 63.

17. Parker, *Old Army*, 94; Lawton to Chief Quartermaster, Nov. 17, 1874, endorsed by Mackenzie, in Wallace, *Mackenzie's Official Correspondence*, 2:167–68; *Army and Navy Journal*, Nov. 6, 1875, 196; Feb. 26, 1876, 464; Mar. 11, 1876, 496; Mar. 17, 1877, 508.

18. Carter, *On the Border*, 146; Ida Lasater Huckaby, *Ninety-four Years in Jack County, 1854–1948*, 106.

19. Mrs. John Herden James, *I Remember: Being the Memoirs of Mrs. John Herden (Maria Aurelia Williams) James Together With Contemporary Historical Events and Sketches of Her Own and Her Husband's Families,* ed. Charles Albert Sloan, 156; *Santa Fe Daily New Mexican,* July 6, Oct. 29, 1882, Mar. 1, 1883; Edward S. Wallace, "General Ranald Slidell Mackenzie, Indian Fighting Cavalryman," *Southwestern Historical Quarterly,* 56 (Jan. 1953): 395.

20. For Mackenzie's one recorded romance, see chapter 13.

21. Carter, *On the Border,* 537–38, states that Mackenzie never drank. The story of the cigars is told by Carter on p. 299. Entries for Nov. 4, 13, 1876, "Diary of Private Earl Smith," quoted in Sherry L. Smith, *Sagebrush Soldier: Private Earl Smith's View of the Sioux War of 1876,* 30–31, 39. I thank Professor Smith for sending me a copy of her paper based on Smith's diary, "With Mackenzie on the Wyoming and Texas Frontiers: A Private's Perspective," which she presented at the Texas State Historical Association convention in Lubbock, Texas, Mar. 3, 1989.

22. Allan A. Stovall, *Breaks of the Balcones; A Regional History,* ed. Wanda Pope and Allan Stovall, 190–91.

23. Carter, *On the Border,* 57; H. H. McConnell, *Five Years a Cavalryman,* 113; Robert G. Carter, "Dust from the Archive: General Ranald Mackenzie," *Corral Dust* (Potomac Corral of Westerners) 2 (Mar. 1957): 6.

24. Carter, "Dust," 6; "R. G. Carter Diary," entry for Apr. 4, 1871; Henry W. Strong, *My Frontier Days and Indian Fights on the Plains of Texas,* 23–24.

25. Parker, *Old Army,* 27–30.

Chapter 6. Bad Hand

1. "Medical History of Fort Richardson, Texas," vol. 26 of *Medical Histories of Posts,* AGO, RG 94; Ernest Wallace, *Ranald S. Mackenzie on the Texas Frontier,* 23.

2. There is a concise history of Indian troubles in Texas up to 1871 in Wallace, *Mackenzie,* chap. 2. Another brief account with more of an Indian perspective can be found in Wilbur S. Nye, *Carbine and Lance: The Story of Old Fort Sill,* chaps. 5 and 6. The standard accounts of the Indians involved are Ernest Wallace and E. A. Hoebel, *The Comanches: Lords of the South Plains,* and Mildred P. Mayhall, *The Kiowas.*

3. "R. G. Carter Diary for 1871," entries for Mar. 1, 4, 5, 6, 7, 1871, National Cowboy Hall of Fame and Western Heritage Center, Oklahoma City.

4. Assistant Adjutant General, Department of Texas (hereafter cited as AAG, DT), to Mackenzie, Mar. 19, 1871, RG 393, National Archives and Records Service, Washington, D.C.; Wallace, *Mackenzie,* 24, 28–29. Wallace errs in denoting the Sixth as being "inexperienced Negro troops."

5. "Mackenzie's Journal of Move to Fort Richardson," May 5, 1871, in Ernest Wallace, ed., *Ranald S. Mackenzie's Official Correspondence,* 1:17–22; "R. G. Carter Diary," entries for Mar. 29, 30, Apr. 1, 7, 1871, and *passim.*

6. Sherman to Ellen Sherman, May 18, 1871, W. T. Sherman Family Papers, University of Notre Dame Archives (microfilm edition); "R. G. Carter Diary," entries for Apr. 9, 28, May 16, 1871. See also Alan Lee Hamilton, *Sentinel of the Southern Plains: Fort Richardson and the Northwest Texas Frontier, 1866–1878*, 28–37.

7. *Austin Daily State Journal*, July 8, 1871, quoted in J'Nell LaVerne Pate, "Colonel Ranald Slidell Mackenzie's First Four Years with the Fourth Cavalry in Texas" (master's thesis, Texas Christian University, 1960), 201; "R. G. Carter Diary," entries for May 4, 7, 10, 12, 1871.

8. Nye, *Carbine and Lance*, 124; Wallace, *Mackenzie*, 28. Marcy's journal can be conveniently consulted in Carl Coke Rister, ed., "Documents Relating to General William T. Sherman's Southern Plains Indian Policy, 1871–1875," *Panhandle-Plains Historical Review* 9, (1936):7–27.

9. Carter, *On the Border*, 76–77.

10. "R. G. Carter Diary," entry for May 18, 1871; Nye, *Carbine and Lance*, 124–31; Benjamin Capps, *The Warren Wagontrain Raid: The First Complete Account of an Historic Indian Attack and Its Aftermath*, 48–54. Capps's account is essentially accurate, although he does allow his considerable talent as a novelist to come into play. Nye's version is important because some of his informants were Indians.

11. Sherman to Mackenzie, May 19, 1871, Wallace, *Mackenzie's Official Correspondence*, 1:23; Mackenzie to McCoy [Sherman's aide], n.d., but "8 miles East Salt Creek," William T. Sherman Papers, Manuscript Division, Library of Congress, Washington, D.C. Capps, *Warren Wagontrain Raid*, 67–70, prints the relevant documents.

12. Mackenzie to AAG, DT, June 16, 1871, Sherman Papers.

13. Lawrie Tatum, *Our Red Brothers and the Peace Policy of President Ulysses S. Grant*, 116–122. Capps, *Warren Wagontrain Raid*, 91–105, offers a suitably dramatic rendering of the arrest. Capps and Nye, *Carbine and Lance*, 126–27, disagree on Satanta's importance in the raid with Nye, relying on his Indian sources, assigning the principal leadership role to a medicine man named Maman-ti or Do-ha-te. Henry W. Strong, *My Frontier Days and Indian Fights on the Plains of Texas*, 21, supports Nye and asserts that Satanta was "only a little chief."

14. Sherman to Mackenzie, May 29, 1871; Sherman to C.O., Fort Richardson, May 28, 1871, both in Sherman Papers.

15. Grierson to Assistant Adjutant General, Department of Missouri, June 9, 1871, in Wallace, *Mackenzie's Official Correspondence*, 1:30–31; Nye, *Carbine and Lance*, 144–47. Capps, *Warren Wagontrain Raid*, 115–25, has an imaginative, but plausible, rendering of this episode.

16. Carter, *Old Sergeant's Story*, 81; Pate, "Mackenzie's First Four Years," 62–63; "R. G. Carter Diary," entry for June 12, 1871.

17. Accounts of the trial can be found in Capps, *Warren Wagontrain Raid*, 160–84; Nye, *Carbine and Lance*, 147–48; and Carter, *On the Border*, 99–104.

18. Robert M. Utley, *Frontier Regulars: The United States Army and the Indian, 1866–1891*, 211; Nye, *Carbine and Lance*, 149.

19. Mackenzie to Sherman, June 15, 1871, Sherman Papers. Parts of this letter are reprinted in Nye, *Carbine and Lance*, 148.

20. Mackenzie to AAG, DT, June 16, 1871, Sherman Papers.

21. A good, brief narrative of the 1868 campaign can be found in Paul Andrew Hutton, *Phil Sheridan and His Army*, 56–114.

22. AAG, DT, to Mackenzie, July 6, 1871, in Wallace, *Mackenzie's Official Correspondence*, 1:35–36; William H. Leckie and Shirley A. Leckie, *Unlikely Warriors: General Benjamin H. Grierson and His Family*, 190; Sherman to Grierson, June 8, 1871, Sherman Papers.

23. Wallace, *Mackenzie*, 39–40; Carter, *On the Border*, 105–106; Hamilton, *Sentinel of the Southern Plains*, 100.

24. "R. G. Carter Diary," entries for July 28, 30, Aug. 2, 1871.

25. Ibid., entries for Aug. 3, 4, 5, 1871; Carter, *On the Border*, 106–18.

26. Carter, *On the Border*, 119–22; "R. G. Carter Diary," entries for Aug. 8, 9, 10, 1871.

27. "R. G. Carter Diary," entries for Aug. 11, 12, 13, 14, 15 (quote), 1871; Carter, *On the Border*, 122–23.

28. Carter, *On the Border*, 123–24, 144; Wallace, *Mackenzie*, 42–43; Grierson to Tatum, Aug. 19, 1871, quoted in Pate, "Mackenzie's First Four Years," 218.

29. Carter, *On the Border*, 124–42. Carter's diary does not mention the night march, stampede, or any contact with Indians.

30. Ibid., 129, 136; "R. G. Carter Diary," entries for Aug. 25 to Sept. 3, 1871.

31. Carter, *On the Border*, 142–43. See 116 for Mackenzie's view of campaign extras. Carter's diary entry for Aug. 5, merely comments, "splendid mess."

32. "R. G. Carter Diary," entries for Sept. 6–13, 1871. Sherman's approval for an expedition "west of Double Mountain" can be found in Wallace, *Mackenzie's Official Correspondence*, 1:38. Quahada has been spelled in a variety of ways, each of which seems equally valid. I like the looks of this spelling.

33. "R. G. Carter Diary," entries for Sept. 19, 29, Oct. 3, 1871; Carter, *On the Border*, 158–59; Wallace, *Mackenzie*, 45–46.

34. "R. G. Carter Diary," entries for Oct. 3, 4, 5, 6, 7, 1871; Carter, *On the Border*, 159–60. Wallace, *Mackenzie*, 46–48, traces the route closely, locating it in relation to modern landmarks; see also Wallace's map opposite p. 66.

35. "R. G. Carter Diary," entries for Oct. 7, 8, 9, 1871.

36. Carter, *On the Border*, 165–68. Possibly the raid on the horse herd was led by Quanah, the famous half-white Comanche chief. See Zoe Tilghman, *Quanah: The Eagle of the Comanches*, 70–71. Nye's Indian informants make no special mention of Quanah, and it is possible that he later exaggerated his role for political reasons; *Carbine and Lance*, 151. The count of missing horses is given in Mackenzie to AAG, DT, Nov. 15, 1871, in Wallace, *Mackenzie's Official Correspondence*, 1:41–42.

37. Carter, *On the Border*, 168–82. Carter was later awarded the Medal of Honor for his part in the fight.

38. Carter, *On the Border*, 185–86.
39. "R. G. Carter Diary," entries for Oct. 10, 11, 1871; Carter, *On the Border*, 188.
40. "R. G. Carter Diary," entry for Oct. 12, 1871; Carter, *On the Border*, 188–94.
41. Carter, *On the Border*, 194–96, first quote on p. 195; "R. G. Carter Diary," entries for Oct. 12, 13, 1871; Mackenzie to AAG, DT, Nov. 15, 1871, in Wallace, *Mackenzie's Official Correspondence*, 1:41–42.
42. Wallace, *Mackenzie*, 46, uses regimental returns to estimate about six hundred men under Mackenzie's command at the beginning of the campaign.
43. Carter, *On the Border*, 198, 202; "R. G. Carter Diary," entries for Oct. 16, 21, 1871.
44. "R. G. Carter Diary," entries for Oct. 24, 29, Nov. 6, 8, 9, 10, 12, 18, 1871; Carter, *On the Border*, 203–207; Wallace, *Mackenzie*, 54–56.
45. James Mooney, "Calendar History of the Kiowa Indians," *Seventeenth Annual Report of the Bureau of American Ethnology.*

Chapter 7. Give Him A Good Swing

1. Allen Lee Hamilton, *Sentinel of the Southern Plains: Fort Richardson and the Northwest Texas Frontier, 1866–1878*, 121; R. W. Wilson, "A Yankee Soldier's Experience on the Texas Frontier," *Hunter's Magazine*, January, 1912, p. 7; Robert G. Carter, *On the Border with Mackenzie; or, Winning West Texas from the Comanches*, 220–22. For a good discussion of the problem of desertion in the Indian-fighting army, see Don Rickey, Jr., *Forty Miles a Day on Beans and Hay: The Enlisted Soldier Fighting the Indian Wars*, 145–55, and Edward M. Coffman, *The Old Army: A Portrait of the American Army in Peacetime, 1784–1898*, 371–75.
2. Carter, *On the Border*, 222–40; Hamilton, *Sentinel of the Southern Plains*, 122–24. "R. G. Carter Diary," entries for Nov. 29 to Dec. 11, 1871, sketches the story of the chase, and *On the Border* fills in the details.
3. Hamilton, *Sentinel of the Southern Plains*, 121–24.
4. Henry W. Strong, *My Frontier Days and Indian Fights on the Plains of Texas*, 80; Ida Lasater Huckaby, *Ninety-Four Years in Jack County, 1854–1948*, 109.
5. Carter, *On the Border*, 111, 336–37; Robert G. Carter, *The Old Sergeant's Story: Fighting Indians and Bad Men in Texas from 1870 to 1876*, 95–96.
6. George W. Cullum, *Biographical Register of the Officers and Graduates of the U.S. Military Academy;* William L. Richter, *The Army in Texas during Reconstruction*, 119–20, 166.
7. Lessing H. Nohl, Jr., "Bad Hand: The Military Career of Ranald Slidell Mackenzie, 1877–1889" (Ph.D. diss., University of New Mexico, 1962), 30–31; Ernest Wallace, *Ranald S. Mackenzie on the Texas Frontier*, 61–62; Reynolds to Assistant Advocate General, Division of the South, July 13, 1872, Letters Sent, Department of Texas, RG 393, NA.
8. Sherman's endorsement on Reynolds to Sherman, Aug. 21, 1871,

William T. Sherman Papers, Manuscript Division, Library of Congress, Washington, D.C.; Nohl, "Bad Hand," 52–55; General Orders No. 66, Nov. 1, 1871, in Ernest Wallace, ed., *Ranald S. Mackenzie's Official Correspondence Relating to Texas, 1873–1879,* 1:40–41. For military purposes the U.S. was divided into four and then three divisions. Each division contained several departments, and the departments were divided into districts and subdistricts. The boundaries changed with more or less frequency, creating possible confusion for the unwary reader.

9. For the story of Reynolds's controversial fight with the Cheyennes under Chief Two Moon, see J. W. Vaughn, *The Reynolds Campaign on Powder River.*

10. Wilbur S. Nye, *Carbine and Lance: The Story of Old Fort Sill,* 152–53.

11. Mackenzie to Assistant Adjutant General, Department of Texas (hereafter cited as AAG, DT), June 4, 1872, in Ernest Wallace, ed., *Ranald S. Mackenzie's Official Correspondence Relating to Texas, 1873–1879, 1:73;* Tatum to Sheridan, July 11, 1872, Philip H. Sheridan Papers, Manuscript Division, Library of Congress, Washington, D.C.; Nye, *Carbine and Lance,* 165.

12. Mackenzie to AAG, DT, Apr. 24, May 1, May 3, 1872, in Wallace, *Mackenzie's Official Correspondence,* 1:54–60.

13. Mackenzie to AAG, DT, Apr. 9, 24, 1872; and Special Order No. 86, Department of Texas, all in Wallace, *Mackenzie's Official Correspondence,* 1:51–52, 53, 54–55. Comfort's offense was not stated.

14. "Recollections of John A. Wilcox," Papers of the Order of Indian Wars, Military History Institute, Carlisle Barracks, Pa.; Strong, *My Frontier Days,* 32. The McKinney and Heyl encounters are described in Hamilton, *Sentinel of the Southern Plains,* 125–26. See Ernest R. Archambeau, ed., "Monthly Reports of the Fourth Cavalry, 1872–1874," *Panhandle-Plains Historical Review* 38 (1965): 99–101, for listings of most of the scouts undertaken.

15. Special Orders No. 102, Department of Texas, May 31, 1872, in Wallace, *Mackenzie's Official Correspondence,* 1:71–72. The Freshwater Fork of the Brazos is now known as the White River. It was sometimes referred to as Catfish Creek.

16. John P. Hatch (C.O. Fort Concho) to C.O., District of New Mexico, Mar. 31, 1872; Hatch to AAG, DT, Apr. 15, 1872; Hatch to AAG, DT, May 16, 1872; McLaughlin's Report, May 15, 1872, all in Wallace, *Mackenzie's Official Correspondence,* 1:45–58, 63–39.

17. Sheridan to Augur, Apr. 20, 1872, in ibid., 1:53; Sheridan to Augur, June 11, 1872, Sheridan Papers.

18. *Galveston Daily News,* June 27, 1872, quoted in J'Nell LaVerne Pate, "Colonel Ranald Slidell Mackenzie's First Four Years with the Fourth Cavalry in Texas, 1871–1874" (master's thesis, Texas Christian University, 1960), 94–95; Townsend to Augur, July 1, 1872, and Augur to Townsend, July 1, 1872, in Wallace, *Mackenzie's Official Correspondence,* 1:98.

19. Mackenzie to AAG, DT, June 28, 1872, and Mackenzie to AAG, DT, July 5, 1872, in Wallace, *Mackenzie's Official Correspondence,* 1:94–95, 100–101.

20. Ibid.; Mackenzie to July 22, 1872, in ibid., 110–23. Wallace, *Mackenzie,* 67–68, traces Mackenzie's route in detail.

21. Mackenzie to AAG, DT, August 7, 1872, in Wallace, *Mackenzie's Official Correspondence*, 1:127–28. Both routes are carefully worked out in Wallace, *Mackenzie*, 69–73.

22. Strong, *My Frontier Days*, 34; Mackenzie to AAG, DT, Aug. 15, 1872, in Wallace, *Mackenzie's Official Correspondence*, 1:129–30.

23. Wallace, *Mackenzie*, 72–73; Mackenzie to AAG, DT, Sept. 3, 1872, in Wallace, *Mackenzie's Official Correspondence*, 1:133–34.

24. *Gainesville Gazette*, Aug. 10, 1872, quoted in Wallace, *Mackenzie*, 77; Grierson to Sherman, Oct. 10, 1872, quoted in Frank M. Temple, "Colonel Grierson in the Southwest," *Panhandle-Plains Historical Review* 30 (1957): 37; Annual Report for 1872, Sept. 28, 1872, in Wallace, *Mackenzie's Official Correspondence*, 1:139.

25. AAG, DT, to Davidson, Oct. 1, 1872, Letters Sent, DT, RG 393, NA; *Galveston Daily News*, Oct. 25, 1872, quoted in Pate, "Mackenzie's First Four Years," 103.

26. G. P. Buel (C.O. Fort Richardson) to AAG, DT, June 18, 1872, and Mackenzie to AAG, DT, June 20, 1872, with endorsement by Sheridan, July 16, 1872, in Wallace, *Mackenzie's Official Correspondence*, 1:87–90.

27. Mackenzie to AAG, DT, Oct. 12, 1872, in Wallace, *Mackenzie's Official Correspondence*, 1:141–42; Charlton to Carter, February, 1921, in Carter, *Old Sergeant's Story*, 85.

28. Mackenzie to AAG, DT, Oct. 12, 1872, in Wallace, *Mackenzie's Official Correspondence*, 1:142; William A. Thompson, "Scouting with Mackenzie," *Cavalry Journal* 10 (1897): 430. Nye, *Carbine and Lance*, 162, gives the Indians' version of the fight.

29. Thompson, "Scouting with Mackenzie," 430; Charlton to Carter, Feb. 1921, in Carter, *Old Sergeant's Story*, 85; Joseph Mills Hanson, "Ranald Slidell Mackenzie," *Cavalry Journal*, Jan.–Feb. 1934, 29.

30. Mackenzie to AAG, DT, Oct. 12, 1872, Wallace, *Mackenzie's Official Correspondence*, 1:142–43. Thompson, "Scouting with Mackenzie," 431, attributes the number fifty-two to Indian sources.

31. Charlton to Carter, Feb. 1921, in Carter, *Old Sergeant's Story*, 86; Mackenzie to AAG, DT, Oct. 12, 1872, in Wallace, *Mackenzie's Official Correspondence*, 1:143.

32. Lawrie Tatum, *Our Red Brothers, and the Peace Policy of President Ulysses S. Grant*, 137–44; Nye, *Carbine and Lance*, 162–63. See also Wallace, *Mackenzie*, 86–87, and Pate, "Mackenzie's First Four Years," 122–24. For Indian troubles in Texas before the Civil War, see Harold B. Simpson, *Cry Comanche* (Hillsboro, Tex.: Hill Junior College Press, 1979).

33. Mackenzie to AAG, DT, Oct. 12, 1872, in Wallace, *Mackenzie's Official Correspondence*, 1:144, Wallace, *Mackenzie*, 84; Charlton to Carter, Jan. 12, 1921, in Carter, *Old Sergeant's Story*, 62.

Chapter 8. Down on the Rio Grande

1. Ernest R. Archambeau, "Monthly Reports of the Fourth Cavalry, 1872–1874," *Panhandle-Plains Historical Review* 38 (1965): 105–110;

Ernest Wallace, *Ranald S. Mackenzie on the Texas Frontier*, 88; Robert G. Carter, *On the Border with Mackenzie;* 394–97.

2. Carter, *On the Border*, 398; Archambeau, "Monthly Reports," 106–109.

3. Wallace, *Mackenzie*, 88; Archambeau, "Monthly Reports," 106–107. The distribution of companies in Jan. 1873 was A, B, C, and E at Fort Richardson; D, G, I, and L at Fort Concho; F and H at Fort Griffin; K at Fort Bliss; and M at Fort Brown.

4. A brief review of the overall problem can be found in Robert D. Gregg, *The Influence of Border Troubles on Relations between the United States and Mexico, 1876–1910*, 11–16. See also J'Nell Pate, "United States–Mexican Border Conflicts, 1870–1880," *West Texas Historical Association Yearbook* 38 (Oct. 1962): 175–94.

5. A. M. Gibson, *The Kickapoos, Lords of the Middle Border*, 201–207.

6. *San Antonio Express*, Aug. 5, 1871; *Austin Tri-Weekly Statesman*, Sept. 9, 1871; Ernest Wallace and Adrian S. Anderson, "R. S. Mackenzie and the Kickapoos: The Raid into Mexico, 1873," *Arizona and the West* 7 (1965): 108–109; Pate, "Border Conflicts," 178–79; Gibson, *Kickapoos*, 234–35.

7. Sherman to Augur, Feb. 5, 1873, in Ernest Wallace, ed., *Ranald S. Mackenzie's Official Correspondence Relating to Texas, 1873–1879*, 1:161–62; Augur to Sherman, Feb. 19, 1873, Letters Sent, Department of Texas, RG 393, NA.

8. Archambeau, "Monthly Reports," 110–11, 116–18.

9. Carter, *On the Border*, 416–17.

10. Ibid., 421.

11. Ibid., 422–23. This is second-hand testimony, but Carter made notes after Mackenzie told him of the conversation, and if the quotes are not exact, there is no doubt that they reflect Sheridan's temperament.

12. Richard A. Thompson, *Crossing the Border with the Fourth Cavalry*, 9, expresses his belief that Grant was in on the plan. See, however, Paul Andrew Hutton, *Phil Sheridan and His Army*, 222–25, 412 n. 58, for a differing opinion. Robert M. Utley, *Frontier Regulars: The United States Army and the Indian, 1866–1891*, 347–49, also doubts that Sheridan had higher approval for the raid.

13. E. B. Beaumont, "Over the Border with Mackenzie," *United Service* 12 (Mar. 1885): 282; Carter, *On the Border*, 425, 427.

14. Beaumont, "Over the Border," 283; Carter, *On the Border*, 424; Wallace, *Mackenzie*, 97; Gibson, *Kickapoos*, 240. Beaumont is the only source for the offer of a reward.

15. Carter, *On the Border*, 430, 426–27.

16. Hutton, *Sheridan and His Army*, 222; Gibson, *Kickapoos*, 240; Mackenzie to AAG, DT, May 23, 1873, in Wallace, *Mackenzie's Official Correspondence*, 1:167–72 (hereafter referred to, with its endorsements, as "Mackenzie's Report"). I presume that the scouts informed Mackenzie that the warriors had departed; I have found no primary source which documents the assertion, but it stands to reason that this was the message, as it explains the great haste with which the expedition was started on its way.

17. Carter, *On the Border,* 429; Beaumont, "Over the Border," 284.

18. Carter, *On the Border,* 429.

19. Carter, *On the Border,* 431, 433; Beaumont, "Over the Border," 286.

20. Beaumont, "Over the Border," 285; Carter, *On the Border,* 335–36. Carter implies that only a few minutes were lost in the delay, but Thompson, *Crossing the Border,* 48, is probably more correct in saying that the halt consumed closer to an hour.

21. Carter, *On the Border,* 440, 447.

22. Ibid., 439–43; Beaumont, "Over the Border," 285–86; "Mackenzie's Report," 168.

23. "Mackenzie's Report," 170; Carter, *On the Border,* 443; Beaumont, "Over the Border," 286. The number and type of wounds are from Mackenzie's account. Carter and Beaumont both mention a man with a broken leg.

24. Carter, *On the Border,* 447–48; Beaumont, "Over the Border," 286.

25. Carter, *On the Border,* 448–53; Beaumont, "Over the Border," 286–87.

26. Carter, *On the Border,* 455–57; Beaumont, "Over the Border," 287.

27. Carter, *On the Border,* 458–60. Beaumont, one of those who supposedly challenged Mackenzie, makes no mention of it in his brief sketch, "Over the Border." Beaumont's failure to mention the conversation does not, of course, prove that it did not take place, but he demonstrates no sign of concern or remorse in his writing.

28. Carter, *On the Border,* 466. Wallace, *Mackenzie,* 104, says that the citations "may seem . . . somewhat out of order in as much as the only defenders were women and a few old men." Utley, *Frontier Regulars,* 349, is rather more severe in judging the action.

29. Mizner to AAG, DT, May 20, 1873, and Sheridan to Belknap, May 22, 1873, in Wallace, *Mackenzie's Official Correspondence,* 1:165–66; Augur to Sheridan, May 22, 1873, Letters Sent, DT, RG 393, NA; Sheridan to Belknap, May 28, 1873; Belknap to Sheridan, May 31, 1873; and Sherman to Sheridan, June 3, 1873, Philip H. Sheridan Papers, Manuscript Division, Library of Congress, Washington, D.C. See Hutton, *Sheridan and His Army,* 23–24, on Sheridan's efforts to ensure government support.

30. Sheridan to Mackenzie, June 2, 1873, Sheridan Papers; Schuhardt to Mackenzie, May 19, 1873, Gilcrease Letterbook; Shafter to Mackenzie, May 21, 1873, and Mackenzie to Augur, May 29, 1873, both in Wallace, *Mackenzie's Official Correspondence,* 1:177–81.

31. Carter, *On the Border,* 460–62.

32. *New York Times,* June 2, 16, 1873; *New York Tribune,* May 26, 1873. J'Nell LaVerne Pate, "Colonel Ranald Slidell Mackenzie's First Four Years with the Fourth Cavalry in Texas" (master's thesis, Texas Christian University, 1960), says that both the *Dallas Herald,* May 31, July 26, 1873, and the *Fort Worth Democrat,* May 23, 1873, expressed reservations about the wisdom of the raid. *Austin Daily Democratic Statesman,* May 23, 1873; *San Antonio Express,* May 23, 1873; *Galveston Daily News,* May 23, 1873; Thompson, *Crossing the Border,* 73–73; Wallace, *Mackenzie's Official Correspondence,* 1:189–90.

33. Mackenzie to Augur, May 23, 29, 1873, and Mackenzie to Schuhardt, May 28, 1873, in Wallace, *Mackenzie's Official Correspondence*, I:174–75, 179–81, 183; Augur to Mackenzie, June 11, 1873, Ranald Slidell Mackenzie Letterbook, U.S. Army Military History Institute, Carlisle Barracks, Pa. (hereafter cited as MHI Letterbook).

34. Mackenzie to Williams, May 22, 1873, Gilcrease Letterbook. The negotiations with the Kickapoos are covered in Gibson, *Kickapoos*, 244–52.

35. Mackenzie to AAG, DT, May 23, 1873, in Wallace, *Mackenzie's Official Correspondence*, 1:173. The Comanche prisoners had been held at Fort Concho until the summer of 1873, when they were taken to Fort Sill and returned to their people; Wilbur S. Nye, *Carbine and Lance: The Story of Old Fort Sill*, 165–66.

36. Williams to Mackenzie, May 28, 1873, and Atkinson to Mackenzie, July 7, 1873, MHI Letterbook; Gibson, *Kickapoos*, 247–50. Gibson says that Mackenzie's raid was decisive in causing the Indians to agree to move.

37. Gibson, *Kickapoos*, 347; Mackenzie to Augur, June 30, 1873, and Williams to Mackenzie, July 7, 1873, MHI Letterbook; Parker (Mackenzie's adjutant) to Augur, Aug. 18, 1873, with enclosures, in Wallace, *Mackenzie's Official Correspondence*, 2:51–52.

38. Mackenzie to Don Victoriano Cepeda, June 2, 1873; Mackenzie to Augur, June 6, 1873; Mackenzie to Williams, June 6, 1873; and Augur to Mackenzie, June 11, 1873, all in MHI Letterbook; Sheridan's endorsement on Mackenzie to Augur, June 6, 1873, in Wallace, *Mackenzie's Official Correspondence*, 2:24.

39. Mackenzie to Augur, June 30, 1873, MHI Letterbook; Mackenzie to Augur, June 28, 1873, with endorsements of Augur, Sheridan, and Sherman, in Wallace, *Mackenzie's Official Correspondence*, 2:33–35.

40. Sheridan to Belknap, May 28, 1873, in Wallace, *Mackenzie's Official Correspondence*, 1:179; Sheridan to Mackenzie, June 2, 1873, MHI Letterbook; Draft of Sheridan's Annual Report, Oct. 27, 1873, Sheridan Papers; Carter, *On the Border*, 462.

41. Mackenzie to AAG, DT, June 1, 1874, Gilcrease Letterbook.

42. Augur to Mackenzie, June 26, 1873, MHI Letterbook, notes report that Mackenzie was "quite ill." Report of Medical Director, Department of Texas, Sept. 12, 1873.

43. Mackenzie to AAG, DT, Sept. 12, 17, 1873; Mackenzie to Adjutant General, U.S. Army, Dec. 4, 1873, all in AGO 3877, ACP 1873, RG 94, NA; Joseph H. Dorst, "Ranald Slidell Mackenzie," *Twentieth Annual Reunion of the Association of Graduates of the United States Military Academy at West Point, New York*, 18.

Chapter 9. The Red River War

1. This account of the beginnings of the Red River War is drawn from Thomas C. Battey, *A Quaker among the Indians;* Wilbur S. Nye, *Carbine and Lance: The Story of Old Fort Sill;* and James L. Haley, *The Buffalo War.* Nye,

following Battey, puts considerable stress on the negative effect of the land survey.

2. Nye, *Carbine and Lance*, 182–87. Nye maintains that the Indians' desire for revenge would have meant war even if other causes had not been present.

3. The most polite English rendition of Isa-tai's name is found in Nye, *Carbine and Lance*, 190. Nye translates it as Rear-End-of-a-Wolf. Ernest Wallace and E. A. Hoeble, *The Comanches: Lords of the South Plains*, 324, give it as Coyote Droppings, while Haley, *Buffalo War*, 52, probably most accurately reflects the blunt-talking Comanches by calling the medicine man Wolf Shit. For the rise of Isa-tai, see Battey, *Quaker among the Indians*, 302–303.

4. For the Adobe Walls fight, T. Lindsay Baker and Billy R. Harrison, *Adobe Walls: The History and Archaeology of the 1874 Trading Post*, is definitive. See Nye, *Carbine and Lance*, 192–200, for the Lost Valley fight.

5. Paul Andrew Hutton, *Phil Sheridan and His Army*, 248; Haley, *Buffalo War*, 105–106.

6. General Order No. 4, July 10, 1874, in Ernest Wallace, ed., *Ranald S. Mackensie's Official Correspondence Relating to Texas, 1873–1879*, 2:77–78; Sherman to Sheridan, July 15, 1874, and Sheridan to Sherman, July 21, 1874, in Joe F. Taylor, "The Indian Campaign on the Staked Plains, 1874–1875: Military Correspondence from the War Department, Adjutant General's Office, File 2815–1874," *Panhandle-Plains Historical Review* 34 (1961): 10, 12; Sheridan to Pope, July 22, 1874, Philip H. Sheridan Papers, Manuscript Division, Library of Congress, Washington, D.C.

7. Augur to Sheridan, July 22, 1874; Augur to Sheridan, July 23, 1874; and Augur to Mackenzie, July 23, 1874, all in Letters Sent, Department of Texas.

8. Augur to Sheridan, July 28, 1874, ibid. This plan was formalized in Augur's written order to Mackenzie, August 28, 1874, in Wallace, *Mackenzie's Official Correspondence*, 2:80–82.

9. Augur's written order to Mackenzie, Aug. 28, 1874, and Mackenzie to Augur, Aug. 28, 1874, in Wallace, *Mackenzie's Official Correspondence*, 2:80–82. Wallace took this from Robert G. Carter, *On the Border, with Mackenzie; or, Winning West Texas from the Comanches*, 476–78. Carter describes the Red River War as if he were a participant, which he was not.

10. Carter, *On the Border*, 473. The supply camp was located about twelve miles southeast of present-day Crosbyton, Texas. See Wayne Parker, "Mackenzie's Supply Camp," *Grain Producer's News* 30, no. 7 (July 1979): 4–7, for an archaeological survey of the site. For Mackenzie's movements, see Wallace, *Mackenzie's Official Correspondence*, 2:112–18, as well as Mackenzie to AAG, DT, Sept. 19, 1874, and "Mackenzie's Journal of Campaign: Part I, The First Expedition, September 20–29, 1874," both in ibid., 2:93, 119–24.

11. Wallace, *Mackenzie's Official Correspondence*, 119–21. See also the account, based on his diary, of C. A. P. Hatfield Folder x-25, Papers of the Order of Indian Wars, U.S. Army Military History Institutes, Carlisle Barracks, Pa. This is similar to an article in the *Tulia Herald*, August 1, 1935, a typescript of which is in the Bruce Gerdes Papers, Panhandle-Plains Historical Museum, Canyon, Tex.

12. Henry W. Strong, *My Frontier Days and Indian Fights on the Plains of Texas*, 56, tells of the taunts shouted by the Indians.

13. Quote from Charlton to Carter, n.d., in Robert G. Carter, *The Old Sergeant's Story: Fighting Indians and Bad Men in Texas from 1870 to 1876*, 107.

14. Quote from Hatfield in Papers of the Order of Indian Wars.

15. Nye, *Carbine and Lance*, 221, tells of Maman-ti's medicine. One veteran's story states that the descending troops were subjected to "a fierce fire," but there is no other account to support this. Eugene M. Beck to R. B. Smyth, Nov. 14, 1938, R. B. Smyth Papers, Panhandle-Plains Historical Museum, Canyon, Tex.

16. Beck to Smyth, November 19, 1938, Smyth Papers. Carter, *On the Border*, 490–91, repeats all three of these stories, indicating Beck as a probable source for Carter.

17. Beaumont to Dorst, Dec. 7, 1905, Joseph Dorst Papers, U.S. Military Academy Archives, West Point, N.Y.; Beck to Smyth, Nov. 19, 1938, Smyth Papers.

18. The sources agree that the movement back to Tule Canyon began by 3:00 P.M. Beaumont to Dorst, Dec. 7, 1905, and Dorst to Adjutant General, U.S. Army, Mar. 12, 1894, Dorst Papers; Hatfield, Papers of the Order of Indian Wars.

19. "Mackenzie's Journal of Campaign, Part I," in Wallace, *Mackenzie's Official Correspondence*, 2:123–24; Strong, *My Frontier Days*, 61; Beck to Smyth, Nov. 19, 1938, Smyth Papers; Charlton to Carter, n.d., in Carter, *Old Sergeant's Story*, 109. Mackenzie, as usual, counted only bodies recovered. There is no reason to believe any of the estimates, but their existence strongly suggests a larger number of Indian dead than the official total. Nye, *Carbine and Lance*, 224, describes the plight of the Indians immediately following the fight.

20. "Mackenzie's Journal of Campaign: Part II, The First Expedition, September 29–October 20, 1874," in Wallace, *Mackenzie's Official Correspondence*, 2:136–42; William A. Thompson, "Scouting with Mackenzie," *Cavalry Journal* 10 (1897), adds some details to Mackenzie's journal report. Those interested in a detailed itinerary of this and the other scouts should consult Ernest Wallace, *Ranald S. Mackenzie on the Texas Frontier*, 150–66 and the map opposite 146.

21. Mackenzie to AAG, DT, Oct. 29, 1874, in Wallace, *Mackenzie's Official Correspondence*, 2:150–53.

22. Mackenzie to AAG, DT, November 9, 1874, in ibid., 157; Dorst to Adjutant General, U.S. Army, Mar. 12, 1894, Dorst Papers.

23. "Mackenzie's Journal of Campaign," in Wallace, *Mackenzie's Official Correspondence*, 2:119–29, 136–42, 154–56, 187–90, gives a good idea of the difficulties of the campaign. Mackenzie to AAG, DT, Nov. 9, 1874, in ibid., 157–58.

24. Captain Stebastian Gunther to Augur, Jan. 6, 1875; Mackenzie to Augur, Nov. 27, 1874; and Mackenzie to Augur, Dec. 2, 1874, all in ibid., 175, 183, 185–86.

25. Strong, *My Frontier Days,* 66.

26. Mackenzie to Augur, Nov. 16, 1874; Mackenzie to Augur, Nov. 27, 1874; and Mackenzie to Augur, Dec. 2, 1874, all in Wallace, *Mackenzie's Official Correspondence,* 2:165, 174, 183.

27. Mackenzie's Journal of Campaign: Part IV," in Wallace, *Mackenzie's Official Correspondence,* 2:187–89; Carter, *On the Border,* 514–17. Warrington received the Medal of Honor for his part in the fray.

28. "Mackenzie's Journal: Part IV," in Wallace, *Mackenzie's Official Correspondence,* 2:189–90.

29. The incident with the sergeant is in Carter, *On the Border,* 518.

30. Neill to Assistant Adjutant General, Department of Missouri, Oct. 4, 1874, and Sheridan to Sherman, Oct. 29, 1874, in Wallace, *Mackenzie's Official Correspondence,* 2:125–26, 153–54; Taylor, "Indian Campaign," 74.

31. Thompson, "Scouting with Mackenzie," 433. For the overall war, see Haley, *Buffalo War;* Robert M. Utley, *Frontier Regulars: The United States Army and the Indian, 1866–1891;* and William H. Leckie, *The Military Conquest of the Southern Plains.* Hutton, *Sheridan and His Army,* 260–61, notes that it had not been "a particularly graceful campaign" but ends by quoting with approval Sheridan's claim that this was "the most successful" of any war against the Indians.

Chapter 10. Jailer to Half-starving Criminals

1. The drift of the discussions regarding Fort Sill and the proposed McClellan's Creek post can be followed in Ernest Wallace, ed., *Ranald S. Mackenzie's Official Correspondence Relating to Texas, 1873–1879,* 2:104, 158–59, 161, 170, 171–72, 177–78.

2. Paul Andrew Hutton, *Phil Sheridan and His Army,* 253; Allen Lee Hamilton, *Sentinel of the Southern Plains: Fort Richardson and the Northwest Texas Frontier, 1866–1878,* 167; Sheridan to Belknap, July 23, Nov. 8, 1874, in Philip H. Sheridan Papers, Manuscript Division, Library of Congress, Washington, D.C. For a defense of Davidson, see Homer K. Davidson, *Black Jack Davidson: A Cavalry Commander on the Western Frontier* (Glendale, Calif.: Arthur H. Clark Co., 1974), 13–14. For Sheridan's relationship with Grierson, see Hutton, *Sheridan and His Army,* 228–30.

3. Sheridan to Belknap, Jan. 2, 1875; Sheridan to Belknap, Feb. 9, 1875; and Sheridan to Belknap, Feb. 24, 1875, all in Sheridan Papers. Hutton, *Sheridan and His Army,* 262–73, deals with the Louisiana situation.

4. "Record of Medical History, Fort Sill, Oklahoma," Mar. 1875, Fort Sill Archives, Fort Sill, Okla. (hereafter cited as Fort Sill Medical History). Description of Fort Sill based on Parker to M. F. Parker, Oct. 4, 1876, and Parker to R. Wayne Parker, Oct. 7, 1876, James Parker Papers, U.S. Military Academy Archives, West Point, N.Y.; quote from last. See also the description in Wilbur S. Nye, *Carbine and Lance: The Story of Old Fort Sill,* 49–50, 280–83.

5. Hutton, *Sheridan and His Army,* 118–20; Richard N. Ellis, *General*

Pope and U.S. Indian Policy, x; Mackenzie to Sheridan, Apr. 17, 1875, Gilcrease Letterbook. James L. Haley, *The Buffalo War,* 206–207, asserts that Miles was behind Pope's effort to split the command.

6. Sheridan to Pope, Mar. 30, 1875, Sheridan Papers; Mackenzie to Sheridan, Apr. 17, 1875, Gilcrease Letterbook. The latter letter, along with a selection of others from the Gilcrease Letterbook, can be found in *American Scene* 8, no. 2 (1967).

7. Sheridan to Pope, Apr. 19, 1875, Sheridan Papers.

8. Mackenzie to Sheridan, Apr. 17, 1875, Gilcrease Letterbook.

9. Pope to Drum, Apr. 21, 1875, transmitting Mackenzie's report, in Joe F. Taylor, "The Indian Campaign on the Staked Plains, 1874–1875: Military Correspondence from the War Department Adjutant General's File 215— 1874," *Panhandle-Plains Historical Review* 35 (1962): 218; William T. Hagan, *United States–Comanche Relations: The Reservation Years,* 115– 16; Fort Sill Medical History, Apr. 1875. On the condition of the Indians, see "Report of J. M. Haworth," in *Report of the Secretary of the Interior,* 44th Cong., 1st sess., H. Exec. Doc. 1680, 1875, 774–75.

10. "Report of Haworth," 774; G. W. Conover, *Sixty Years in Southwest Oklahoma,* 73–74; Bill Neeley, *Quanah Parker and His People,* 107–10; Mackenzie to Pope, May 15, 25, 1875, in Gilcrease Letterbook; Fort Sill Medical History, June 1875.

11. Hutton, *Sheridan and His Army,* 258–60. For officers' attitudes toward the Indians, see Richard N. Ellis, "The Humanitarian Soldiers," *Journal of Arizona History* 10, no. 2 (Summer 1969): 53–66, and Thomas C. Leonard, "Red, White, and the Army Blue: Empathy and Anger in the American West," *American Quarterly* 26 (1974), reprinted in Peter Karsten, ed., *The Military in America: From the Colonial Era to the Present,* 2d ed. (New York: The Free Press, 1986). On who was punished, see Hagan, *United States–Comanche Relations,* 120.

12. James Parker, *The Old Army,* 48–49; Neeley, *Quanah,* 112–13; Lessing H. Nohl, Jr., "Bad Hand: The Military Career of Ranald Slidell Mackenzie, 1877–1889" (Ph.D. diss., University of New Mexico, 1962), 151. Quote by Quanah from John Edward Weems, *Death Song: The Last of the Indian Wars,* 229.

13. Parker, *Old Army,* 49–50. The story can be found in Ernest Wallace, *Ranald S. Mackenzie on the Texas Frontier,* 170–71, and Cynthia Ann Chamberlain, "Colonel Ranald Slidell Mackenzie's Administration of the Western Section of the Indian Territory, 1875–1877" (master's thesis, Texas Tech University, 1965), 39–40.

14. Mackenzie to Pope, Sept. 5, 1875, Gilcrease Letterbook. For the common military opinion of Haworth, see Nye, *Carbine and Lance,* 164–65, 200–201, and Davidson, *Black Jack Davidson,* 182–86.

15. Sheridan to Augur, Nov. 27, 1874, and Sheridan's endorsement of report, Apr. 10, 1877, Sheridan Papers; Mackenzie's endorsement on Lieutenant Francis W. Mansfield to Post Adjutant, May 4, 1875, Taylor, "Indian Campaign," 240–42.

16. The relevant documents regarding the purchase of the sheep can be

found in Taylor, "Indian Campaign," 247–53. For the goats, see Mackenzie to Assistant Adjutant General, Department of the Missouri, Apr. 24, 1876, Letters Sent, Fort Sill Archives, Fort Sill, Okla. For the distribution and fate of the sheep, see James Mooney, "Calendar History of the Kiowa Indians," 339–40, and Hagan, *United States–Comanche Relations*, 128. Nye, *Carbine and Lance*, 249–50, perfectly captures the Indians' attitude toward the woolly animals.

17. Chamberlain, "Colonel Mackenzie's Administration," 58–60; James Parker to R. W. Parker, Oct. 7, 1876, Parker Papers; Nye, *Carbine and Lance*, 250. Nye noted on his p. 253 that some individual Indians such as Tabananica and Quanah did become successful stockmen.

18. Mackenzie to Pope, Sept. 5, 1875, Gilcrease Letterbook.

19. Jean L. Zimmerman, "Colonel Ranald S. Mackenzie at Fort Sill," *Chronicles of Oklahoma* 42 (Spring 1966):12–21, covers this problem thoroughly. Quote from Mackenzie to Assistant Adjutant General, Department of the Missouri, June 6, 1876, Letters Sent, Fort Sill Archives. On the Cheyenne breakout, see George Bird Grinnell, *The Fighting Cheyennes*, 398–413.

20. Joseph H. Dorst, "Ranald Slidell Mackenzie," *Twentieth Annual Reunion of the Association of Graduates of the United States Military Academy at West Point, New York*, 12; orders for Lieutenant Mason, May 10, 1876, Letters Sent, Fort Sill Archives; Haworth's report to Commissioner, Sept. 20, 1875, in Carl Coke Rister, ed., "Early Accounts of Indian Depredations," *West Texas Historical Association Yearbook* 2 (June 1926): 61.

21. Lillian Gunter, "Life of Julian Gunter," Lillian Gunter Papers, Panhandle-Plains Historical Museum, Canyon, Texas. Mackenzie to Lieutenant Alexander Rodgers, July 19, 1877, Letters Sent, Fort Sill Archives.

22. Fort Sill Medical History, reports for Apr., May, June, July 1875.

23. Fort Sill Medical History, report for Sept. 1875, describes the foreign visitors. The Eisenring story is in Zimmerman, "Mackenzie at Fort Sill," 16–17.

24. Barbara A. Neal Ledbetter, *Fort Belknap, Frontier Saga: Indians, Negroes, and Anglo-Americans on the Texas Frontier*, 54; A. C. Greene, *The Last Captive*, 133.

25. Mackenzie to Pope, Dec. 18, 1875, and Pope to Mackenzie, Dec. 7, 1875, in Gilcrease Letterbook.

26. *New York Times*, Apr. 7, 1876.

27. 44th Cong., 1st sess., H. Exec. Doc. 175, serial 1691, 1–3.

28. Ibid., 4; *New York Times*, May 27, 1876.

29. *Army and Navy Journal*, Apr. 1, 1876. This item is copied into the Gilcrease Letterbook just before Mackenzie to Sherman, April 23, 1876, defending himself.

30. *New York Times*, Apr. 8, 1876; Mackenzie to Sherman, Apr. 30, 1876, Gilcrease Letterbook; Sheridan to Mackenzie, May 3, 1876, Sheridan Papers.

31. Mackenzie to Sheridan, May 11, 1876, Gilcrease Letterbook; Mackenzie to Sherman, May 22, 1876, William T. Sherman Papers, Manuscript

Division, Library of Congress, Washington, D.C. For the Belknap affair, see Hutton, *Sheridan and His Army*, 305–10. For Reynolds's misfortunes, see J. W. Vaughn, *The Reynolds Campaign on Powder River.*

32. Mackenzie's concern that some might think him "irrational" is in Mackenzie to Sherman, May 22, 1876, Sherman Papers.

33. Mackenzie to Sheridan, Mar. 29, 1877, Gilcrease Letterbook; Sheridan to Sherman, Apr. 20, 1878, Sheridan Papers.

34. Mackenzie to Sherman, May 9, June 3, Sept. 4, 1875, all in Sherman Papers.

35. Sherman to Sheridan, Nov. 12, 1875, Sheridan Papers.

36. Mackenzie to Sheridan, June 9, 1879, Gilcrease Letterbook. Mackenzie mentions his go-around with malaria in Mackenzie to Sherman, Apr. 23, 1876, ibid.

Chapter 11. The Very Man for the Job

1. John S. Gray, *Centennial Campaign: The Sioux War of 1876,* is a good, generally well reasoned account of the war. For shorter versions, consult Robert M. Utley, *Frontier Regulars: The United States Army and the Indian, 1866–1891,* 236–91, and Paul Andrew Hutton, *Phil Sheridan and His Army,* 282–330.

2. Gray, *Centennial Campaign,* 258–61; Hutton, *Sheridan and His Army,* 322–23; Paul L. Hedren, *Fort Laramie in 1876: Chronicle of a Frontier Post at War,* 135; Mackenzie to Sheridan, Aug. 1, 1876, Gilcrease Letterbook.

3. Gray, *Centennial Campaign,* 260–63; Sherman to Mackenzie, Aug. 22, 1876, and Mackenzie to Crook, Sept. 9, 1876, both in Gilcrease Letterbook.

4. Mackenzie to Crook, Sept. 30, 1876, Gilcrease Letterbook; George W. Manypenny, *Our Indian Wards,* 344.

5. Mackenzie to Crook, Sept. 9, 1876, Gilcrease Letterbook; Hutton, *Sheridan and His Army,* 325; George Bird Grinnell, *The Fighting Cheyennes,* 360; Mackenzie to Crook, Oct. 18, 1876, Gilcrease Letterbook.

6. For this and the following paragraph, see Grinnell, *Fighting Cheyennes,* 360–61; Luther North, *Man of the Plains: Recollections of Luther North, 1856–1882,* 201–204; George Bird Grinnell, *Two Great Scouts and Their Pawnee Battalion: The Experiences of Frank J. North and Luther H. North,* 249–50, 253–55. North called the third chief Yellow Leaf, but he is apparently the same as Red Leaf.

7. John G. Bourke, "Mackenzie's Last Fight with the Cheyennes: A Winter Campaign in Wyoming and Montana," *Journal of the Military Service Institution* 2 (1890): 31–35.

8. See Hutton, *Sheridan and His Army,* 123–29, for a good brief character sketch of Crook. Quotes from John F. Finerty, *War-Path and Bivouac; or, the Conquest of the Sioux,* 291 and Bourke, "Mackenzie's Last Fight," 3. Mackenzie's dress was described by Sergeant James McClellan in *Motor Travel,* Feb. 1931, as quoted in Fred H. Werner, *The Dull Knife Battle,* 77–78. The idea that Mackenzie was reckless was refuted by Luther North.

9. These episodes are from Private Smith's diary and are quoted in Sherry

L. Smith, *Sagebrush Soldier: Private William Earl Smith's View of the Sioux War of 1876*, 36–37, 46, 54, 38.

10. Bourke, "Mackenzie's Last Fight," 33.

11. Diary of Richard I. Dodge, Nov. 16, 1876, Newberry Library, quoted in Smith, *Sagebrush Soldier*, 47–48.

12. James B. Kincaid, "Diary of Sgt. James B. Kincaid, Co. B, 4th Cav., Aug. 5, 1876 to 1881," *Winners of the West* 16, no. 6 (July 1939): 3.

13. Smith Diary, Nov. 23, 1876, in Smith, *Sagebrush Soldier*, 59; Special Field Orders No. 3, on Crazy Woman's Fork, Nov. 22, 1876, Joseph Dorst Papers, U.S. Military Academy Archives, West Point, N.Y.

14. Mackenzie gives the distance as fifteen to twenty miles; Mackenzie's report to Crook, *Army and Navy Journal*, Dec. 16, 1876, 293; North, *Man of the Plains*, 21–12; "McClellan's Journal," in Werner, *Dull Knife Battle*, 69.

15. Grinnell, *Fighting Cheyennes*, 369. Smith, *Sagebrush Soldier*, 68–69, gives as good an explanation of the Cheyenne actions as we are likely to have.

16. North, *Man of the Plains*, 21–13; Smith Diary, Nov. 25, 1876, in Smith, *Sagebrush Soldier*, 66.

17. Smith Diary, Nov. 25, 1876, in Smith, *Sagebrush Soldier*, 66; Joe DeBarthe, *The Life and Adventures of Frank Grouard, Chief of Scouts, U.S.A.*, 327; Bourke, "Mackenzie's Last Fight," 45–46; Dorst to Adjutant General, U.S. Army, Mar. 12, 1894, Dorst Papers.

18. Bourke, "Mackenzie's Last Fight," 45–46; Dorst to Adjutant General, U.S. Army, Mar. 17, 1894, Dorst Papers; Grinnell, *Two Great Scouts*, 271; Smith Diary, Nov. 25, 1876, in Smith, *Sagebrush Soldier*, 77.

19. Mackenzie's report to Crook, *Army and Navy Journal*, Dec. 16, 1876, 243; Grinnell, *Two Great Scouts*, 271–72; Bourke, "Mackenzie's Last Fight," 198–99.

20. It is not clear which scout was sent to talk to the Cheyennes. Kincaid, "Diary," 5, and Smith Diary, Nov. 25, 1876, in Smith, *Sagebrush Soldier*, 80, say that it was Frank Grouard. Bourke, "Mackenzie's Last Fight," 199, and Luther North, quoted in Werner, *Dull Knife Battle*, 38, say the scout was Bill Roland (or Rowland). Bourke, "Mackenzie's Last Fight," 200, lists the Seventh Cavalry items recovered at the encampment.

21. Smith Diary, Nov. 25, 1876, in Smith, *Sagebrush Soldier*, 88, 91. Luther North claimed that the temperature never got above twenty-five degrees below zero during the campaign; North, *Man of the Plains*, 217 n. For Mackenzie's reaction to Mckinney's death, see Robert G. Carter, *On the Border with Mackenzie; or, Winning West Texas from the Comanches*, 340.

22. Smith, *Sagebrush Soldier*, 92–93; Bourke, "Mackenzie's Last Fight," 218–19; North, *Man of the Plains*, 216–17.

23. North, *Man of the Plains*, 218; "McClellan's Journal," in Werner, *Dull Knife Battle*, 58.

24. Smith, *Sagebrush Soldier*, 93–94.

25. "McClellan's Journal," in Werner, *Dull Knife Battle*, 59; Smith, *Sagebrush Soldier*, 100–102.

26. Mackenzie's Report to Crook, *Army and Navy Journal*, Dec. 16, 1876, 273; Dull Knife quoted in Ernest Wallace, *Ranald S. Mackenzie on the Texas*

Frontier, 174, from *New York Tribune,* Apr. 23, 1877; Sheridan's Annual Report, Oct. 25, 1877, in *Report of the Secretary of War,* 45th Cong., 2d sess., H. Exec. Doc. 1795, 1877, 56.

27. Dodge Diary, Nov. 29, 1876, in Smith, *Sagebrush Soldier,* 99–100. The remark about suicide seems to be hearsay. I have found no other suggestion that Mackenzie was ever again suicidal.

28. Dodge Diary, Dec. 5, 1876, ibid., 124; reference supplied by Dr. Sherry L. Smith.

29. Smith, *Sagebrush Soldier,* 121.

30. "Mackenzie's Record of Service," in Ernest Wallace, Jr., *Ranald S. Mackenzie's Official Correspondence Relating to Texas, 1873–1879,* 14; Joseph H. Dorst, "Ranald Slidell Mackenzie," *Twentieth Annual Reunion of the Association of Graduates of the United States Military Academy of West Point, New York,* 18; Hutton, *Sheridan and His Army,* 278–80. The classic account of the electoral crisis is C. Vann Woodward, *Reunion & Reaction* (Boston: Little, Brown & Company, 1951).

31. Sheridan to Sherman, Feb. 1877, Philip H. Sheridan Papers, Manuscript Division, Library of Congress, Washington, D.C.; Utley, *Frontier Regulars,* 278–79.

32. Mackenzie to Sheridan, Mar. 29, 1877, Gilcrease Letterbook.

33. Mackenzie to Sherman, n.d., 1877, William T. Sherman Papers, Manuscript Division, Library of Congress, Washington, D.C.

11. Sherman to E. O. C. Ord, July 14, 1875, Sherman Papers; Steele to Maxey, May 30, 1876, in Wallace, *Mackenzie's Official Correspondence,* 2:199; Wallace, *Mackenzie,* 174–75. See also Utley, *Frontier Regulars,* 350–53.

35. Sheridan to Sherman, Nov. 24, 29, 1877, Sherman to Sheridan, Nov. 29, 1877, Sheridan Papers; General Orders No. 10, Dec. 3, 1877, in Wallace, *Mackenzie's Official Correspondence,* 2:201–202; James Parker, *The Old Army,* 86–92, all quotes.

36. Parker, *Old Army,* 99; Lessing H. Nohl, Jr. "Bad Hand: The Military Career of Ranald Slidell Mackenzie, 1877–1889" (Ph.D. diss., University of New Mexico, 1962), 245; Mackenzie to AAG, DT, Apr. 26, 1878, Gilcrease Letterbook.

37. Mackenzie to AAG, DT, n.d., May 22, 28, 1878, Gilcrease Letterbook.

38. General Orders No. 7, June 11, 1878, William B. Shafter Papers, Stanford University Library, Stanford, Calif.

39. Mackenzie to AAG, DT, June 23, 1878, in Wallace, *Mackenzie's Official Correspondence,* 2:204–209; Nuncio's note is given on p. 209.

40. Daniel Cosio Villegas, *United States versus Porfirio Diaz,* trans. Nettie Lee Benson, 179; Sheridan to Sherman, June 24, 1878, Sheridan Papers.

41. Mackenzie to AAG, DT, July 1, 1878, Gilcrease Letterbook; Wallace, *Mackenzie,* 180.

42. Mackenzie to AAG, DT, Sept. 9, 1878, in Wallace, *Mackenzie's Official Correspondence,* 2:218–20; Mackenzie to Young, Sept. 16, 1878, and Young to Assistant Adjutant General, District of the Nueces, Sept. 22, 1878,

S. B. M. Young Papers, U.S. Army Military History Institute, Carlisle Barracks, Pa. For brief descriptions of the entire situation, see Utley, *Frontier Regulars*, 349–56; Wallace, *Mackenzie*, 174–82.

43. Sheridan to Sherman, June 24, 1878, Sheridan Papers; Utley, *Frontier Regulars*, 355; Wallace *Mackenzie*, 182; Josefina Zoraida Vazquez and Lorenzo Meyer, *The United States and Mexico* (Chicago and London: University of Chicago Press, 1985), 82–83; Karl K. Schmitt, *Mexico and the United States, 1921–1973: Conflict and Coexistence* (New York: John Wiley & Sons, 1974), 93–96.

Chapter 12. Last Campaigns

1. Deed Records, Kendall County, Texas, 4: 414, 640, and 5: 184, 493, 494, 571, 572; Records of the General Land Office of Texas, files Bexars-27501, 1989, 2464. I owe special thanks to Katherine Skinner-Klee of Boerne, Texas, for locating these records and supplying me with other information about Kendall County. Elaine H. Schoenfeld of the Archives and Records Division of the General Land Office clarified the way Mackenzie obtained the patent lands. The *Texas Almanac* for 1867 gave the price of land in Kendall County as between two and five dollars an acre.

2. C. Hugo Claus, "Boerne and the Cibolo Valley in Kendall County," *Schuetze's Yarbuch fuer Texas, 1882,* 29–31. Translation on file in the Boerne Public Library. For strangers to the area, it should be noted that Boerne is pronounced "Burney."

3. Ibid.; *San Antonio Daily Express*, March 5, 1887.

4. Robert H. Thonhoff, *San Antonio Stage Lines, 1847–1881,* Southwestern Studies Monograph No. 29 (El Paso: Texas Western Press, 1871), describes the stage connection. Parker to brother, Nov. 12, 1878, and Parker to mother, Jan. 26, 1876, James Parker Papers, U.S. Military Academy Archives, West Point, N.Y., tell of the arrival of Mackenzie's family.

5. Mackenzie to Adjutant General, U.S. Army, Sept. 1, 1884, AGO 3877, ACP 1873, RG 94, NA; Deed Records, Kendall County, Texas, 70: 511–15.

6. The story of the Ute war can be found in Wilson Rockwell, *The Utes: A Forgotten People,* and in much more detail in Marshall Sprague, *Massacre: The Tragedy at White River.* Robert M. Utley, *Frontier Regulars: The United States Army and the Indian, 1866–1891,* 332–42, covers the war concisely.

7. Utley, *Frontier Regulars*, 338–39; Rockwell, *Utes,* 165–66.

8. Sheridan to Ord, Oct. 3, 1879, and C. Upson to Secretary of War, Oct. 4, 1879, in Ernest Wallace, ed., *Ranald S. Mackenzie's Official Correspondence Relating to Texas, 1873–1879,* 2:223, 224.

9. Report for Oct. 1879, Post Returns, Fort Garland, Colorado, Returns from U.S. Military Posts, 1800–1916, Record Group 393, National Archives, Washington, D.C. (cited hereafter as RG 393, NA).

10. Mackenzie to Hatch, Nov. 7, 1879, and Mackenzie to Pope, Nov. 12, 1879, both in Gilcrease Letterbook.

11. Ibid. See also Mackenzie to Pope, Nov. 21, 1879, *ibid.,* for more in the same vein.

12. Mackenzie to Dunn, Dec. 27, 1879; Mackenzie to Pope, Feb. 19, 1880; and Mackenzie to Dunn, Mar. 26, 1880, all in Gilcrease Letterbook.

13. Special Field Order No. 1, May 16, 1880, Joseph Dorst Papers, U.S. Military Academy Archives, West Point, N.Y.; Report for May 1880, Post Returns, Fort Garland, RG 393, NA; James Parker, *The Old Army,* 127; Mackenzie to Pope, June 29, 1880, Gilcrease Letterbook.

14. Lieutenant F. H. French to Miss Warner, July 12, 1880, F. H. French Papers, U.S. Military Academy Archives, West Point, N.Y.; Report for July 1880, Post Returns, Fort Garland, RG 393, NA; Parker, *Old Army,* 130–31; *Army and Navy Journal,* Aug. 28, 1880.

15. Report for Oct. 1880, Post Returns, Fort Garland, RG 393, NA; Mackenzie to Chief of Ordnance, Jan. 6, 1881, and Mackenzie to Pope, Jan. 6, 1881, both in Gilcrease Letterbook.

16. Reports for Apr., May, June, 1881, Post Returns, Fort Garland, RG 393, NA.

17. Parker, *Old Army,* 50–54, 132–35; Joseph H. Dorst, "Ranald Slidell Mackenzie," *Twentieth Annual Reunion of the Association of Graduates of the United States Military Academy at West Point, New York,* 13–15; Pope's Report in *Report of the Secretary of War,* 47th Cong., 1st sess., H. Exec. Doc. 2011, 115–17 (hereafter referred to as Pope's Report).

18. Parker, *Old Army,* p. 53. Colorow's futile resistance is recorded in Sprague, *Massacre,* 315–16, and Rockwell, *Utes,* 174, although they differ on the day the episode took place. Pope's Report, 116, is almost indignant about the eagerness of the whites to benefit from the removal of the Indians.

19. Pope's Report, 117; Sheridan's Annual Report, 1881, p. 3, Philip H. Sheridan Papers, Manuscript Division, Library of Congress, Washington, D.C.

20. Ralph H. Ogle, "Federal Control of the Western Apaches, 1848–1886," *New Mexico Historical Review* 15 (July 1940): 296; James T. King, *War Eagle: A Life of General Eugene A Carr,* 216.

21. King, *War Eagle,* 206–15; Ogle, "Federal Control of the Apaches," 294–96. Utley, *Frontier Regulars,* 369–74, has a succinct account of this affair. Nocadecklinny is one of several variations of the medicine man's name.

22. Parker, *Old Army,* 335–77; King, *War Eagle,* 217–20; Ogle, "Federal Control of the Apaches," 296–98.

23. Mackenzie to Pope, Oct. 12, 1881, Gilcrease Letterbook.

24. Warren to Adjutant General, U.S. Army, Oct. 29, 1880, and Pope to Secretary of War, Sept. 1, 1880, AGO 3877, ACP 1873, RG 94, NA.

25. Letters of support all in AGO 3877, ACP 1873, RG 94, NA. For Ord's dismissal, see Utley, *Frontier Regulars,* 355–56.

26. "Military Service Record," in Wallace, *Mackenzie's Official Correspondence* 2:14.

27. Mackenzie to Assistant Adjutant General, Department of the Missouri (cited hereafter as AAG, DM), Nov. 1, 1881; Mackenzie to AAG, DM, Nov. 15, 1881; Mackenzie to Pope, Feb. 16, 1882; Assistant Adjutant General, District of New Mexico (cited hereafter as AAG, DNM), to Commanding Officer, Fort Cummings, N.M., Nov. 19, 1881; AAG, DNM, to C.O., Fort

Cummings, Nov. 22, 1881, all in Letters Sent, District of New Mexico, Records of U.S. Army Continental Commands, RG 393, National Archives (hereafter cited as Letters Sent, DNM).

28. Mackenzie to C.O., Fort Craig, N.M., Feb. 20, 1882, ibid.

29. Mackenzie to Quartermaster General, U.S. Army, Nov. 4, 16, 1881; AAG, DNM, to C.O., Fort Stanton, Mar. 2, 1882, both in ibid.

30. Mackenzie to Pope, Feb. 16, 1882, Gilcrease Letterbook; Mackenzie to Pope, May 9, 1882, and Report of Disturbance at Taylor Ranch, Aug. 25, 1882, in Letters Sent, DNM.

31. Mackenzie to Llewellyn, Jan. 9, 1882; Mackenzie to AAG, DM, Jan. 10, 1882; Mackenzie to C.O., Fort Stanton, Jan. 10, 1882, all in Letters Sent, DNM.

32. Mackenzie to Llewellyn, Mar. 21, 1882; Mackenzie to Adjutant General, Department of the Missouri (cited hereafter as AG, DM), Mar. 31, 1882; Mackenzie to AG, DM, Apr. 2, 1882; Mackenzie to AG, DM, May 24, 1882, all in ibid. A report of Mackenzie's trip to the agency can be found in the *Santa Fe Daily New Mexican*, Apr. 6, 1882.

33. Mackenzie to AAG, DM, Dec. 3, 1881, Letters Sent, DNM.

34. Mackenzie to Forsyth, Jan. 12, 1882, and Mackenzie to Fuero, Jan. 21, 1882, both in ibid.; Mackenzie to Pope, Jan. 20, 1882, Gilcrease Letterbook.

35. Brief accounts can be found in Utley, *Frontier Regulars*, 375–76, and Dan L. Thrapp, *The Conquest of Apacheria*, 248–49. See also George A. Forsyth's version in *Thrilling Days in Army Life*.

36. Forsyth to Mackenzie, May 4, 1882, and Mackenzie to Pope, May 6, 1882, both in Gilcrease Letterbook. Both Thrapp, *Conquest*, 249, and Ogle, "Federal Control of the Apaches," 304, state that Forsyth's retelling of the incident in *Thrilling Days* was the first published account.

37. Mackenzie to Forsyth, May 3, 1882; Mackenzie to Forsyth, Mizner, and Lawton, May 17, 1882; Mackenzie to Fuero, May 17, 1882, all in Letters Sent, DNM; Pope's Report, 99–100; Sheridan to Drum, May 4, 1882, quoted in Robert D. Gregg, *The Influence of Border Troubles on Relations between the United States and Mexico, 1876–1910*, 148.

38. Sherman to Garfield, Dec. 20, 1880, quoted in Utley, *Frontier Regulars*, 367; Sheridan to Lincoln, Dec. 8, 1881, Sheridan Papers. See also, Paul Andrew Hutton, *Phil Sheridan and His Army*, 353.

39. Sheridan to Lincoln, Oct. 4, 1882, Sheridan Papers; Parker to Arthur, Oct. 4, 1882; Sheldon to Arthur, Oct. 4, 1882; Hill to Arthur, Oct. 5, 1882; Luna to Arthur, Oct. 16, 1882, all in AGO 3877, ACP 1873, RG 94, NA; Dorst, "Mackenzie," 18, asserts Grant's influence. That the former president was a major force in Mackenzie's selection was apparently well known; see, for example, *Santa Fe Daily New Mexican*, Nov. 3, 1882, and *Army and Navy Journal*, Oct. 28, 1882, quoting the *San Francisco Chronicle*, which states that many officers thought Mackenzie got the promotion because of "favoritism."

40. Resignation Order, Oct. 26, 1882, in *Santa Fe Daily New Mexican*, Nov. 3, 1882.

41. Mackenzie to Assistant Adjutant General, U.S. Army, Nov. 2, Dec. 7, 1882, AGO 3877, ACP 1873, RG 94, NA; Sherman to Sheridan, Nov. 3, 1882, Sheridan Papers; *Santa Fe Daily New Mexican*, Dec. 7, 1882.

42. *Santa Fe Daily New Mexican,* Feb. 22, Apr. 28, 29, 1883. The obituary on Apr. 28 makes clear that Mackenzie's family was with him throughout most of his New Mexico tour of duty.

43. Sheridan to Lincoln, Sept. 25, Oct. 7, 1883, Sheridan Papers.

44. *San Antonio Light,* Oct. 15, 1883; *San Antonio Express,* Nov. 1, 1883.

Chapter 13. Perfect Peace

1. General Order No. 27, Oct. 23, 1883, Joseph Dorst Papers, U.S. Military Academy Archives, West Point, N.Y.; Mackenzie to Quartermaster General, U.S. Army, Nov. 1, 1883; Mackenzie to Adjutant General, U.S. Army, Nov. 5, 1883; Mackenzie to Benet, Nov. 27, 1883, all in Letters Sent, DT.

2. Charles Judson Crane, *The Experiences of a Colonel of Infantry,* 139–40; Vincent to AG, DM, Dec. 19, 1883, Letters Sent, DT. Most of the correspondence is duplicated in AGO 3877, ACP 1873, RG 94, NA.

3. J. M. Skaggs, "The Insanity and Death of General Ranald S. Mackenzie," *True West,* Sept.–Oct. 1971, 25; *Saint Louis Globe-Democrat,* Dec. 29, 1883. The official report simply states that Mackenzie "engaged in an altercation, in which he was more or less injured"; Vincent to AG, DM, Dec. 19, 1883, Letters Sent, DT.

4. Vincent to AG, DM, Dec. 19, 1883 (a separate message from the one above); Memorandum, Dec. 19, 1883; Vincent to AG, DM, Dec. 20, 21, 22, 1883, all in Letters Sent, DT.

5. Vincent to AG, DM, Dec. 24, 1883; Vincent to Vice-President, Missouri-Pacific Railroad, Dec. 24, 1883; Adjutant General, U.S. Army, to Vincent, Dec. 25, 1883; Vincent to Adjutant General, U.S. Army, Dec. 26, 1883, all in ibid.

6. Note by Rodgers, n.d., AGO 3877, ACP 1873, RG 94, NA; Journal entry, n.d., p. 357, S. B. M. Young Papers, U.S. Army Military History Institute, Carlisle Barracks, Pa.; Harriet Mackenzie to Lincoln, Dec. 29, 1883; H. Mackenzie to Sheridan, Dec. 29, 1883; Sheridan to H. Mackenzie, Dec. 29, 1883, all in AGO 3877, ACP 1873, RG 94, NA.

7. Middleton to Adjutant General, U.S. Army, Dec. 28, 1883; Adjutant General, U.S. Army, to Middleton, Dec. 29, 1883; Nichols to Sheridan, Feb. 27, 1884; and Sheridan to Lincoln, Feb. 27, 1884, all in AGO 3877, ACP 1873, RG 94, NA. Sheridan to Nichols, n.d., Philip H. Sheridan Papers, Manuscript Division, Library of Congress, Washington, D.C.

8. Proceedings of Retiring Board, March 5, 1884, AGO 3877, ACP 1873, RG 94, NA.

9. See George W. Henry, "Organic Mental Disease," in *A History of Medical Psychology,* ed. George Zilboorg (New York: W. W. Norton & Company,

1941), 526–51, for a history and description of the disease. The attack in New Mexico is mentioned in Vincent to AG, DM, Dec. 19, 1883, Letters Sent, DT.

10. Dr. Bonnie Baird of the University of Texas Health Science Center at San Antonio picked the brains of her colleagues and offered these possibilities in a letter to the author dated Apr. 5, 1988. Joseph Mills Hanson, "Ranald Slidell Mackenzie," *Cavalry Journal*, Jan.–Feb. 1934, p. 32, offers a nice capsule of older explanations.

11. Frederick C. Chabot, *With the Makers of San Antonio* (San Antonio: Artes Graficas, 1937), 338, gives a brief biography of Warwick Tunstall. Mackenzie's supposed treks to see Florida are described in Edward S. Wallace, "General Ranald Slidell Mackenzie, Indian Fighting Cavalryman," *Southwestern Historical Quarterly* 56 (January 1953): 378–96. Lessing H. Nohl, "Bad Hand: The Military Career of Ranald Slidell Mackenzie, 1877–1889" (Ph.D. diss., University of New Mexico, 1962), covers the early affair in some detail.

12. Shafter to Mackenzie, May 26, 1873, in Ernest Wallace, ed., *Ranald S. Mackenzie's Official Correspondence Relating to Texas, 1873–1879*, 2:182; Shafter to Mackenzie, June 27, 1873, MHI Letterbook. The *San Antonio Light*, Dec. 18, 1883, contains the first mention of the upcoming wedding. A notice also appeared in the *Galveston Daily News* on the same day suggesting that the rumors had been circulating for some time. The confusion of dates is shown in the *San Antonio Light*, Dec. 20, 27, 1883.

13. See Wallace, "Indian Fighting Cavalryman," 396, for the suggestion that the excitement of the engagement unhinged Mackenzie. The army wives' tale is a condensation of a much longer version supplied by Wanda Hoffman. Mrs. Hoffman heard the story in China shortly after World War II from the wives of American military advisors to Chiang Kai-Shek. Her main informant was Angelia Rodriquez, who was married to a senior officer, both of whom had deep roots in San Antonio and strong military ties. It helps to remember that Mrs. Sharpe lived until 1946, so many of the army wives could have known her.

14. I have not read Mrs. Sharpe's recollections, but Nohl in "Bad Hand" and in a letter to me dated Jan. 21, 1987, states that Mackenzie is not mentioned. See Edward Wallace, "Border Warrior," *American Heritage*, June, 1958, 104, for the assertion that Mackenzie bought the land after his engagement. A copy of Harriet D. Mackenzie's will is on file in the county clerk's office, Kendall County, Texas. Morris R. S. Mackenzie's will, a copy of which can be found in the same place, makes no mention of paying the legacy.

15. Mackenzie to Drum, Apr. 4, June 6, Sept. 1, 1884, all in AGO 3877, ACP 1873, RG 94, NA.

16. Williams College, "1859 Class Reports," 1887, copy in the Williamsiana Collection, Williams College Library, Williamstown, Mass.; Death of R. S. Mackenzie, Certificate No. 2568, Municipal Archives, City of New York. Harriet Mackenzie accepted the official verdict in H. Mackenzie to Drum, Feb. 1, 1889, AGO 3877, ACP 1873, RG 94, NA.

17. *New York Daily Tribune*, Jan. 20, 1889; *New York Times*, Jan. 20, 1889.

18. Joseph H. Dorst, "Ranald Slidell Mackenzie," *Twentieth Annual Reunion of the Association of Graduates of the United States Military Academy at West Point, New York,* 19; Dorst to J. M. Lee, July 11, 1906, Dorst Papers; *Morristown Jerseyman,* Jan. 25, 1889. Lawton and Young are quoted in James Parker, *The Old Army,* 45.

19. Description of Mackenzie's funeral is from the *Army and Navy Journal* 26:447–48.

BIBLIOGRAPHY

Manuscript Materials

Birnie, William A. H. "The Social Organization of Williams College." Term paper, Williams College, 1924. Williamsiana Collection, Williams College Library, Williamstown, Mass.

Brasher, John. "Morristown, New Jersey, 1850–1860." Paper, 1969. Free Joint Public Library of Morristown and Morris County, Morristown, N.J.

Cadet Application Papers. U.S. Military Academy Archives, West Point, N.Y.

Carter, Robert Goldwaith. Diary. Typescript edited by B. Byron Price. National Cowboy Hall of Fame and Western Heritage Center, Oklahoma City.

Chamberlain, Cynthia Ann. "Colonel Ranald Slidell Mackenzie's Administration of the Western Section of Indian Territory, 1875–1877." Master's thesis, Texas Tech University, Lubbock, 1964.

Cornell, Greta. "Mount Pleasant Academy, 1814–1925." Paper. Ossining Historical Society, Ossining, N.Y.

Dorst, Joseph. Papers. U.S. Military Academy Archives, West Point, N.Y.

duPont, Henry A. Papers. Hagley Museum and Library, Wilmington, Del.

French, F. H. Papers. U.S. Military Academy Archives, West Point, N.Y.

Gerdes, Bruce. Papers. Panhandle-Plains Historical Museum, Canyon, Texas.

Gunter, Lillian. Papers. Panhandle-Plains Historical Museum, Canyon, Texas.

Hatfield, C. A. P. Account of Battle of Palo Duro Canyon. Papers of the Order of Indian Wars. U.S. Army Military History Institute, Carlisle Barracks, Pa.

Loomis, Leslie George. "The Non-Fraternity Man at Williams College, 1868–1943." Seminar paper. Williamsiana Collection, Williams College Library, Williamstown, Mass.

McCrea, Tully. Papers. U.S. Military Academy Archives, West Point, N.Y.

Mackenzie, Catherine. Biographical Sketch of Alexander Slidell Mackenzie. Duyckinck Papers. Rare Books and Manuscripts Division, New York Public Library.

Mackenzie, Ranald Slidell. Letterbook. Thomas Gilcrease Museum, Tulsa, Okla.

————. Letterbook. U.S. Army Miltary History Institute, Carlisle, Barracks, Pa.

Nohl, Lessing H., Jr. "Bad Hand: The Military Career of Ranald Slidell Mackenzie, 1877–1889." Ph.D. diss., University of New Mexico, 1962.

Parker, James. Papers. U.S. Military Academy Archives, West Point, N.Y.

Pate, J'Nell LaVerne. "Colonel Ranald Slidell Mackenzie's First Four Years with the Fourth Cavalry in Texas, 1871–1874." Master's thesis, Texas Christian University, 1960.

Perry, Arthur Latham, "Recollections and Diaries." Ed. Bliss Perry. Unpublished typescript in Williamsiana Collection, Williams College Library, Williamstown, Mass.

"Register of Delinquencies." Vol. 11. U.S. Military Academy Archives, West Point, N.Y.

Shafter, William B. Papers. Stanford University Library, Stanford, Calif.

Sheridan, Philip H. Papers. Manuscript Division, Library of Congress, Washington, D.C.

Sherman, William T. Family, Papers. University of Notre Dame Archives, West Bend, Ind. (microfilm edition).

———. Papers, Manuscript Division, Library of Congress, Washington, D.C.

Smith, Sherry L. "With Mackenzie on the Wyoming and Texas Frontiers: A Private's Perspective." Paper presented at the Texas State Historical Association Convention, Lubbock, March 1989.

Smyth, R. B. Papers. Panhandle-Plains Historical Museum, Canyon, Tex.

U.S. Adjutant General's Office. Records. Record Group 94. National Archives and Records Service, Washington, D.C.

U.S. Army Commands. Records. Record Group 393. National Archives and Records Service, Washington, D.C.

———. Records of Fort Sill. Archives, Fort Sill, Okla.

U.S. Bureau of the Census. Eighth Census of the United States. Population Schedules.

———. Seventh Census of the United States. Original Returns of the Assistant Marshals, First Series.

Wilcox, John A. "Recollections of John A. Wilcox." Papers of the Order of Indian Wars. U.S. Military History Institute, Carlisle Barracks, Pa.

Williams College. "1859 Class Reports." Williamsiana Collection, Williams College Library, Williamstown, Mass.

———. "Oath Register for 1845–46." Williamsiana Collection, Williams College Library, Williamstown, Mass.

———. "Obituary Record." Williamsiana Collection, Williams College Library, Williamstown, Mass.

Wimberly, Russell E. "Ranald Slidell Mackenzie, Union Officer of the Civil War." Seminar paper. Southwest Collection, Texas Tech University, Lubbock.

Young, S. B. M. Papers. U.S. Army Military History Institute, Carlisle Barracks, Pa.

Government Documents

Ainsworth, Fred C., and Kirkley, Joseph, comps. *The War of the Rebellion: A Compilation of the Official Records of the Union and Confederate Armies,* 4 series, 130 vols. Washington, D.C.: Government Printing Office, 1901.

Annual Report of the United States Secretary of War, 1867–83.

Annual Report of the United States Secretary of the Interior, 1870–83.

Mooney, James. "Calendar History of the Kiowa Indians." In *Seventeenth Annual Report of the Bureau of American Ethnology.* Washington, D.C.: Government Printing Office, 1898.

Official Register of the U.S. Military Academy, 1859, 1860, 1861, 1862. Association of Graduates, U.S. Military Academy, West Point, N.Y.

Published Diaries, Letters, Memoirs, and Miscellaneous Documents

Anderson, Edward W. "Letters of a West Pointer." Ed. Frances Sullivan. *American Historical Review* 33 (1928): 602–16.

Archambeau, Ernest R. "Monthly Reports of the the Fourth Cavalry, 1872–1874." *Panhandle-Plains Historical Review* 38 (1965): 95–153.

Battey, Thomas C. *A Quaker among the Indians.* Boston: Lee & Shepard, 1891.

Beaumont, E. B. "Over the Border with Mackenzie." *United Service* 12 (Mar. 1885): 281–88.

Bourke, John G. "Mackenzie's Last Fight with the Cheyennes: A Winter Campaign in Wyoming and Montana." *Journal of the Military Service Institution* 2 (1890): 29–49, 198–221.

Carter, Robert G. "Dust from the Archives: General Ranald Mackenzie." *Corral Dust* (Potomac Corral of the Westerners) 2 (Mar. 1957), no. 1.

——. *The Old Sergeant's Story: Fighting Indians and Bad Men in Texas from 1870 to 1876.* 1926. Reprint, Bryan, Tex., and Mattituck, N.Y.: J. M. Carroll & Company, 1982.

——. *On the Border with Mackenzie; or, Winning West Texas from the Comanches.* 1935. Reprint, New York: Antiquarian Press, 1961.

Catalog of Mount Pleasant Academy: A Department of the University of the State of New York. Ossining-on-Hudson: n.p., 1917.

Charlton, John B. "The Battle of Palo Duro Canyon." *Winners of the West,* April 28, 1942. 1–2.

Church of the Redeemer in Morristown, New Jersey: A Memoir. Morristown, N.J.: n.p., 1914.

Conover, G. W. *Sixty Years in Southwest Oklahoma.* Anadarko, Okla.: N. T. Plummer, 1927.

Conway, Walter E., ed. "Colonel Edmund Schriver's Inspector-General's Report on Military Posts in Texas, November, 1872–January, 1873." *Southwestern Historical Quarterly* 67 (Apr. 1964): 559–83.

Crane, Charles Judson. *The Experiences of a Colonel of Infantry.* New York: The Knickerbocker Press, 1923.

Dorst, Joseph H. "Ranald Slidell Mackenzie." *Twentieth Annual Reunion of the Association of Graduates of the United States Military Academy at West Point, New York.* East Saginaw, Mich.: Evening News Printing and Binding House, 1889.

duPont, Henry A. *The Campaign of 1864 in the Valley of Virginia and the Expedition to Lynchburg.* New York: National Americana Society, 1925.

Floyd, Dale E., ed. *"Dear Friends at Home . . . ": The Letters and Diary of Thomas James Owen, Fiftieth New York Volunteer Engineer Regiment, during the Civil War.* Washington, D.C.: Government Printing Office, 1985.

Forsyth, George A. *Thrilling Days in Army Life.* New York: n.p., 1900.

Gladden, Washington. *Recollections.* Boston and New York: Houghton Mifflin company, 1909.

Grant, Ulysses S. *Personal Memoirs of U. S. Grant.* 2 vols. in one. 1885. Reprint, New York: Bonanza Books, n.d.

Hilen, Andrew, ed. *The Letters of Henry Wadsworth Longfellow.* 6 vols. Cambridge: The Belknap Press of Harvard University Press, 1966–82.

Hinton, Howard. *My Comrades, or School Days at Mt. Pleasant.* Ossining, N.Y.: n.p., 1909.

Hone, Philip. *The Diary of Philip Hone, 1828–1851.* Ed. Allen Nevins. 2 vols. in one. 1889. Reprint, New York: Arno Press and the *New York Times,* 1970.

Huckaby, Ida Lasater. *Ninety-Four Years in Jack County, 1854–1948.* 1948. Reprint, Waco, Tex.: Texian Press, 1974.

Irving, Pierre Munroe. *The Life and Letters of Washington Irving.* 4 vols. New York: G. P. Putnam, 1862–64.

James, Mrs. John Herndon. *I Remember: Being the Memoirs of Mrs. John Herndon (Maria Aurelia Williams) James together with Contemporary Historical Events and Sketches of Her Own and Her Husband's Families.* Ed. Charles Albert Sloan. San Antonio: The Naylor Company, 1938.

Kincaid, James B. "Diary of Sgt. James B. Kincaid, Co. B, 4th Cav., August 5, 1876 to 1881." *Winners of the West* 16, no. 6 (July 1939): 2–3.

Letters about the Hudson River and Its Vicinity, Written in 1835–1837. 3rd ed. New York: Freeman Hunt & Co., 1837.

Longfellow, Fanny Appleton. *Mrs. Longfellow: Selected Letters and Journal of Fanny Appleton Longfellow, 1817–1861.* Ed. Edward Wagenknecht. New York, London, Toronto: Longmans, Green and Co., 1956.

McConnell, H. H. *Five Years a Cavalryman.* Jacksboro, Tex.: n.p., 1889.

McDonald, James R. "Social Life of Williams." *Lippincott's Magazine,* October 1887: 12–15.

Manypenny, George W. *Our Indian Wards.* 1880. Reprint. New York: DeCapo Press, 1972.

North, Luther. *Man of the Plains: Recollections of Luther North, 1856–1882.* Ed. Donald F. Danker. Lincoln: University of Nebraska Press, 1961.

Notson, William M. *Fort Concho Medical History, January 1869 to July 1872.* San Angelo: Fort Concho Preservation and Museum, 1974.

Parker, James. *The Old Army.* Philadelphia: Dorance and Co., 1929.

Porter, Horace, "Five Forks and the Pursuit of Lee." In *Battles and Leaders of the Civil War,* 4:708–22. Ed. Robert U. Johnson and Clarence C. Buel. New York: Thomas Yoseloff, 1956.

Reynolds, Florence Leary, comp. *Reminiscences of Ossining.* Ossining, N.Y.: Moran-Register Press, 1922.

Rister, Carl Coke. "Documents Relating to General W. T. Sherman's Southern Plains Indian Policy, 1871–1875." 2 parts. *Panhandle-Plains Historical Review* 9 (1936): 48–63; 10 (1937): 7–27.

Rowland, Thomas, "Letters of a Virginia Cadet at West Point, 1859–1861." *South Atlantic Quarterly,* May 1915–Sept. 191–6.

San Antonio City Directory. 1877–78, 1883–84 (on microfilm at San Antonio Public Library).

Schaff, Morris. *The Spirit of Old West Point, 1858–1862.* Boston: Houghton, Mifflin and Company, 1907.

Sheridan, Philip H. "Record of Engagements with Hostile Indians in Texas, 1868 to 1882." *West Texas Historical Association Yearbook* 9 (1933): 101–18.

Smith, Sherry L. *Sagebrush Soldier: Private William Earl Smith's View of the Sioux War of 1876.* Norman and London: University of Oklahoma Press, 1989.

Strong, Henry W. *My Frontier Days and Indian Fights on the Plains of Texas.* Jacksboro, Tex.: n.p., 1924.

Tatum, Lawrie. *Our Red Brothers and the Peace Policy of President Ulysses S. Grant.* 1899. Reprint, Lincoln: University of Nebraska Press, 1970.

Taylor, Joe F. "The Indian Campaign on the Staked Plains, 1874–1875: Military Correspondence from the War Department Adjutant General's File 1874–1875." *Panhandle-Plains Historical Review* 34 (1961): 1–216; 35 (1962): 215–357.

Thompson, W. A. "Scouting with Mackenzie." *Cavalry Journal* 10 (1897): 429–33.

Vail, Dudley Landon. *The County Regiment: A Sketch of the Second Regiment of Connecticut Volunteer Heavy Artillery.* Litchfield, Conn.: County University Club, 1908.

Vail, Theodore F. *History of the Second Connecticut Volunteer Heavy Artillery.* Winsted, Conn.: Winsted Printing Company, 1868.

Wallace, Ernest. "The Journal of Ranald S. Mackenzie's Messenger to the Kwahadi Comanches." *Red River Valley Historical Review* 3, no. 3 (Spring 1978): 227–46.

Wallace, Ernest, ed. *Ranald S. Mackenzie's Official Correspondence Relating to Texas, 1873–1879.* 2 vols. Lubbock: West Texas Museum Association, 1968.

Newspapers and Periodicals

Army and Navy Journal
Austin Statesman.
Galveston Daily News.
Morristown The Jerseyman.
New Orleans Times-Picayune.
New York Times.
New York Tribune.
San Antonio Daily Herald

San Antonio Express.
San Antonio Light.
Santa Fe Daily New Mexican.

Books

Ambrose, Stephen A. *Duty, Honor, Country: A History of West Point.* Baltimore: Johns Hopkins University Press, 1966.

Bacon, Edgar Mayhew. *Chronicles of Tarrytown and Sleepy Hollow.* New York and London: G. P. Putnam's Sons, 1902.

Baker, T. Lindsay, and Harrison, Billy R. *Adobe Walls: The History and Archaeology of the 1874 Trading Post.* College Station: Texas A&M University Press, 1986.

Barnes, Charles Merritt. *Combats and Conquests of Mortal Heroes Sung in Song and Told in Story.* San Antonio: Guessaz & Ferlet Company, 1910.

Beach, Edward L. *The United States Navy: 200 Years.* New York: Henry Holt and Company, 1986.

Bedford, Hilory G. *Texas Indian Troubles: The Most Thrilling Events in the History of Texas.* Dallas: Hargreaves Printing Co., 1905.

Berthrong, Donald J. *The Southern Cheyennes.* Norman: University of Oklahoma Press, 1963.

Best, Isaac O. *History of the 121st New York State Infantry.* Chicago: n.p., 1921.

Bierschwale, Margaret. *Fort McKavett, Texas: Post on the San Saba.* Salado, Tex.: Anson Jones Press, 1966.

Bigelow, John, Jr. *The Campaign of Chancellorsville: A Strategic and Tactical Study.* New Haven: Yale University Press, 1910.

Brady, Cyrus Townsend. *Indian Fights and Fighters.* 1913. Reprint, Lincoln and London: University of Nebraska Press, 1971.

Capps, Benjamin. *The Warren Wagontrain Raid: The First Complete Account of an Historic Indian Attack and Its Aftermath.* New York: The Dial Press, 1974.

Chabot, Frederick C. *With the Makers of San Antonio.* San Antonio: Artes Graficas, 1937.

Coffman, Edward M. *The Old Army: A Portrait of the American Army in Peacetime, 1784–1898.* New York and Oxford: Oxford University Press, 1986.

Coles, G. W.; Roper, John L.; and Archibald, Henry C. *History of the Eleventh Pennsylvania Volunteer Cavalry, Together with a Complete Roster of the Regiment and Regimental Officers.* Philadelphia: Franklin Printing Co., 1902.

Cosio Villegas, Daniel. *The United States versus Porfirio Diaz.* Trans. by Nettie Lee Benson. Lincoln: University of Nebraska Press, 1963.

Cullum, George W. *Biographical Register of the Officers and Graduates of the U.S. Military Academy.* 2 vols. New York: n.p., 1898.

Cutler, Ralph H., Jr., and Scherzer, Carl B., eds. *Morristown and Morris*

Township: A Guide to Historical Sites. Morristown: The Washington Association of New Jersey, 1975.

Davis, Burke. *To Appomattox: Nine April Days, 1865.* New York: Rinehart & Company, 1959.

De Barthe, Joe. *The Life and Adventures of Frank Grouard, Chief of Scouts, U.S.A.* 1894. Reprint, New York: Time-Life Books, 1982.

Ellis, Richard N. *General Pope and U.S. Indian Policy.* Albuquerque: University of New Mexico Press, 1970.

Finerty, John F. *War-Path and Bivouac; or, the Conquest of the Sioux.* Chicago: M. A. Donohue & Co., 1890.

Foote, Shelby. *The Civil War: A Narrative.* 3 vols. New York: Random House, 1958–74.

Forman, Sidney. *West Point: A History of the United States Military Academy.* New York: Columbia University Press, 1950.

Gibson, A. M. *The Kickapoos, Lords of the Middle Border.* Norman: University of Oklahoma Press, 1963.

Gray, John S. *Centennial Campaign: The Sioux War of 1876.* Fort Collins, Colo.: The Old Army Press, 1976.

Green, Bill. *The Dancing Was Lively: Fort Concho, Texas, A Social History, 1867–1882.* San Angelo, Tex.: Fort Concho Sketches Publishing Co., 1974.

Greene, A. C. *The Last Captive.* Austin, Tex.: The Encino Press, 1972.

Gregg, Robert D. *The Influence of Border Troubles on Relations between the United States and Mexico, 1876–1910.* New York: DeCapo, 1970.

Griffin, Ernest Freeland, ed. *Westchester County and Its People: A Record.* New York: Lewis Historical Publishing Company, 1946.

Grinnell, George Bird. *The Fighting Cheyennes.* 1915. Reprint, Norman: University of Oklahoma Press, 1956.

———. *Two Great Scouts and Their Pawnee Battalion: The Experiences of Frank J. North and Luther H. North.* 1928. Reprint: Lincoln: University of Nebraska Press, 1973.

Hagan, William T. *United States–Comanche Relations: The Reservation Years* New Haven, Conn.: Yale University Press, 1976.

Haley, J. Evetts. *Fort Concho and the Texas Frontier.* San Angelo, Tex.: San Angelo Standard Times, 1952.

Haley, James L. *The Buffalo War.* Garden City, N.Y.: Doubleday & Company, 1976.

Hamblin, Deborah. *Brevet Major-General Joseph Eldridge Hamblin, 1861–1865.* Boston: n.p., 1902.

Hamilton, Allen Lee. *Sentinel of the Southern Plains: Fort Richardson and the Northwest Texas Frontier, 1866–1878.* Fort Worth: Texas Christian University Press, 1988.

Hedren, Paul L. *Fort Laramie in 1876: Chronicle of a Frontier Post at War.* Lincoln and London: University of Nebraska Press, 1989.

Heitman, Francis B. *Historical Register and Dictionary of the United States Army, 1789–1903.* Washington, D.C.: Government Printing Office, 1903.

Hendrick, Burton J. *Statesmen of the Lost Cause.* New York: Literary Guild of America, 1939.

Herr, John K., and Wallace, Edward. *The Story of the U.S. Cavalry.* Boston: Little, Brown and Company, 1953.

Hutton, Paul Andrew. *Phil Sheridan and His Army.* Lincoln and London: University of Nebraska Press, 1985.

Kimble County Historical Survey Committee. *Recorded Landmarks of Kimble County.* Junction, Tex.: Kimble County Historical Survey Committee, 1971.

King, James T. *War Eagle: A Life of General Eugene A. Carr.* Lincoln: University of Nebraska Press, 1963.

Knowlson, James S., et al., comps. *A Biographical Record of the Kappa Alpha Society in Williams College, Williamstown, Mass., from Its Foundation to the Present Time, 1833-1881.* New York: S. W. Green's Son, 1881.

Langstaff, John Brett. *New Jersey Generations: Macculloch Hall, Morristown.* New York: Vantage Press, 1964.

Leckie, William H. *The Military Conquest of the Southern Plains.* Norman: University of Oklahoma Press, 1963.

————, and Leckie, Shirley A. *Unlikely Warriors: General Benjamin H. Grierson and His Family.* Norman: University of Oklahoma Press, 1984.

Ledbetter, Barbara A. Neal. *Fort Belknap, Frontier Saga: Indians, Negroes and Anglo-Americans on the Texas Frontier.* Burnet, Tex.: Eakin Press, 1982.

Longfellow, Samuel, ed. *Life of Henry Wadsworth Longfellow with Extracts from His Journals and Correspondence.* 3 vols. Boston: Ticknor and Company, 1886.

McFarland, Philip. *Sea Dangers: The Affair of the Somers.* New York: Schocken Books, 1985.

Mayhall, Mildred P. *The Kiowas.* Norman: University of Oklahoma Press, 1962.

Merrill, Samuel Hill. *The Campaigns of the First Maine and First District of Columbia Cavalry.* Portland, Maine: Bailey & Notes, 1866.

Morison, Samuel Eliot. *"Old Bruin": Commodore Matthew C. Perry, 1794-1858.* Boston and Toronto: Little, Brown and Company, 1967.

Muller, William G. *The Twenty Fourth Infantry, Past and Present.* Fort Collins, Colo.: The Old Army Press, 1972.

Neeley, Bill. *Quanah Parker and His People.* Slaton, Tex.: Brazos Press, 1986.

Norton, Oliver Wilcox. *The Attack and Defense of Little Round Top, Gettysburg, July 2, 1863.* New York: The Neale Publishing Co., 1913.

Nye, Wilbur S. *Carbine and Lance: The Story of Old Fort Sill.* 2d ed. Norman: University of Oklahoma Press, 1942.

Peskin, Allan. *Garfield.* Kent, Ohio: Kent State University Press, 1978.

Pirtle, Caleb, III, and Cusack, Michael F. *The Lonely Sentinel, Fort Clark: On Texas's Western Frontier.* Austin, Tex.: Eakin Press, 1985.

Richter, William L. *The Army in Texas during Reconstruction, 1865-1870.* College Station: Texas A&M University Press, 1987.

Rickey, Don, Jr. *Forty Miles a Day on Beans and Hay: The Enlisted Soldier Fighting the Indian Wars.* Norman: University of Oklahoma Press, 1963.

Rister, C. C. *Fort Griffin on the Texas Frontier.* Norman: University of Oklahoma Press, 1956.

Rockwell, Wilson. *The Utes: A Forgotten People.* Denver: Sage Books, 1956.

Scoville, Joseph A. *The Old Merchants of New York City.* 5 vols. New York: John W. Lovell Company, 1885.

Sears, Louis Martin. *John Slidell.* Durham, N.C.: Duke University Press, 1925.

Sergent, Mary Elizabeth. *They Lie Forgotten: The United States Military Academy, 1856–1861, together with a Class Album for the Class of May, 1861.* Middletown, N.Y.: The Prior King Press, 1986.

Spring, Leverett Wilson. *A History of Williams College.* Boston: Houghton Mifflin Co., 1917.

Sprague, Marshall. *Massacre: The Tragedy at White River.* Boston: Little, Brown & Company, 1957.

Stackpole, Edward J. *Sheridan in the Shenandoah: Jubal Early's Nemesis.* Harrisburg, Pa.: The Stackpole Company, 1961.

———. *They Met at Gettysburg.* 1956. Reprint, New York: Bonanza Books, 1961.

Stovall, Allan A. *Breaks of the Balcones: A Regional History.* Ed. Wanda Pope and Allan Stovall. Austin, Tex.: Firm Foundation Publishing House, 1967.

Taylor, Emerson Gifford. *Gouverneur Kemble Warren: The Life and Letters of an America Soldier, 1830–1882.* Boston and New York: Houghton Mifflin Company, 1932.

Thompson, Gilbert. *The Engineer Battalion in the Civil War.* Occasional Papers of the Engineer School No. 44. Washington, D.C.: Press of the Engineer Society, 1910.

Thompson, Richard A. *Crossing the Border with the Fourth Cavalry.* Waco, Tex.: Texian Press, 1986.

Thrapp, Dan L. *The Conquest of Apacheria.* Norman: University of Oklahoma Press, 1967.

Tilghman, Zoe. *Quanah: The Eagle of the Comanches.* Oklahoma City: Harlow Publishing Co., 1939.

Utley, Robert M. *Frontier Regulars: The United States Army and the Indian, 1866–1891.* 1973. Reprint, Lincoln and London: University of Nebraska Press, 1984.

Van de Water, Frederick F. *The Captain Called It Mutiny.* New York: Ives Washburn, 1954.

Vandiver, Frank E. *Jubal's Raid: General Early's Famous Attack on Washington in 1864.* New York, Toronto, London: McGraw-Hill, 1960.

Various authors. *History of Morris County, New Jersey, with Illustrations and Biographical Sketches of Prominent Citizens and Pioneers.* 1887. Reprint, Morristown, N.J.: Morris County Historical Society, 1973.

Vaughn, J. W. *The Reynolds Campaign on Powder River.* Norman: University of Oklahoma Press, 1961.

Wallace, Ernest. *Ranald S. Mackenzie on the Texas Frontier.* Lubbock, Tex.: West Texas Museum Association, 1964.

————, and Hoebel, E. A. *The Comanches: Lords of the South Plains.* Norman: University of Oklahoma Press, 1952.

Weems, John Edward. *Death Song: The Last of the Indian Wars.* Garden City, N.Y.: Doubleday & Company, 1976.

Werner, Fred H. *The Dull Knife Battle.* Greeley, Colo.: Werner Publications, 1981.

Wert, Jeffry D. *From Winchester to Cedar Creek: The Shenandoah Campaign of 1864.* Carlisle, Pa.: South Mountain Press, 1987.

Willson, Beckles. *John Slidell and the Confederates in Paris (1862–65).* 1932. Reprint, New York: AMS Press, 1970.

Worcester, Donald E. *The Apaches: Eagles of the Southwest.* Norman: University of Oklahoma Press, 1979.

Articles

Albee, Allison. "The Case of the Missing Castle." *The Westchester Historical Journal* 45, no. 4 (Fall 1969): 78–86.

Anderson, Adrian N. "The Last Phase of Colonel Ranald S. Mackenzie's 1874 Campaign against the Comanches." *West Texas Historical Association Yearbook* 30 (1964): 71–82.

Becker, Daniel. "Comanche Civilization with History of Quanah Parker." *Chronicles of Oklahoma* 1 (June 1923): 243–52.

Carlson, Paul H. "William R. Shafter Commanding Black Troops in West Texas." *West Texas Historical Association Yearbook* 50 (1974): 104–16.

Chapman, John. "Fort Concho." *Southwest Review* 25 (Apr. 1940): 258–85.

Cole, Roy W. "South of the Border." *Cavalry Journal,* Mar. 1940, pp. 144–48.

Crane, R. C. "The Settlement in 1874–75 of Indian Troubles in West Texas." *West Texas Historical Association Yearbook* 1 (1925): 3–15.

Crimmins, M. L. "Fort McKavett, Texas." *Southwestern Historical Quarterly* 38 (July 1934): 28–39.

————. "General Mackenzie and Fort Concho." *West Texas Historical Association Yearbook* 10 (1934): 16–31.

————. "General Ranald S. Mackenzie." *Frontier Times,* Aug. 1945, pp. 316–19.

Ellis, Richard N. "The Humanitarian Soldiers." *Journal of Arizona History* 10 (Summer 1969): 53–66.

Hanson, Joseph Mills. "Ranald Slidell Mackenzie." *Cavalry Journal,* Jan.–Feb. 1934, pp. 25–32.

Hatfield, Charles A. P. "The Comanche, Kiowa, and Cheyenne Campaign in Northwest Texas and Mackenzie's Fight in Palo Duro Canyon, September 26, 1874." *West Texas Historical Association Yearbook* 5 (1929): 128–33.

Leckie, William H. "The Red River War." *Panhandle-Plains Historical Review* 29 (1956): 78–100.

Liebling, A. J. "The Navy's Only Mutiny." *The New Yorker,* Feb. 18, 1939, pp. 35–38.

Ogle, Ralph H. "Federal Control of the Western Apaches, 1848–1886." *New Mexico Historical Review* 15 (July 1940): 269–335.

Parker, Wayne. "Mackenzie's Supply Camp." *Grain Producer's News,* July 1979, pp. 4–7.

Pate, J'Nell. "United States–Mexican Border Conflicts, 1870–1880." *West Texas Historical Association Yearbook* 38 (1962): 175–94.

Skaggs, J. M. "The Insanity and Death of General Ranald S. Mackenzie." *True West,* Sept.–Oct. 1971: 3–5, 41.

Sullivan, Jerry M. "Fort McKavett, 1852–1883." *West Texas Historical Association Yearbook* 45 (1969): 138–149.

Temple, Frank M. "Colonel Grierson in the Southwest." *Panhandle-Plains Historical Review* 30 (1957): 27–54.

Wallace, Edward. "Border Warrior." *American Heritage,* June 1958, pp. 22–25, 101–104.

————. "General Ranald Slidell Mackenzie, Indian Fighting Cavalryman." *Southwestern Historical Quarterly* 56 (Jan. 1953): 378–96.

Wallace, Ernest. "Colonel Ranald S. Mackenzie's Expedition of 1872 across the South Plains." *West Texas Historical Association Yearbook* 38 (1962): 3–18.

————, and Anderson, Adrian S. "R. S. Mackenzie and the Kickapoos: The Raid into Mexico, 1873." *Arizona and the West* 7 (1965): 105–26.

Wolfe, George D. "The Indians Named Him Bad Hand." *True West,* Nov.–Dec. 1961, pp. 16–18, 49–50.

Zimmerman, Jean L. "Colonel Ranald S. Mackenzie at Fort Sill." *Chronicles of Oklahoma,* 42 (Spring 1966): 12–21.

INDEX